Punishing the Vulnerable

Punishing the Vulnerable

Discrimination in American Prisons

Jeremiah Wade-Olson

PRAEGER™

An Imprint of ABC-CLIO, LLC
Santa Barbara, California • Denver, Colorado

Library of Congress Cataloging-in-Publication Data

Names: Wade-Olson, Jeremiah, author.
Title: Punishing the vulnerable : discrimination in American prisons / Jeremiah Wade-Olson.
Description: Santa Barbara, California : Praeger, [2019] | Includes bibliographical references and index.
Identifiers: LCCN 2018058134 (print) | LCCN 2019000278 (ebook) | ISBN 9781440858093 (eBook) | ISBN 9781440858086 (hardcopy : alk. paper)
Subjects: LCSH: Discrimination in criminal justice administration—United States. | Imprisonment—United States. | Criminals—United States—Social conditions. | Prisoners—United States—Social conditions. | Alternatives to imprisonment—United States.
Classification: LCC HV9950 (ebook) | LCC HV9950 .W324 2019 (print) | DDC 365/.60973—dc23
LC record available at https://lccn.loc.gov/2018058134

ISBN: 978-1-4408-5808-6 (print)
978-1-4408-5809-3 (ebook)

23 22 21 20 19 1 2 3 4 5

This book is also available as an eBook.

Praeger
An Imprint of ABC-CLIO, LLC

ABC-CLIO, LLC
147 Castilian Drive
Santa Barbara, California 93117
www.abc-clio.com

This book is printed on acid-free paper ∞

Manufactured in the United States of America

Portions of this book have been revised and updated from the following, with permission:

Olson, Jeremiah C. "Race and Punishment in American Prisons." *Journal of Public Administration Research and Theory* 26, no. 4 (October 2016): 758–68. https://doi.org/10.1093/jopart/muw026

Wade-Olson, Jeremiah. "Race, Staff, and Punishment: Representative Bureaucracy in American State Prisons." *Administration and Society* (October 10, 2016). https://doi.org/10.1177%2F0095399716667156

Wade-Olson, Jeremiah. "Social Construction and Political Decision Making in the American Prison System(s)." PhD diss., University of Kentucky, 2013. https://uknowledge.uky.edu/cgi/viewcontent.cgi?referer=&httpsredir=1&article=1005&context=polysci_etds

To my two favorite people, Patrice Wade Olson and Vijaykant Nadadur

Contents

Acknowledgments ix

A Brief Note on Language and Identity xi

Introduction: America's Prisons: A Portrait of the Vulnerable xiii

Chapter 1 "Crime" and Moral Panics 1

Chapter 2 Discretion and Punishment 23

Chapter 3 Punishing the Poor 36

Chapter 4 Punishing the Sick 56

Chapter 5 Punishing Race 69

Chapter 6 Punishing Immigrants 79

Chapter 7 Punishing Drug Use 95

Chapter 8 Punishing Families 108

Chapter 9 Instead of Prisons 121

Technical Appendix 135

References 143

Index 163

Acknowledgments

This book is the result of a long road that began at Jail North in Charlotte, North Carolina. The jail, located at 5235 Spector Drive, is where I underwent training as a detention officer and where I first interacted with inmates. It was my first experience with the criminal justice system, but not my last. I worked at Jail Central, an eight-story complex in Uptown Charlotte; I've been inside prisons and jails in Kentucky and Pennsylvania, but the journey really began at Jail North. Through movies and television, I was taught that jails and prisons were filled with violent predators and monsters. At Jail North, most of the inmates I interacted with were poor, young men. The most dangerous people I interacted with had mental illnesses that rendered communication difficult. For the most part, I felt that they were people in need of medical care and were not super predators. The jails in my hometown of Charlotte were full of vulnerable people, and I assumed that Charlotte couldn't be too different from the rest of the country.

Like many people who find themselves in jail, I sought my escape. Although I write this mostly in jest, two people enabled my escape from Jail North to academia. John Szmer and Martha Kropf represent many things to me. They are mentors, graduate assistant advisers, a source of income (they declared that my detention guard experience made me uniquely equipped to babysit their children), friends, and, most importantly, family. John and Martha encouraged me to go back to school and get my PhD. They have supported me emotionally and intellectually for over a decade. My debt to them cannot be expressed in words. I hope they enjoy this book and that they feel proud. I love them both, even if John argues too much.

Next, I need to thank those who have trained and guided me. I had the pleasure of studying under Richard Waterman, Richard Fording, Mark Peffley, and Nicolai Petrovsky at the University of Kentucky. Richard Fording was my first intellectual hero, and his work on incarceration made me think that a political scientist could study prisons. I am not sure if I can claim to be his intellectual offspring, because he is a much better writer than me, but I hope that this book makes a fraction of the impact that his work has. I would also like to thank Clayton Thyne, Stephen Voss, and Emily Beaulieu for helping to whip me into shape to be at least an adequate member of the professoriate.

I must also thank my editor, Jessica Gribble. The original idea behind this book was quite narrow, focused mostly on patterns of racial discrimination. Jessica helped me to move beyond race to a broader conception of vulnerability that is at the heart of this book. Jessica also engaged in some hand-holding as I began my first book (an admittedly terrifying prospect). My previous work has been published in academic journals, whose process seems to be submission, soul-crushing criticism, revise and resubmit, more soul-crushing criticism, and then publication, maybe. My experience with Jessica has been the polar opposite. Throughout the process, Jessica was warm, friendly, and understanding.

My family also helped me survive the book-writing process. My wife, Patrice Wade Olson, was encouraging, sometimes critical, and always helpful. She helped me tone down some language that my dissertation committee would have called "overly normative." She's the optimist to my pessimist, the organized to my chaos, the rock to my moral ambiguity. I'm not sure what I did before her, but I wasn't as happy. I also need to thank my brothers, some genetically related and others chosen: Josh, Jason, Michael, Zechariah, Vijaykant Nadadur, Tanner Talley, Hunter Driscoll. I must also thank my mother, Penelope; my nieces, Lydia and Sawyer; and my nephew, Reese. And, of course, I have to thank the newest family member, our beagle, Bogota.

Finally, many of my colleagues have helped me work through the issues related to this book. Four stand out as providing friendship and friendly arguments: Doug Anthony and Nina Kollars at Franklin and Marshall College, Andrea Malji at Hawai'i Pacific University, and Amelia Biehl at Florida Gulf Coast University. I have also greatly benefited from my colleagues at the University of Michigan, Flint. They will be listed alphabetically, because I do not yet have tenure! Special thanks to Dauda Abubakar, Kimberly Bender, Daniel Hummel, Peggy Kahn, Jason Kosnoski, Kenneth Litwin, Derwin Munroe, and Kimberly Saks McManaway. One last set of thank-yous, to Adam Lutzker for his mentorship, sense of humor, and NBA opinions, and to Suzanne Shivnen, who listens to me complain without complaint, even when I tell her stories about Patrice and our dog.

A Brief Note on Language and Identity

This book examines and explains prison punishment through a social construction lens. Social construction theory argues that knowledge is shared and that language can help shape reality. Indeed, much of public policy in the United States is decided in part by fights over framing and language. The word choices in this book are the author's and are a reflection of biases, both known and unknown. I have attempted to match the terminology of other scholars in the field and/or what seemed most professional.

This issue particularly affects the word choices related to race, immigration, and "crime." I use the terms "African American" and "Latino/a" throughout the book. Other scholars have used terms like "Hispanic" (potentially inappropriate because not all people from "Latin" America are of Spanish descent), "black," "Black," and, regrettably, "blacks." I recently reviewed work at a political science conference where a paper referred to discrimination against "the blacks." In cases where racial or homophobic slurs were used, I have chosen not to repeat the exact words. Instead of using slurs, I will either state that a slur was used or partially censor the word with an em dash (e.g., r— s— for "racial slur"). I recently had a student complain about the jarring effect of reading multiple racial slurs in Thomas Sugrue's classic *The Origins of the Urban Crisis*, which has made me more cognizant of the effects of reading multiple, repetitive racial slurs. I have also used "America" and "United States" interchangeably (sorry PK).

When discussing immigration detention, I use the term "undocumented immigrant" rather than more politically charged definitions. There are other politically charged terms that I do not use. Some scholars have referred to prison cells as "cages" and have referred to the criminal (in)justice system. I do not necessarily think those categorizations are incorrect, but I feel that both phrases are too charged and are a little distracting. Finally, I use "crime" and crime (with and without quotation marks) interchangeably. Crime is not an objective concept that societies or groups within societies can agree on. Crime is a social construction, perhaps the ultimate social construction. I do not want to give "crime" more weight than it deserves, but at the same time, continually using quotation marks around "crime" reduces readability (and leads to other issues; should I put quotation marks around "criminal justice" and "law enforcement"?, should I refer to "prisoners" or "inmates" or something else?).

Writing a book like this is difficult because I cannot completely capture the complexity of group and/or individual identities. Chapters in this book are organized thematically, with chapters on race, poverty, physical and mental illness, immigration status, and so on. By this, I do not mean to suggest that the categories are discrete and/or comprehensive. There is overlap between poverty and mental illness, between poverty and race, between immigration status and poverty, and so on. This book relies largely on quantitative data rather than ethnography, but that does not mean that I do not recognize the rich, complex, and interconnected nature of modern identities. There are also aspects that are important for prison punishment, including the personality of the correctional officers and the personality of inmates, which are difficult to conceive of, let alone measure. This book is an attempt to build on previous research and some of the more important features related to criminal justice punishment, but there will always be additional pieces to add to the puzzle.

The 32nd chapter of the *Tao Te Ching* illustrates our dilemma: "When you have names and forms, know that they are provisional" (Mitchell 1988, p. 32). I acknowledge that language is imprecise and provisional and that my word choices are, in part, a reflection of my personal biases. I am aware that language continues to change. I am aware that identities continue to change. It is up to the reader to decide whether the language and framing in this book is convincing. If it inspires some researchers to write more nuanced material or to include variables omitted here, so much the better.

Introduction

*America's Prisons: A Portrait of the Vulnerable**

> On the horizon are tens of thousands of severely morally impoverished juvenile super-predators. They are perfectly capable of committing the most heinous acts of physical violence for the most trivial reasons . . . they will do what comes "naturally": murder, rape, rob, assault, burglarize, deal deadly drugs, and get high.
>
> —John Dilulio Jr., November 27, 1995, "The Coming of the Super-Predators"

> They are not just gangs of kids anymore. They are often the kinds of kids that are called "superpredators." No conscience, no empathy. We can talk about why they ended up that way but first we have to bring them to heel.
>
> —Former Democratic presidential candidate Hillary Clinton, January 25, 1996

On February 24, 2016, a Black Lives Matter activist named Ashley Williams confronted presidential candidate Hillary Clinton about the above quote from 1996. Williams insisted that Clinton owed an apology for mass incarceration. Williams declared, "I'm not a 'superpredator,' Hillary Clinton. Can you apologize to black people for mass incarceration?" Mrs. Clinton replied that no one had asked her that question before (Scott 2016). After receiving that nonanswer, Williams was led away. A month and a half later, on April 7, 2016, former president Bill Clinton publicly expressed his

* For additional information, including original content and an analysis of the 2016 Bureau of Justice Statistics Survey of Inmates data set (due out in 2019), please visit www.punishingthevulnerable.com.

feelings about the Ashley Williams incident. Defending his wife, he stated, "I don't know how you would describe the gang leaders who got thirteen-year-olds hopped up on crack and sent them out in the streets to murder other African American children! Maybe you thought they were good citizens. [Hillary] didn't. You are defending the people who kill the lives you say matter" (Robinson 2016).

While the rhetoric of the Clintons has not aged well, the negative portrayal and fear of prisoners has not ended. President Donald Trump complained of "burning and crime-infested inner cities" and infamously equated Mexican immigrants with rapists and drug dealers (Feldscher 2017; Phillips 2017), while in his 2006 book, *The Audacity of Hope*, future president Barack Obama talked about the need for punishment "when a gangbanger shoots indiscriminately into a crowd" (p. 215). Popular conceptions of crime and prison are not any better. News media focus on rare, heinous events, while popular television shows emphasize violence, drug dealing, and often sexually transgressive narratives. Quotes from political officials combine with narratives from shows like *Criminal Minds*, *Law and Order*, *Breaking Bad*, and *Lockup: Raw* to create a sense of fear in the population. These quotes and shows are misleading, emphasizing violence and extreme events rather than the common, low-level infractions that land most inmates in prison.

This book offers a counternarrative to that framing. Rather than holding a vast array of amoral master criminals, prisons in the United States are filled with the poor, the less educated, the physically and mentally ill, immigrants, the marginalized, and racial minorities. Prisoners in the United States are, in a word, vulnerable. The vulnerable fill American prisons, and the vulnerable are further harmed by treatment inside prisons. Families are broken up as inmates are sent hundreds of miles away from their hometowns, mental illness and substance abuse issues are exacerbated and sometimes created by harsh conditions, rehabilitative programs range from inadequate to nonexistent, and prison punishment, including solitary confinement, strips the incarcerated of their dignity, rights, and, in some cases, their sanity. Prisons in the United States of America are not filled with "super predators"; American prisons are filled with the vulnerable.

Who are the vulnerable? Dictionary definitions of "vulnerable" include being easily hurt, influenced, or attacked; being capable of being physically or emotionally wounded; and being open to attack or damage. The vulnerable are easier to send to prison because of their disadvantages, and the vulnerable are more likely to be poorly treated in prison because of those same disadvantages. Kimberle Crenshaw (1989) writes of those who are "multiply burdened," those who have multiple disadvantages and often face multiple forms of discrimination. Most inmates in the United States are multiply burdened; they often come from impoverished backgrounds *and* are poorly educated *and* have a physical or mental limitation *and* are members of a marginalized racial or ethnic group. These individuals can face significant cumulative disadvantages that leave them open to attack from the state, both inside and outside of prison.

My use of the term "vulnerable" is largely in line with public health conceptions of vulnerability. Public health scholars argue that the vulnerable are those who are exposed to disproportionate burdens or risks (Aday 1994; Chang et al. 2004; Frohlich and Potvin 2008; Mechanic and Tanner 2007; Osgood, Foster, and Courtney 2010; Wilson and Neville 2009). Individuals are vulnerable for a variety of personal, psychological, geographic, and economic characteristics. Vulnerability may take the form of a mental illness, poverty, a lack of strong familial ties, historical discrimination, contemporary discrimination, and/or personal characteristics. The various risk factors are often interconnected and correlated with each other, leading to multiple burdens or multiple disadvantages.

Lu Ann Aday (1994) discusses group identities that, on average, are correlated with vulnerability. White Americans are generally less vulnerable than African Americans, Latino/as, Native Americans, and Asian Americans; married individuals are generally less vulnerable than single individuals; those with strong social ties are less vulnerable than those with weak ties; those with a high school education are less vulnerable than those with less than a high school education; the middle and upper classes are less vulnerable than the poor; those in white-collar jobs are less vulnerable than the unemployed or blue-collar workers; and those with adequate housing are less vulnerable than those with inadequate housing. In the context of American prisons, we can add that the mentally healthy are less vulnerable than the mentally ill, U.S. citizens are less vulnerable than noncitizens, and people who don't use drugs are less vulnerable than drug users.

Some of these identities are likely more important in a prison context than others. Based on previous scholarship and my own experience in detention/correctional settings, race, poverty, immigration status, and mental health may be the most critical factors. This is not to say that vulnerabilities determine treatment. Some inmates may have certain vulnerable characteristics and escape punishment, while other inmates may have relatively privileged identities and be subjected to punishment. However, on average, we would expect the vulnerable to face worse treatment in prison. Indeed, that is the case, both in this book and in the broader literature on criminal justice policy. What is especially critical to keep in mind is that none of these vulnerabilities are related to the specific crime that the inmate was convicted of. These vulnerabilities remain even after taking into account the inmate's criminal history. The hand of the state is certainly heavy, but it does not fall on every group equally.

Societies must determine what to do with the most vulnerable members of their populations. What can be done with the poor, the less educated, those with mental illnesses, those who are marginalized and live at the edge of society's boundaries? Two broad options are available: managing vulnerable populations through the provision of government services and managing vulnerable populations through punishment. A country can provide a thick safety net, with generous welfare benefits and programs for those in need. The poor can receive assistance; the homeless, housing; the mentally ill, treatment. Or a country can use police and prisons to disrupt marginalized groups. Arrest the poor, incarcerate the mentally ill, and put the difficult, most vulnerable members of society behind bars. The United States has tried both options, generosity and punishment; indeed, we still try both. However, the past decades have seen the former in decline and the latter in ascendance. Our focus on punishment has led the United States to become the world's premier prison state. Along the way, criminal justice policies have served to make the lives of the vulnerable more precarious and unsafe.

The reach of the American prison system is tremendous. The U.S. prison population is the largest in the world in absolute numbers and is second in terms of incarceration rates (Walmsley 2016). At the end of 2014, 2.3 million people were held in America's jails and prisons, and 6.9 million people are currently under some form of correctional supervision, including probation and parole (Kaeble et al. 2015). If the total correctional population were a city, it would be the fifth-largest city in the United States, slightly larger than the population of Houston, Texas. It would be the 50th-largest city in the world, with a larger population than Toronto, Baghdad, Madrid, or Singapore (World Atlas 2017). More people are locked up in American federal and state prisons than live in Philadelphia, Detroit, Charlotte, or San Diego. There are more people living in solitary confinement (approximately 100,000 inmates) than there are people living in my hometown of Concord, North Carolina, or my place of employment, Flint, Michigan.

The American prison state is incredibly expensive. State spending on corrections in 2011 was estimated at $51 billion, representing about 3 percent of total expenditures (National Association of State Budget Officers 2011). Another $8.5 billion is spent annually by the Federal Bureau of Prisons (U.S. Department of Justice 2006). The Vera Institute of Justice (2017) estimates that local jails spend a further $22.2 billion. It takes a little over 12 years for the United States to spend $1 trillion on incarcerating the vulnerable. The opportunity costs of mass imprisonment are rarely noted. The $81.7 billion we spend on prisons and jails could instead pay for an additional 1.5 million elementary schoolteachers or to nearly quintuple the federal government block grant program Temporary Assistance to Needy Families, which provides assistance to poor families. Our fixation on punishment has crowded out opportunities for rehabilitation, education, and other programming.

Mass incarceration has resulted in American correctional departments becoming one of the country's largest bureaucracies. Over 750,000 people are employed in state correctional departments, working at 1,721 different prisons (Stephan 2008). There are an additional 3,200 local and county jails. In fact, there are more prisons and jails in the United States than there are colleges (Ingraham 2015). There is a great deal of variation across prisons, including differences in security levels, financial resources, educational programming, health care opportunities, and punishment options. Equally important, there is variation within prisons, with some inmates facing harsher conditions than others, even within the same facility. "Doing time" is not a uniform experience, even for inmates in the same prison (Lerman 2014). Just as everyone is not equally likely to be placed in prison, inmates vary in their likelihood of being punished while incarcerated.

This introduction focuses on a profile of American prisons and prisoners. Far from being the "super predators" maligned by politicians of both major political parties, most prisoners are drawn from the weakest, most isolated, most disadvantaged areas of society. We take the vulnerable, punish them severely, and then blame them for any failures. After decades of blaming "criminals" and "super predators," it is my hope that we can examine our own culpability. That examination must begin with better knowledge of the realities of modern American prisons.

American Prisons

For nearly six decades, criminal justice policy in the United States has undergone a dramatic transformation, reflecting a shift in the values and assumptions guiding the treatment of "crime" and "criminals." The United States has shifted from a system focused on rehabilitation to a system focused on punishment, from a system that viewed crime as primarily society's failure to a system that views crime as an individual failure. This change has enjoyed bipartisan support from presidents such as Lyndon Johnson, Ronald Reagan, and Bill Clinton (Alexander 2010; Hinton 2016; Simon 2007; Western 2006). The placement of millions of vulnerable Americans behind bars, and their subsequent harsh treatment inside prison, is a direct consequence of this switch from rehabilitation to punishment.

The most obvious manifestation of the switch to a more punitive model has been the historic increase in the imprisonment rate. The mainstream narrative has argued that the historic increase in incarceration is based on a corresponding increase in crime. Presidents Johnson, Nixon, Reagan, and Clinton all warned of increasing crime and the dangers of lawlessness (Alexander 2010; Hinton 2016; Simon 2007; Western 2006). Sometimes the dangers were posed by "rioters" and sometimes by the "crack epidemic," but the drumbeat against crime was unrelenting. Unfortunately for the vulnerable, this narrative, rather than more objective information, has dominated criminal justice policy.

Scholars will often reproduce graphs of both incarceration and crime rates. The graphs are somewhat well known, and the lines on the graphs do not perfectly match. Although the violent and property crime rates fluctuate and have followed a downward trajectory since the 1990s, the incarceration rate increases dramatically; it doubled between 1960 and 1980 and then doubled again by 1991. The incarceration rate in 2012 was 70 percent higher than in 1991. In a little over 50 years, the American prison population grew by 600 percent. The massive increase in the incarceration rate is a historical phenomenon and one that seemed unlikely prior to the 1970s. From 1925 until the early 1970s, the U.S. prison population stood at or below 200,000 inmates. Today, the solitary confinement population alone is at 100,000 inmates.

Despite the fact that imprisonment rates have increased in all 50 states since 1960, there has been significant variation in that growth and the extent to which states have embraced the crime control model. As a result, a large literature has emerged that aims to explain variation in state imprisonment rates. Contrary to conventional wisdom, these studies have consistently concluded that the use of imprisonment is not solely determined by the level of crime. Indeed, several studies have found that crime rates are only weakly related to imprisonment rates, if they are related at all (Jacobs and Jackson 2010; Wacquant 2009; Western 2006). Rather, these studies conclude that variations in state imprisonment rates are largely explained by the social and political context in a state. More specifically, state imprisonment rates are highest in states with high levels of racial diversity (especially large African American populations) and in ideologically conservative states where the state Republican Party has had significant influence on state policy making (e.g., Jacobs and Helms 1996; Jacobs and Carmichael 2001; Smith 2004; Stucky, Heimer, and Lang 2005; Yates and Fording 2005). Incarceration is not simply a response to crime; incarceration is a political response largely divorced from objective measurements of crime.

The implementation and enforcement of criminal laws is based in part on which groups are suspected of committing crime, not simply an objective reading of events. Equivalent behavior can result in selective enforcement. Between 1880 and 1929, there were at least 15 major riots in which white city residents tried to remove Chinese or African American residents, the most famous example being the Tulsa race riot. Smaller riots with similar motivations took place in at least 30 small towns. Those riots did not lead to criminal charges or a negative stereotype that white Americans are lawless rioters. Race riots *against* African Americans have been interpreted differently than rioting *by* African Americans. Similarly, concerns about drug use tend to be associated with racial minorities and/or the poor. One can compare the hysteria over crack cocaine and methamphetamine use with the more compassionate narratives surrounding "opioid addiction." It is not to say that drug use or rioting are not problematic but rather that rioting or drug use by certain groups is considered more threatening than rioting or drug use by other groups.

Mass incarceration is a historical phenomenon; for the first 200 years of U.S. history, prisons were rarely used. Mass incarceration is also a geographically limited phenomenon; most countries in the world incarcerate far fewer people at a much lower rate. The level of incarceration in the United States is unparalleled in the modern world. (Incarceration rates are technically highest in the Seychelles, a group of islands in the Indian Ocean off the coast of east Africa. The population of the Seychelles is 92,900. Between 2008 and 2012, the incarceration rate of the Seychelles doubled, from 297 prisoners to 628 prisoners. It is possible that the massive growth in the Seychelles incarceration rate is a random historical blip. Data on the Seychelles is often omitted by other scholars, but I have included it.) Our high levels of imprisonment are sometimes taken for granted as an inevitable consequence of modern society. However, the United States is an outlier in its use of imprisonment. There is nothing normal about mass incarceration when viewed from a historical or geographic perspective. Table I.1 presents the incarceration rate for select countries (Walmsley 2016).

In terms of incarceration rates, the United States has strange bedfellows. While the United States is a wealthy democracy, our incarceration rate is

Table I.1 Select countries' incarceration rate

Country	People Incarcerated per 100,000
Canada	115
China	118
United Kingdom	143
Mexico	169
Average	175
Russian Federation	419
Rwanda	434
Guam (USA)	438
Thailand	476
Cuba	510
Virgin Islands (USA)	542
Turkmenistan	583
El Salvador	598
United States of America	666
Seychelles	738

similar to countries with autocratic governments, such as Turkmenistan, Cuba, Russia, and El Salvador. Our incarceration rate is over three times the world average and is much higher than for American allies and fellow democracies, such as the United Kingdom and Canada. The high level of incarceration in the United States begs several questions: Is crime really a bigger problem in the United States than in El Salvador or Turkmenistan? Is the United States really more dangerous than Rwanda or Russia? Are American criminals really six times as threatening as Canadian criminals? Compared to similar countries, the United States' carceral binge makes it an outlier.

As previous research has shown, the mainstream explanation that mass incarceration is based on crime rates is flawed. Crime rates are not strictly predictive of incarceration rates. There have been periods of American history with low incarceration rates and relatively high levels of crime, such as the outburst of organized crime and violence related to alcohol prohibition in the 1920s, and there have been periods of high incarceration rates and low crime, such as the 1990s. The United States is not faced with the extreme levels of violence of places like Mexico and El Salvador. Most of the people in prison in the United States are there for relatively minor offenses. Vulnerability is a better predictor of imprisonment than objective threat. Once incarcerated, vulnerability is a strong predictor of punishment inside prison as well.

According to the Bureau of Justice Statistics, in 2015, 53 percent of state inmates were incarcerated for a violent offence, 19 percent for a property crime offense, 16 percent for a drug offense, and about 12 percent for a public order offense. In federal prisons, nearly half of all inmates (49.5 percent) are in for drug offenses, 7 percent for violent crime, 6 percent for property crime, and 36 percent for public order offenses. Table I.2 has a detailed breakdown of the offenses inmates are imprisoned for at the state and federal levels.

Far from being the super predators painted by DiIulio and American politicians, the majority of inmates at the combined federal and state levels are not in prison for a violent offense. Fifty-three percent of state prison inmates are incarcerated for a violent offense, while 7 percent of federal inmates are serving time for violence. Nearly 800,000 (792,188) individuals are locked up for a nonviolent offense. A minority of state prison inmates are incarcerated for the more serious charges of murder and rape/sexual assault. At the state and federal levels, out of a total prison population of 1.5 million inmates, over 1.3 million people are serving a sentence for a crime other than murder. When it comes to the most serious crime, the United States subjects murderers to much longer sentences than do most other countries in the world.

The United States has more than 41,000 people serving a life-without-parole sentence, compared to 59 people in Australia, 41 in England, and 37

Table I.2 Prisoners by offense type (2015)

Type of Crime	State	Federal
Violent	52.9	7.4
Murder	13	1.5
Manslaughter	1.3	
Rape/sexual assault	12.4	
Robbery	12.8	3.7
Aggravated/simple assault	10.2	
Other	3.2	2.1
Property	19	6
Burglary	10.1	0.2
Larceny theft	3.6	
Motor vehicle theft	0.8	
Fraud	2.3	4.7
Other	1.1	1.1
Drug	15.7	49.5
Drug possession	3.5	
Other	12.2	
Public Order	11.6	36.3
Weapons	3.9	16.3
Driving under the influence	2.1	
Other	5.6	12
Immigration		8

in the Netherlands. Most countries in Latin America do not have a life-without-parole sentence, and Mexico will not extradite defendants who face such sentences. Western Europeans regard a sentence of 10 or 12 years as extremely long (and the United States, in previous decades, felt similarly; 50 years ago in Louisiana, inmates with a life sentence were eligible for release after 10.5 years). Punishment in the United States is out of step with most of the world (Segura 2012). A large percentage of those with life sentences in American prisons would be released if they were in another country. Many of those convicted of even the most heinous crimes may be able to reintegrate into society. Many inmates who were convicted of murder suffered from a substance abuse addiction and/or a mental health issue. It is difficult to recommend leniency on people convicted of murder, but it is worth keeping in mind that it is more difficult to recommend in an American context than in a Western European or Latin American context.

Common wisdom suggests that prisons hold convicted criminals, and thus prisons have a negative impact on crime. However, the vast majority of crimes go unreported, and a majority of those crimes that are reported go unsolved. Forty-six percent of violent crimes are reported, and 35 percent of property crimes are reported. Forty-six percent of violent crime cases lead to an arrest, while 20 percent of property crime cases lead to an arrest (Gramlich 2017). RAINN (2017), an advocacy association for victims of sexual assault, estimates that out of 1,000 robberies, 619 are reported to police, 167 lead to an arrest, 37 get referred to prosecutors, 22 lead to a felony conviction, and 20 lead to prison sentences. For assault and battery, out of 1,000 cases, 627 are reported to police, 255 lead to an arrest, 105 are referred to prosecutors, 41 lead to a conviction, and 33 lead to a prison term. For rape, out of 1,000 cases, 310 are reported to police, 57 lead to arrest, 11 get referred to prosecutors, 7 lead to a felony conviction, and 6 lead to a prison term. This effectively means that perpetrators of nonmurder violent crime have a 0.6 to 4.4 percent chance of serving a prison sentence (RAINN 2017).

Even if we only consider the most serious violent crime—murder—large numbers of murders go unsolved. The homicide clearance rate, the percentage of solved crimes that lead to arrest, is 64 percent. Which, of course, means that 36 percent of murders do not lead to an arrest. Since 1980, more than 211,000 homicides have gone unsolved (*Economist* 2015a). According to the Bureau of Justice Statistics, 70 percent of murder arrests lead to a conviction (Reaves 2013). Since only 64 percent of murders lead to arrest, and 70 percent of those arrests lead to conviction, less than half of murders (45 percent) lead to a prison sentence. In some cities, the clearance rate is much lower. Chicago police solve about 30 percent of the city's homicides (Heinzmann 2016), while the clearance rate in New Orleans is 22 percent (Daley 2017).

Statistically speaking, many crimes go unsolved, up to and including murder. Popular crime novels and television shows imply that police spend most of their time investigating crimes and that those investigations are mostly successful. While there are specialized detective units for major crimes in many police agencies, rank-and-file police officers do not spend the majority of their time solving crimes. Police spend most of their time on patrols, filling out paperwork, and responding to radio calls. "Stop and frisk" tactics and car-based patrols are more common than dedicated crime solving. Indeed, solving crimes is not the primary purpose of police forces. Scholars such as Didier Fassin have argued that the job of policing is to enforce social order, not to solve crimes (Fassin 2013).

Most crimes go unsolved, and therefore only a small percentage of criminal activity results in a prison sentence. I argue that what distinguishes those who are incarcerated from those who are not is largely a difference in vulnerability. American prisoners tend to be poorer, less educated, more marginalized, and subject to severe disadvantages like mental illness, substance abuse, and lack of citizenship. Once incarcerated, the vulnerable are punished a second time. This book seeks to highlight two important facts: first, that the vulnerable are disproportionately sent to prison, and second, while in prison, the vulnerable are disproportionately punished.

Russian novelist Fyodor Dostoyevsky, himself a former prisoner in imperial Russia, is quoted as saying, "The degree of civilization in a society can be judged by entering its prisons" (Shapiro 2006). Jesus of Nazareth, perhaps the world's most famous victim of capital punishment, was also deeply concerned about prisoners. The New International Version translation of Matthew 25:35–40 reads,

> For I was hungry and you gave me something to eat, I was thirsty and you gave me something to drink, I was a stranger and you invited me in, I was in prison and you came to visit me. Then the righteous will answer him "Lord, when did we see you hungry and feed you, or thirsty and give you something to drink? When did we see you a stranger and invite you in, or needing clothes and clothe you? When did we see you sick or in prison and go to visit you?" The King will reply, "Truly I tell you, whatever you did for one of the least of these brothers and sisters of mine, you did for me."

This book tries to rely more on empirical evidence than on moral pleadings. Indeed, one principal argument of this book is that morality is socially constructed and varies geographically and temporally. Yet the "least of these" quote has stuck with me from a young age. I believe that the way a government treats its most vulnerable citizens is crucial to understanding a society. Concern about the conditions of prisons and of prisoners go back thousands of years and across multiple continents.

How do we treat the "least of these"? How do we treat the vulnerable? This book is about that treatment. It tries to conceptualize prisoners as a vulnerable population in need of help rather than as dangerous predators or amoral villains. The vulnerable end up in prison because they are politically weak and are viewed negatively by society. The vulnerable are punished in prison because prisons are overcrowded and prison guards rely on stereotypes and heuristics when deciding who to punish. Our prison population exploded at a specific place and time and was caused by political, psychological, and cultural conditions. This book wrestles with some of the causes and effects of mass incarceration.

Plan of the Book

If incarceration isn't a simple response to crime, why do we send certain people to prisons? I argue that crime is socially constructed and varies both geographically and temporarily. This can be clearly seen in the evolution of crime and prisons in the United States: from concerns about religious crimes to concerns about managing African American and immigrant populations to modern concerns about drug use. When fear of crime is focused on certain groups or behaviors, societies often engage in "moral panics." These moral panics, divorced from objective statistics, cause societies to severely punish vulnerable groups. Chapter 1, "'Crime' and Moral Panics," focuses on both the social construction of crime and on moral panics.

Much of the decision-making authority for determining who is arrested and who is punished in prison rests in the hands of police and prison guards. Chapter 2, "Discretion and Punishment," discusses the discretionary authority of both police and prison guards. Building on psychological theories of implicit bias and heuristics in decision making, I argue that prison guards do not treat prisoners as individuals but rather as representatives of groups. Although this form of decision making is driven more by convenience and ease than explicit animus, it is extremely susceptible to cognitive biases. The chapter includes original interviews with prison guards and their responses to questions about interacting with inmates. After discussing the biases and heuristics that police and prison guards use, the remainder of the book provides evidence of discrimination against vulnerable groups.

Perhaps the most significant form of vulnerability that leads to incarceration is poverty. Extreme poverty is a common disadvantage that American prison inmates face. Chapter 3, "Punishing the Poor," focuses on punishment of the economically disadvantaged. Although only 1–2 percent of the American population is homeless, the homeless make up 15 percent of the U.S. jail population. Homeless inmates are more likely to have previous involvement with the criminal justice system, to have a substance abuse and/or mental health issue, to be less educated, and to be unemployed. Incarceration and homelessness appear to increase the risk of one another (Greenberg and Rosenheck 2008).

Many of those inmates who have not suffered from homelessness nevertheless face difficult economic challenges. Loic Wacquant (2009) found that two-thirds of detainees lived on a household income of less than $1,000 a month, and 45 percent had household incomes of less than $600 a month. Lower-income individuals are more likely to end up in prison. Individuals who are incarcerated made significantly less than comparable groups prior to being placed in prison. On release from prison, wages are further depressed (Western 2006). Contrary to popular opinion, most inmates were working legal jobs prior to their incarceration (Wacquant 2009; Western 2006). The working poor are more vulnerable to incarceration because they cannot afford quality legal defense and their lack of political power makes them easier to punish. Using multiple measures of economic disadvantage, I find that poor inmates receive worse treatment in prison.

Issues of poverty often intersect with issues of poor health. American prison inmates are in worse physical and mental health than the general population. Chapter 4, "Punishing the Sick," discusses punishment of those with physical and mental illnesses. Mental health and substance abuse issues are a common experience for many American prison inmates. The Bureau of Justice Statistics reports that more than half of all prison and jail inmates have a mental health problem. In 2005, this included 705,600 inmates in state prisons, 78,800 in federal facilities, and 479,900 in local jails. This represents 56 percent of state prisoners, 45 percent of federal prisoners, and 64 percent of jail inmates (James and Glaze 2006). There is a large treatment gap in receiving mental health services. Only a third of state prisoners, a fourth of federal prisoners, and less than an eighth of local jail inmates with a mental illness were treated since their admission to prison. Inmates also struggle with substance abuse problems. Sixty-six percent of state prison inmates and 74 percent of mentally ill state prison inmates had an issue with substance abuse or dependence. The vulnerability is so great, in fact, that only 19 percent of state prison inmates do not have a substance abuse or mental health issue (James and Glaze 2006). Eighty-one percent of inmates face formidable mental health and substance abuse challenges. These inmates are more likely to be punished inside prison than are their healthier counterparts.

Female inmates are especially vulnerable to physical and mental illnesses. Many prisoners, but especially female inmates, face horrific levels of violence in their home environments. The Bureau of Justice Statistics estimates that 1.5 million women in the United States are victims of domestic violence every year, while the Department of Justice estimates 5.3 million instances of domestic violence occur annually. Sixty-eight percent of incarcerated African American women report having experienced domestic violence, and 36 percent report sexual abuse (Richie 2012). Violent victimization continues while in prison. It is common for women to complain about guards groping them during "pat down" searches, inserting objects during a "cavity search," or taunting them in sexually explicit terms while they are bathing or dressing.

A 1996 Human Rights Watch survey found that at least half of all female prisoners have experienced some form of sexual abuse prior to incarceration and that 60 percent of women in state prisons were physically or sexually abused in the past. Women have filed charges against prison guards in 41 percent of state and federal prisons (Richie 2012). Rather than being seen as in need of special help, these inmates are singled out for punishment. In many cases, when it is discovered that a prisoner has been sexually victimized by prison staff, the inmate is placed in solitary confinement while the prison staff are unpunished.

Imagine how we would view prisons if middle-class and upper-class white women were regularly sexually assaulted by prison guards. Race and punishment are closely tied in U.S. criminal justice policy. Chapter 5, "Punishing Race," discusses racial discrimination in American prisons. The fact that African American, Native American, and Latino/a individuals are disproportionately incarcerated has slowly reached mainstream consciousness. Significant critical scholarship has established the various forms of racial prejudice in the American criminal justice process. This book extends that scholarship and examines treatment decisions inside prisons. African American, Native American, and Latino/a individuals are not only disproportionately sent to prison but also disproportionately punished while inside prison.

The net of incarceration has widened, and it falls heavily on new residents in the United States. Chapter 6, "Punishing Immigrants," focuses on the discrimination faced by migrant communities. Immigrants, and specifically vulnerable immigrants, are targeted and punished in American prisons. Immigration detainees are the fastest-growing segment of the prison population (Kubrin, Zatz, and Martinez 2012). Immigration officers target migrants from certain countries (Haiti, Mexico) or who practice certain religions (Islam). Immigrants complain of being humiliated, harassed, physically abused, and placed in solitary confinement for minor offenses (Dow 2004). Immigration scholars argue that punitive laws rather than security threats have driven the rise in immigration detention (Macias-Rojas 2016). Jails and prisons can also make money off immigrants through daily rate reimbursements from the federal government.

Another well-known vulnerability is related to drug use. U.S. criminal justice policy has punished some forms of drug use and some drug users more than others. Most infamously, cannabis is illegal, while objectively more harmful drugs such as alcohol and tobacco are legal. In some states, medical cannabis programs allow the middle and upper classes access to legal cannabis, while poor users are still targeted for arrest and incarceration. Drug use among the wealthy and politically powerful is largely ignored, while drug use by the poor is subject to draconian enforcement. In addition, those with the most serious drug addictions and dependencies are sent to prison, while more casual users are able to escape incarceration. This differential enforcement dates back to at least the law enforcement efforts during the prohibition of alcohol in the 1920s. Chapter 7, "Punishing Drug Use," discusses the negative treatment of drug users in American prisons.

Chapter 8, "Punishing Families," considers the collateral damage of American prisons—the horrific impact that incarceration has on American families. Eight million children are affected by parental incarceration. Families are devastated by incarceration as parents are separated from their children and the pains of incarceration lead spouses to divorce. Many parents lose their custody rights because of incarceration. Prisons make it difficult for parents to maintain contact with their children due to expensive phone calls, unfriendly and sometimes hostile visitation environments, and sheer distance from many population centers. Despite official government rhetoric prioritizing families, prison actively destroys familial bonds.

The book concludes with a discussion of the urgent need to reform American prisons. While each substantive chapter ends with suggestions for reform, chapter 9 summarizes and expands on those earlier suggestions. Reforms include the reclassification of most criminal laws, an end to cash bail and monetary sanctions, alternative placements for inmates with mental health and/or substance abuse issues, the legalization or decriminalization of drugs, improvements in access for inmates' families, and massive decarceration. Although any policy change may have negative consequences, some of which are unintended, there can be no doubt that the American prison system as currently constructed is seriously flawed.

Incarceration affects millions of prisoners and their loved ones. The burdens of incarceration and punishment do not fall evenly; they fall disproportionately on the poor, the sick, racial minorities, immigrants, and other marginalized groups. The American prison system does not simply punish crime; it punishes the vulnerable.

CHAPTER ONE

"Crime" and Moral Panics

I often ask my students to tell me what a crime is. The students are usually incredulous that I would ask such a seemingly obvious question. Sometimes they suggest that a crime is something that is illegal or immoral. However, after discussing that thought as a class, we usually agree that there are many behaviors that are illegal, such as speeding or fishing without a license, that are not immoral. There are also behaviors that seem immoral, like lying, hateful speech, and adultery, that are in most cases legal. Even if morality and legality were synonymous, we would be left with the problem of laws changing dramatically over time. Why would, for example, slavery be legal in one era and not in another?

Next, I will ask my students to tell me what murder is. At this point, the students are generally annoyed. Everyone knows what murder is! It's when one person kills another person! Unfortunately, this neat conceptualization falls apart quickly. In some cases, especially during times of war, killing another person is not only legal and moral but also virtuous. Former Navy Seal sniper Chris Kyle had 160 confirmed kills during the Iraq War. Some people considered Kyle a hero, and before his death, Kyle's exploits were the subject of a best-selling book and movie. After his death, supporters immortalized Kyle with a statue (McCoy 2014). Others see the Iraq War as a largely immoral fight.

Instead of limiting himself to the 160 kills credited by the military, Kyle claimed to have killed 255 people in Iraq, an additional 30 "looters" during Hurricane Katrina, and 2 men who attempted to rob him in Texas. The looting and robbery stories are unsubstantiated (McCoy 2014). In his book, *American Sniper*, Kyle wrote, "People ask me all the time, 'how many people have you killed?' My standard response is 'Does the answer make me less, or more, of a man? The number is not important to me. I only wished I had killed more'" (McCoy 2014). The movie adaptation of Kyle's book, *American*

Sniper, was the top grossing film of 2014 and has made over $500 million (Zeitchik 2015).

Was Chris Kyle's behavior heroic? The number of deaths may be disputed, but the fact that Kyle killed over 100 people is not. If you believe that every killing was justified, Kyle's actions were heroic. There are even some people who would justify his alleged killing of "looters" during Hurricane Katrina or of the attempted thieves in Texas. However, one can imagine other perspectives. Kyle's supporters built a statue to honor the man after his death. An Iraqi who had a family member killed by Kyle is unlikely to build a similar statue. While some people may view Chris Kyle as a hero, there are likely others who would not want to associate with someone who said, "I only wished I had killed more."

While the case of Chris Kyle is extreme, differing views on violence are common. One study found that 35 percent of parents in the United States practice corporal punishment on infants, over half of parents hit children at age 12, a third at age 14, and 13 percent at age 17. Twenty-eight percent of children between the age of 5 and 12 are hit with a belt or paddle (Straus and Stewart 1999). There is widespread disagreement on the appropriateness of corporal punishment for children. Support or disapproval for corporal punishment varies by race, socioeconomic status, and religious belief (Flynn 1996). We cannot agree, as a society, as to the appropriateness of hitting a child with a belt, paddle, or "switch."

A switch is a stick. It is common practice in some parts of the country to force a child to go into a yard and pick out the stick that he or she will then be beaten with. Proponents of the practice will point to Proverbs 13:24, which states, "Whoever spares the rod hates their children, but the one who loves their children is careful to discipline them." In 2014, National Football League running back Adrian Peterson was suspended for hitting his four-year-old with a switch, causing "visible swelling, marks and cuts" on the child's ankles, limbs, back, buttocks, and genitals (O'Connor 2014). There is still debate on the validity of corporal punishment of children. For his part, after a suspension from the National Football League, Adrian Peterson himself said, "I won't ever use a switch again. There's different situations where a child needs to be disciplined as far as timeout, taking their toys away, making them take a nap. There's so many different ways to discipline your kids" (Pelissero 2014).

There is not an objective measure to determine whether or not a specific form of violence is acceptable. Hitting a child is unacceptable, unless it is a form of discipline that will improve the child's moral character. Punching, choking, and wrestling another adult is unacceptable, unless it is in a professional fight, in which case Americans will spend millions of dollars to watch the spectacle. Killing another human is illegal, sometimes. Killing another human is heroic, sometimes. Causing someone's death by selling a dangerous product, such as cigarettes or alcohol, is legal and morally acceptable. Killing someone in the course of one's job, such as a soldier or a police officer, rarely leads to legal ramifications. The water crisis in the city of Flint, Michigan, where I work, likely caused at least 12 deaths due to a Legionnaires' disease outbreak. This is in addition to the significant long-term health problems associated with lead poisoning during the water crisis (Ganim 2017). Would we be justified in labeling the Legionnaires' disease outbreak as murder?

There is no objective, universal standard of harm. Killing someone through the consumption of a product, such as cigarettes or alcohol, is generally not considered murder. Causing someone's death through neglect is rarely punished. Politicians are rarely held accountable for a lack of generosity toward the poor, which causes premature deaths. For some pro-life people, killing a fetus is murder. For some pro-choice people, a fetus is not fully equal to a human life. Both groups fight over language; some refer to a "fetus," while others refer to an "unborn child" or an "unborn baby." The pro-life and pro-choice communities are also divided on when and under what conditions or motivations a pregnancy can morally be ended.

Other forms of killing are generally accepted. For the vast majority of Americans, eating meat is taken for granted as a relatively ethical decision. For others, killing an animal is murder. Some people argue that hunting is immoral while factory farming is acceptable, while their opponents argue the opposite. There are vegans who wear leather shoes and belts. Even in cases that are not related to the consumption of animals, we end up inadvertently killing animals. Free ranging domestic cats kill between 1 and 4 billion birds and between 6 and 22 billion mammals annually (Loss, Will, and Mara 2013). Building houses or businesses destroys the habitats needed by nonhuman animals. Presumably, few people have cats or buy houses so that nonhuman animals will be killed. However, even if the death is inadvertent, a life is still lost.

We can also think about the opportunity costs inherent in our decision making; for example, I have spent hundreds of dollars on products for my dog, money that I could have used to buy meals for a homeless person. I left a job working directly with inmates; I probably would have been most helpful to inmates if I had stayed as a detention officer. Treating an inmate with respect may have a more measureable positive effect than this book will. In some ways, the opportunity costs point out how easy it is to punish the vulnerable. I could give money to people suffering from severe poverty, but those people don't live in my neighborhood, and it's more fun to buy something for my dog. My dog's life matters more to me than the lives of the chickens that died in part to be ground up into dog food. My dog seems to be more important to me than panhandlers in Flint or Pontiac, judging by my generosity. It is much easier to focus on those around me than to think about people who may need help. Through my spending, I suggest which lives matter more or less to me.

Rhetoric over which lives matter has spawned movements and countermovements related to police brutality. (Of course, the use of the phrase "police brutality" has its own normative underpinnings.) Supporters of policing reform have decried the deaths of mostly young, mostly unarmed African American and Latino men, while their opponents have emphasized the sometimes dangerous nature of modern policing. Whether police homicides are a necessary response to a dangerous society or an unjust example of systematic discrimination is in some ways a political question. We tend to let our political beliefs determine our interpretation of facts rather than let objective facts determine our political beliefs (Kahneman 2011). It is difficult to know what is moral in a world where the difference between a homicide and a justified shooting is in part a political question.

Sometimes students will point to the Bible or to a text like the Ten Commandments. They will argue that morality is determined by religion and that laws should be determined by religion. Of course, the Bible, like many religious texts, condones practices that are anathema to modern American society. The Bible sanctions slavery, polygamous marriage, the inferior status of women, and the death penalty for many infractions that we would not recognize as worthy of capital punishment today. The Ten Commandments implore us not to covet; comedian George Carlin famously declared that coveting is what keeps the economy going. The Ten Commandments implore us to keep the Sabbath holy; yet more Americans watch National Football League broadcasts than go to church (Green 2016; Frankovich 2015). Religious texts may be too demanding, too open to interpretation, or simply too impractical to be the basis of modern American law.

Morality is not straightforward. It is not based solely on logic or reason or religious texts. Morality may be influenced by all those things, but morality is also an evolving, ever-changing process. What was legal in biblical-era Palestine is not necessarily legal in the United States. What was legal in the United States in 1800 is not necessarily legal in today's United States. What is legal in Alabama is not necessarily legal in California. "Crime" is an amorphous, malleable concept. There are two consistencies in American morality and punishment: first, that we always assume that our current morality is the correct and natural one, and second, that we punish the same groups of people regardless of what excuse we use for the punishment. We punish those who are too vulnerable and too weak to fight back.

Crime is a social construct. This means that crime is not an independent, objective concept but an ambiguous one that varies by society and time period. Human societies are culturally variable. We have a series of beliefs, values, proverbs, and stories that inform "what everybody knows" about a social world. People produce society together; we decide collectively what is right and what is wrong (Berger and Luckmann 1966). To use one example, laws against interracial marriages were passed in Maryland and Virginia in the 1600s. Interracial marriage was illegal in the United States until 1967. Mississippi law declared interracial marriage a felony punishable by a life sentence in prison. An 1840 Indiana law punished interracial marriage with a $1,000 to $5,000 fine and 10 to 20 years in prison (Pascoe 2010). Such laws were viewed as vital until 1967; today such laws are viewed as offensive and immoral.

Why were interracial marriages illegal prior to 1967? Why are such marriages acceptable today? Changes in our views on race are inextricably tied to changes in the law. In 1968, 75 percent of white Americans opposed interracial marriage. By the 1990s, that number had dropped to 16 percent (Pascoe 2010). Similar dynamics can be observed with the changing support for same-sex marriages. In 2001, Americans opposed same-sex marriages by a margin of 57 to 35 percent. By 2017, 62 percent of Americans reported support for same-sex marriage, while 32 percent oppose it (Pew Research Center 2017).

Marriage relationships did not change. Interracial and same-sex couples get married for the same complicated reasons as other couples. The nature of interracial and same-sex relationships did not change; our views on interracial and same-sex couples changed. We might think that modern Americans have it right and that older generations were bigoted, but that reflects our current biases. Humans are sometimes supportive of and sometimes appalled by slavery, interracial relationships, and same-sex relationships. Morality is a reflection of a society's values at a certain place and time. Morality is not an independent, objective value. We may think that we are correct, but other cultures thought they were correct as well.

Erich Goode and Nachman Ben-Yehuda (2009, pp. 111–112) write,

> Morality is relative geographically and culturally, historically and temporally, situationally and subculturally. Adulterers could be stoned to death in Iran, yet in Sikhism, adultery is tolerated, often encouraged and even, upon occasion, rewarded. An assassination on one side of a border or against the member of a particular group is seen as murder, a brutal act of butchery and cowardice; on the other side, or against the member of another group, the same killing may be regarded as laudable, an act of heroism, liberation and triumph. Ancient Aztec priests cut open the chest of a human sacrifice and tore out his still-beating heart; in contemporary Mexico, the same act would be cause for arrest, prosecution, possibly commitment to a mental institution.

Cultures shape what behaviors are considered acceptable and unacceptable. Much of our cultural knowledge is shaped on the basis of language.

Language helps build classification schemes (Berger and Luckmann 1966). We can say that certain behaviors, products, or groups are good or bad. The people who play football are strong; the people who play chess are weak. Or the people who play football are brutes, while the people who play chess are intelligent. I was taught that Americans are the best, except for Yankees. And that Southerners are the best, except that North Carolina is better than South Carolina. And that North Carolinians are the best, except for Charlotte or the neighboring high school. We used to burn, in effigy, the mascot of the rival high school during pep rallies. We used to have a rivalry week with a high school in Kannapolis, North Carolina, that was based on, basically, nothing. Yet we were able to define another group of high school students as the "other" and as less than us, mainly because of a line that said this side is Concord, that side is Kannapolis.

The language that we use quickly identifies classes of people. Language defines some groups in opposition to others: liberals in opposition to conservatives, men in opposition to women, vegetarians against meat eaters, Southerners against Northerners, Americans in opposition to the rest of the world. When I was in high school in North Carolina in the 1990s, it was common to hear people use racial and homophobic slurs. Those slurs classified certain people (African Americans, gay people) as bad and other people (white Americans, heterosexuals) as good. This differentiation may reflect major differences (e.g., evangelical Christian versus atheist) or minimal differences (e.g., Michigan versus Ohio). Differences may objectively be minor but nevertheless be important to a society.

Classification allows us to put some behaviors or people into one group and other behaviors or people into another group. Once classified, an individual becomes totally identified with his or her socially assigned stereotype (Berger and Luckmann 1966). Patrice is an African American woman, therefore she represents and will act according to the stereotypes of an African American woman. Michael is a prisoner, therefore he represents and will act according to the stereotypes of a prisoner. The classification process reduces an individual; the individual becomes nothing but the assigned category (Berger and Luckmann 1966). This process of treating individuals as merely representative of a group makes the decision-making process much easier but at the cost of tremendous measurement error, since few individuals perfectly match the stereotypes associated with their group.

The language that we use and the groups that we lump people into both suggest the value we place on those groups and what society should do to those groups. The introduction to this book discussed a recent controversy in which former president Bill Clinton defended his wife's use of the term "super predator" to describe young African Americans. By using the term "super predator," Clinton suggests that those young African Americans are dangerous and not valued by society. Indeed, predators are usually put down violently or otherwise removed. If the United States is faced with super predators, the only logical option is to neutralize those super predators.

Similarly, President Donald Trump has made repeated derogatory statements about Muslim and Latino/a immigrants. This suggests that President Trump does not value Muslim and Latino/a immigrants and will do what he can to punish those groups. President Clinton's and President Trump's statements effectively separate African Americans and Muslim and Latino/a immigrants from the rest of American society. Following that logic, those groups are dangerous and not really American; therefore, it is acceptable and even moral to punish those groups. Any complaints about the treatment of marginalized groups can be ignored. If someone is in support of a marginalized group, and that group is bad, the person in support is also bad. One can think of the common slur in the Old South that white Americans who supported African Americans as equals were "n-word lovers," or the overly simplistic "with us or against us" framing of the war on terror.

These classifications help governments decide which groups to help and which groups to punish. Ann Schneider and Helen Ingram (1993) suggest that groups in society can be divided based on their degree of political power and their group reputation. Groups with negative reputations and little political power, such as "criminals," drug users, and communists, are considered "deviants." Deviants are bad people and as such should be punished. If a politician advocates services for criminals, that politician can be accused of being "soft on crime." Conversely, severe punishment of criminals can lead to electoral support (Schneider and Ingram 1993). The consequence, in the United States at least, has been mass incarceration, as politicians compete with each other to be the harshest enemies of "deviants."

Concerns about deviants have frequently resulted in extreme, unbalanced public policies. This deep concern can lead to a form of mass hysteria, known as a moral panic. After constructing the categories "criminal" or "super predator," politicians are under immense pressure to punish those categories. Imagine a politician saying, "There are super predators, but we should just ignore them," or "They are monsters; let's rehabilitate them." These policies are based more on fear than objective harm and can rapidly spiral out of control. Constructing prisoners as "criminals" and "super predators" rather than as the "vulnerable" or "needy" has led the United States to engage in a decades-long campaign against these populations.

Moral Panics

A moral panic is an explosion of fear and concern at a particular time and place about a specific perceived threat (Goode and Ben-Yehuda 1994). The classic example is the moral panic over witches. In Europe between 1400 and 1650, hundreds of thousands of people were judged to have "consorted with the devil" and were put to death. Eighty-five percent of people killed were women, a vulnerable group with less power (Goode and Ben-Yehuda 1994). While it may seem quaint, outdated, or even comical, an obsession with witchcraft led to the death of hundreds of thousands of people in spite of a lack of evidence that witches existed.

I would argue that war on crime is itself a moral panic. In our postindustrial economy, it is difficult to know how to manage immigration, expanded civil rights, changing gender and sexual norms, mental health issues, and poverty. The cost of successfully integrating those populations is likely high. Societies can try to integrate the marginalized through extensive social services or isolate the marginalized with severe criminal justice policies. Instead of rebuilding the social safety net and trying to integrate marginalized populations, we have placed millions of vulnerable people in prisons.

The war on drugs is a more familiar moral panic within the larger panic that has driven incarceration. We have greatly exaggerated the threat that illicit drugs such as cocaine, heroin, and cannabis pose. Chapter 7 will go into greater detail about the punishment of drug use, but it will suffice to say that many illicit drugs are in fact less harmful than legal drugs such as alcohol and tobacco. And many people in prison for drugs have substance abuse problems, which means they have less control over their decision to use or keep using drugs. Why do we have a war on drugs but not a war on tobacco? Why don't we try to rehabilitate those with substance abuse problems? It is partially because we subjectively view illicit drug use as sinful and as more harmful to society.

The moral panic aspect of the war on drugs can be seen through government and media propaganda about drug use. Government and media propaganda has a long and varied history in the United States. Newspapers have claimed that Chinese opium addicts were sexually seducing substantial numbers of middle-class white women; that cocaine caused African Americans to have superhuman strength and violent tendencies; that cannabis caused users to become crazy and violent; that LSD caused chromosomal damage and insanity; that PCP caused users to become superhumanly strong, violent, and crazy; that crack cocaine produced instant addiction and permanent damage to babies exposed to it; and that methamphetamine also caused instant addiction (Goode and Ben-Yehuda 2009). Some of the more sensational claims may seem ridiculous, but at the time the claims were viewed as credible.

Drugs do pose different societal problems under various circumstances. However, the objective existence of a harmful condition does not, in and of itself, constitute a social problem. Extremely harmful situations may not be viewed as a problem, while relatively benign circumstances are viewed as extremely dangerous (Goode and Ben-Yehuda 1994). The top news stories of 2017 included sexual misconduct allegations against movie producer Harvey

Weinstein; a mass shooting in Las Vegas, Nevada; an investigation into Russian election interference; and the protests against police brutality by members of the National Football League (Winsor 2017). While each of those stories is culturally important, it is unlikely that those stories objectively represent the most important events or problems in the United States in 2017.

A problem does not even have to exist to cause a moral panic. Moral panics have occurred over issues such as witchcraft, cannabis overdoses, a link between autism and vaccinations, and modern American voter fraud. Goode and Ben-Yehuda (1994, p. 151) write that "definitions of social problems derive from or are produced by specific sociocultural circumstances, groups and categories, social structures, historical eras, individuals and/or classes." If a problem is real to a society, that society will address the problem, whether or not it is an objective issue. It does not matter that there is not conclusive evidence that witches exist or that vaccines cause autism; it only matters if people believe witches exist or vaccines cause autism.

Problems are defined socially. Once a problem is identified, societies find someone to blame for the problem. Societies often need someone to scapegoat for their issues. In each case, a specific agent or group is thought to be responsible for the threat (Goode and Ben-Yehuda 1994). The groups that are blamed are deviants or "folk devils." "Folk devils" are people who are viewed as engaging in evil practices that threaten society's culture, way of life, and/or central values. Moral panics usually generate widespread anxiety and increased hostility toward folk devils. There is an increased division between us (good, decent, respectable folk) and them (the deviants, bad guys, criminals) (Goode and Ben-Yehuda 2009).

The use of folk devils reinforces our stereotypes about who is evil. Roy Baumeister (1997, p. 6) argues that "evil exists primarily in the eye of the beholder, especially in the eye of the victim." Popular depictions of evil in film, television, news coverage, and religion depict evil people as sadistic or egotistical. Villains in children's cartoons are evil for evil's sake and rarely have motives to explain their behavior. The bad guys are portrayed as the enemies of peace and order (Baumeister 1997). As these portrayals seep into the broader culture, it is very difficult for politicians to embrace prisoners' rights or rehabilitation. If criminals are evil, sadistic enemies of the peace, how could they be rehabilitated?

Popular myth views evil or bad people as having a few features in common. Evil people intentionally inflict harm on the innocent; evil is unchangeable and has existed forever; evil people have difficulty controlling their emotions, especially anger and rage. Again, this suggests that evil people are genuinely evil and cannot be rehabilitated. Evil people also function as an "other." Films and television tend to portray evil people as having foreign accents, as opposed to heroes who speak perfect English. "The myth of pure evil depicts malicious, alien forces intruding on the world of well-meaning, unsuspecting, virtuous people" (Baumeister 1997, p. 89). The view of outsiders as being evil also makes it easier to lead a moral panic, because the panic is directed at groups that are already disliked in American society.

Moral panics are not new; the United States has a long history of moral panics, including our own witch trials. In the 1800s, there was a hysteria about the "white slave trade," when Asian conspirators supposedly kidnapped small-town women and forced them into lives of prostitution. Congress passed the Mann Act, making it a crime to assist or entice women to cross state lines to engage in prostitution. During the period, no one managed to discover a single instance of such kidnapping and forced prostitution (Goode and Ben-Yehuda 2009). It is not an accident that concerns about sex slavery used a racial minority as a scapegoat. It is common to blame societal problems on marginalized groups.

In the early 2000s, similar concerns emerged over "sex slavery" in the United States. The State Department estimated that 50,000 sex slaves were entering the United States, while the Justice Department estimated the number to be 100,000. Despite spending over $150 million, very few victims have been found. Estimates from the Departments of State and Justice seem to be based on very little empirical evidence. Although women are forced into sexual slavery in many poorer countries, the practice in the United States is "extremely rare, virtually nonexistent" (Goode and Ben-Yehuda 2009). Again, it does not matter if the problem objectively exists; it matters if society perceives there to be a problem.

Politicians and media help fuel moral panics. Media can inflame and even generate public opinion. Moral panics help media companies sell content. Because of this, media outlets focus on the most extreme stories. Homicide is the most prominent crime in news stories in spite of the fact that 90 percent of crimes are nonviolent offenses (Goode and Ben-Yehuda 2009). The media provides saturation coverage of certain cases, for example, the disappearances of Laci Peterson, Elizabeth Smart, and Natalee Holloway. The media's fascination with missing women who are white, young, pretty, and relatively affluent has been dubbed "missing white woman syndrome." Nearly 2,000 print and broadcast stories were devoted to Natalee Holloway (Liebler 2010). Coverage of Holloway dwarfed coverage of the contemporaneous Darfur, Sudan, genocide.

Media outlets have even published stories about disturbing-sounding behavior that never took place. Media outlets reported about Satanic ritual abuse that never happened. In the early 1980s, many fundamentalist Christians came to believe that Satanists were torturing and killing tens of thousands of children every year, despite a lack of evidence. Media outlets have also published inaccurate stories claiming that over 50,000 children are kidnapped by a stranger annually, when a more realistic estimate is 200 to 300 children. By publicizing false information, it is easy to start a moral panic about child kidnapping or Satanic abuse (Goode and Ben-Yehuda 2009). It also helps demonize strangers as a dangerous other. It is easier to believe in devious strangers than to address the difficult reality of child abuse in our own families.

Moral panics do not always occur. The United States has chosen to emphasize certain crimes committed by certain populations. Other crime, for example, business fraud and violence committed by police officers, is largely ignored. White-collar offenders are much less likely to be detected, prosecuted, and sentenced in criminal court. When they are convicted, the penalties mostly exclude incarceration. At the beginning of the 1980s, 96 percent of those convicted of robbery were punished by a prison sentence averaging 60 months, while only 31 percent of those convicted of the white-collar crime of embezzlement were sent to prison, and that minority served an average of 11 months (Wacquant 2009).

The New York Securities and Exchange Commission revealed that only 12 percent of those who committed proven fraud were brought to criminal court, 6 percent were charged, and 3 percent were eventually sent to prison. The 2,500 bank directors and managers convicted after the late 1980s Savings and Loan Association scandals were sanctioned to an average of 18 months in prison despite costing the country an estimated $1 trillion. Michael Milken, a "junk-bond king responsible for billions of dollars in illegal stock maneuvers on Wall Street" served the longest prison sentence in the country's history for insider trading as of 2000: a total of 22 months in a minimum security prison (Wacquant 2009, p. 127).

More recent enforcement of white-collar crime is even less stringent than during the savings and loan scandals. Only 9 percent of federal cases in 2010–2012 involved white-collar crime. The Justice Department focuses on reaching settlements rather than seeking prison sentences for white-collar criminals. Despite the billions of dollars in banking fraud that caused the Great Recession, the *New York Times* reported that, by 2014, only one top banker was sent to prison, for a 30-month sentence (Eisinger 2014). By contrast, in the state of Michigan, where I am writing this book, the penalty for possessing any amount of cannabis is a year in prison; the penalty for cultivating a cannabis plant is four years in prison.

While the punishment of white-collar crime is minimal, the punishment of police homicides is virtually nonexistent. Extreme violence perpetrated by police and other law enforcement officers is treated very differently than violence perpetrated by the vulnerable. Statistics vary by source, but between 950 and 1,250 people are killed by police annually. The *Washington Post*, which has more conservative estimates than other organizations, estimated that 991 people were killed by police in 2015 and a further 963 were killed in 2016 (Calacal 2016). Despite rhetoric that suggests otherwise, police officers pose a greater threat to society than society poses to police. In 2012, a total of 105 police officers died on the job, nearly half in traffic accidents. Police use violence nine times as often as they face violence. Annually, an estimated 991,930 people experienced some level of police use of force (including threats). Over half, 546,000 people, were subject to physical force (Williams 2015). Another way to think about these numbers is that over a decade, nearly 10 million people will be subjected to police use of force, and over 5 million people will be subjected to physical force.

Use of force is concentrated in a small number of neighborhoods and among a small number of officers (Vitale 2017). Use of force is more common in neighborhoods that are politically vulnerable and less capable of mounting a successful legal suit or protest movement against a police department. One can think of the relative political risk, to a police officer, of using force against a well-dressed, affluent person compared to using force against a poor or homeless person. Aggressive policing is only politically feasible in vulnerable, marginalized communities. It is also likely that aggressive policing deteriorates the relationship between the police and the community, making future aggressive policing more likely.

The level of police violence in the United States is not matched in other democracies. England and Wales, with a population of 57 million people, have seen 55 fatal police shootings in the past 24 years. In the United States, 59 people were killed by police officers in the first 24 days of 2015 (Lartey 2015). Even using the low estimate of 950 people killed by police annually in the United States, that would equate to 22,800 fatal killings of citizens, a rate 414 times that of England and Wales. Adjusting for population, the United States would still have 22,800 fatal killings in comparison to 305 killings, a rate that is 75 times higher. Canada, which has a relatively high level of gun ownership, experiences 25 fatal police shootings a year. Even after adjusting for population, the police homicide rate in the United States is more than four times higher than the rate in Canada (Lartey 2015).

Even when police officers are found guilty of misconduct, discipline rarely follows (Williams 2015). In 2015, not a single police officer was tried for manslaughter for killing a civilian in the line of duty. Since 2005, there have only been 13 police officers convicted of murder or manslaughter for an on-duty killing of a civilian (Ferner and Wing 2016). If the *Washington Post*'s conservative estimate is accurate, on average 977 people are killed by the police annually, or 11,724 people since 2005. It does not seem plausible that out of 11,724 instances, police officers acted wrongly 13 times (an error rate of .0011). It seems unlikely that the police were completely justified in 99.9989 percent of cases.

Police brutality is likely more common than people realize, in large part because most incidences of violence go unreported. In addition, few instances are caught on video or have other newsworthy attributes. Less than 5 percent of people who believed the police behaved improperly filed a complaint. Few victims of police abuse feel comfortable complaining to the same department that was responsible for the abuse (Williams 2015). There is moral outrage about police brutality, especially with the Black Lives Matter movement, but that movement does not have mainstream acceptance and is belittled by All Lives Matter and Blue (police) Lives Matter rhetoric. The larger point is that our moral panics have focused on drug- and poverty-related crimes, while business crime and violence by state actors is mostly ignored.

Once a problem is identified, societies must come up with a response. In most instances, institutions arise to help punish deviants (Berger and Luckmann 1966). Police and prisons are the dominant institutions of punishment in the modern United States. While both institutions seem omnipresent, both are relatively new inventions. American prisons have undergone multiple transformations and have experienced great regional variability. Instead of an objective, rational assessment of harm and punishment for those harms, American prisons have responded to the fears and moral panics of different regions and different times.

Institutions all have a history, and an institution cannot be understood without knowing its history (Berger and Luckmann 1966). The following is a brief history of how prisons in the United States have evolved and changed. It is not just that the United States in 2018 is more punitive than most countries in the world; the United States in 2018 is also more punitive than earlier points of the country's history. A Louisiana politician from the 1960s would be considered too "soft on crime" to be elected in even a relatively liberal state in 2018. Our current model of punishment is only one of many; it is not an inevitable result but the outcome of specific historical processes. It is the result of political choices and responses to moral panics.

A Brief History of American Prisons

Prisons and the widespread use of incarceration are relatively new phenomena. In small communities, such as those in early colonial America, it was easy to rely on social pressure and surveillance to make sure people conformed to social norms. In colonial America few punishments involved jail sentences, and the jails that did exist were no different architecturally than any other house in the community. Offenders were housed in rooms, rather than cells, and there was no attempt to separate offenders by gender, age, or the severity of their crime. The warden and his wife were expected to live in the jail, and there were no uniforms to distinguish offenders from the rest of society. Colonial jails were "overcrowded, disorderly and unsanitary, and there were few or no security measures to prevent escapes" (Blomberg and Lucken 2010, p. 22). Offenders were expected to pay for their own food and clothing, and the indigent sometimes starved in early American jails (Banks 2005).

In colonial Boston, on average less than 2 percent of punishments involved a jail sentence. From 1710 to 1719, zero jail sentences were issued in Essex and Middlesex counties (Blomberg and Lucken 2010). This is not to suggest that punishment was rare but that the equivalent of incarceration was rare. Colonial Americans were indeed punished, but public and physical punishments were the norm. Monetary fines were the most common punishment, but other options included floggings, banishment, shaming techniques, and bondage or slavery. Methods of shaming included branding, the stocks, the pillory, mutilation, and the public cage (Banks 2005). The community was expected to take part in the punishment, for example, by throwing rotten food on offenders placed in the stocks. The death penalty was the harshest punishment available in colonial America, and large crowds gathered to watch the spectacle of a public execution.

Although punishment practices resembled those in England, geographic separation meant that the colonies only needed to "establish laws not contrary to those of England" (Blomberg and Lucken 2010, p. 59). Religion was very important, and crimes were viewed as synonymous with sin. "Crimes" included "profanity, drunkenness, flirting, gossiping, blaspheming and practicing witchcraft" (Banks 2005, p. 14). However, what constituted a crime varied according to religion and geography. In New England there was a focus on moral offenses, while South Carolina ignored the same offenses. Punishment varied as well. In Massachusetts, 25 offenses were listed as punishable by death, while in Pennsylvania only murder was punishable by death (Blomberg and Lucken 2010). The list of sinners/criminals who could be executed included "recidivists, murderers, arsonists, horse thieves and incorrigible youth" (Blomberg and Lucken 2010, p. 45).

Rapid population growth in the late 18th and early 19th centuries helped undermine the colonial system of punishment. From 1790 to 1830, the population of Massachusetts doubled, the population of Pennsylvania tripled, and the population of New York increased fivefold. Western expansion and immigration on the East Coast helped undermine the tight bonds of earlier communities (Blomberg and Lucken 2010). The influx of new residents made community surveillance and attempts at enforcing absolute conformity impractical. A new diversity of opinions and views interfered with the prosecution of moral offenses. It became more difficult to punish the sinner/criminal once religious views became heterogeneous.

At the same time, new ideas from Enlightenment thinkers challenged the colonial model. Colonial punishments were severe and inconsistent. Since the death penalty was an option for even minor offenses, the "criminal" was often acquitted even if the judge or jury thought the offender was guilty (Blomberg and Lucken 2010). An Italian philosopher, Cesare Beccaria, wrote perhaps the most thorough repudiation of the pre-Enlightenment model of criminal justice, denouncing torture and capital punishment, the inconsistency in enforcement, the lack of deterrence, and the lack of proportionate punishment. Beccaria (1764, p. 28) wrote, "The end of punishment, therefore, is no other than to prevent the criminal from doing further injury to society, and to prevent others from committing the like offence. Such punishments, therefore, and such a mode of inflicting them, ought to be chosen, as will make the strongest and most lasting impressions on the minds of others, with the least torment to the body of the criminal."

Following Beccaria and other Enlightenment thinkers, a new model of punishment developed. By the 1820s, most states reformed their penal codes. New York repealed the death penalty for all offenses except murder and arson, Virginia reserved the death penalty for murder and some offenses committed by slaves, while Maine and Vermont abolished the death penalty altogether (Blomberg and Lucken 2010). Physical punishments also declined, with Pennsylvania banning the act of branding in 1791 (Blomberg and Lucken 2010). The public spectacle of colonial-era punishment was replaced by a new institution: the prison.

The first attempts at incarceration were largely a failure. The first prisons, including Newgate in New York, Walnut Street Jail in Pennsylvania, and Castle Island in Boston Harbor, were overcrowded and inadequate for the care of inmates. As a consequence of these failures, states began constructing larger facilities. Massachusetts opened a state prison with a capacity for 300 inmates in 1805, Pennsylvania opened Western Penitentiary in 1818 and Eastern State Penitentiary in 1823, while New York opened what would become known as Sing Sing Prison in 1828 (Banks 2005). It is important to remember that prisons, which seem omnipresent today, have only existed in the United States for a couple of centuries. It is also worth noting that since their inception, prisons have struggled to provide adequate care.

The early prisons were penitentiaries with two common types: the Pennsylvania and Auburn models. In the Pennsylvania system, each inmate was placed in a single cell that was linked to a small courtyard. Inmates were completely alone while in their cell and wore hoods whenever they left their cell. Other than the Bible, no reading materials were provided, and labor was considered a privilege. When an inmate was given work, the labor was conducted in isolation. Occasionally, the warden or members of the community would stop by an inmate's cell, providing the inmate an opportunity to confess his or her transgressions (Banks 2005). The motivation behind the Pennsylvania system was to reform the inmate through quiet reflection and repentance, hence the term "penitentiary."

The Auburn system offered an alternative form of incarceration. During the day, inmates worked together in prison workshops, while at night the inmates were separated into solitary cells. At all times, inmates were expected to be silent. Strict discipline was enforced by lockstep marching and whippings. The daily routine of Auburn system inmates was heavily regulated.

The goal of the Auburn system was not the reform of the inmate but rather to break the inmate's spirit and foster a state of complete submission to authority (Banks 2005). The ghosts of the Auburn and Pennsylvania systems are still with us; the emphasis on prison labor, strict discipline, and isolation is common in American prisons, including in solitary confinement units and in specially constructed maximum security prisons, some of which retain the name "penitentiary."

The push to build penitentiaries was not universal. Southern states in particular were reluctant to adopt prisons. In the South, slavery kept the majority of the poor under control, and religious concerns sparked opposition from evangelical ministers. The Bible advocated "swift, severe, and bloody punishments," which matched the old colonial model better than the new prison model. Southern states were also concerned about mixing white and free African Americans in penitentiaries, a process that was thought to injure white and boost African American pride (Banks 2005). These concerns made incarceration a less viable option in the South.

A system of convict leasing largely replaced penitentiaries in the South. In 1858, Virginia became the first state to lease its convicts to private businesses (in this case railroad and canal companies). The practice of leasing convicts spread to Georgia in 1866, Arkansas in 1867, and Florida and South Carolina in 1877. By the time Virginia returned to a penitentiary system in 1879, all the other Southern states leased out all or some of their convicts to private companies. The life expectancy of leased convicts was incredibly low, with 41 percent of leased convicts in Alabama dying in 1870. By 1883, one Alabama doctor reported that most leased convicts died within three years (Banks 2005).

The view of convicts at that time is shocking to contemporary ears. In his outstanding book on convict leasing, *Slavery by Another Name*, Douglas Blackmon quotes correctional officials saying, "The Negroes die off every few years, though it is said that in time each hand also makes enough to buy two more in his place," and even more horrifically, "N—is cheap" (Blackmon 2008, p. 43). Since prisoners were leased at cheap rates instead of owned, prison administrators had little reason to invest much in the care of convicts. Leased convicts in some ways represented a more dysfunctional form of labor than slavery; for all its horrors, slave owners at least had an incentive to keep their slaves alive.

Companies used African American laborers to build railroads, farm cotton, and work in mines. At one mine, inmates were required to remove eight tons of coal every day (Blackmon 2008). Convict labor helped to rebuild the South after the devastation of the Civil War. Prison systems have frequently scapegoated inmates for society's problems while ignoring the significant economic contributions that inmates provide. Leased prisoners were often killed by overwork, inadequate food, inadequate health care, and the brutality of guards. Convicts who died were unceremoniously buried (Blackmon 2008). The wealth and benefits derived from prison labor went to companies and various levels of government, while the memory of the providers of that labor is obliterated beneath thousands of unmarked graves.

An 1882 inspection of a prison where convicts were leased found that the prisons were "totally unfit for use, without ventilation, without adequate water supplies, crowded to excess, filthy beyond description." Prisoners were "poorly clothed and fed . . . excessively and sometimes cruelly punished; there were no hospitals; the sick were neglected; and they were so much intimidated that it was next to impossible to get from them anything touching on their treatment." One prison had no floors or toilets. Prisoners were fed only meat and bread (Blackmon 2008, p. 73). Prisoners in convict lease camps faced food scarcity, disease, work injuries, excruciating labor demands, violence, and death (Haley 2016).

Convict leasing could be particularly devastating to women. Women were victims of sexual assault before and after their incarceration. Women were whipped while naked and sometimes raped in view of other prisoners. W. E. B. Du Bois reported, "A young girl at camp Hardmont, Georgia, in 1895, was repeatedly outraged by several of her guards, and finally died in childbirth while in the camp" (Haley 2016, p. 19). In this instance, "outraged" referred to repeated sexual assaults. None of the guards were ever prosecuted for rape (Haley 2016). This lack of accountability for sexual violence is still, unfortunately, a feature of American prisons today.

Similar to modern prisons, the convict lease system represented an end point that began with rampant racial discrimination. African American women were arrested and imprisoned at much higher rates than were white women. In Atlanta, African American women were nearly six times more likely to be arrested than white women. Amazingly, in Georgia there were more African American women in convict camps than white men. While the media was sympathetic to imprisoned white women, imprisoned African American women were vilified. African American women were perceived as ugly, willing to fight, unable to control their children, and generally vulgar (Haley 2016).

African Americans were targeted for minor infractions. Of 86 African American women arrested in Atlanta, 45 were arrested for arguing or using profanity. Other common charges were drunk and disorderly conduct and occupying/keeping a house of ill repute. African American women could be sent to convict lease camps for failing to abate a nuisance or for dumping dirty water in the streets. African American women who had poor relationships with their employers were particularly vulnerable to arrest (Haley 2016). Similar to modern incarceration, "offenses" were minor, and placement in convict lease camps fell disproportionately on the poor and on racial minorities. Convict leasing served to make labor more docile and available while positing the vulnerable as folk devils.

The convict leasing system also enabled the South to limit the political power of African Americans. Law enforcement played a critical role; local police enforced poll taxes and other voter-suppression efforts (Vitale 2017). Convict leasing and the threat of arrest also helped force African Americans into subservient economic roles. Vagrancy laws were used to force African Americans to accept employment in the sharecropping system (Vitale 2017). These practices enabled a system of racial control that mirrors the petty arrests and "workfare" requirements of the contemporary United States.

While the Southern states adopted convict leasing, the rest of the country adopted different reforms. The 1870 meeting of the American Prison Society in Cincinnati, Ohio, led to a declaration of principles for reform. The recommendations included scientific treatment of offenders and individualized care. Academic and vocational training, improved classification, indeterminate sentencing, and parole were some of the other hallmark recommendations. By 1876, Elmira Reformatory was built in New York State. Reformatories offered a new model of prison governance. Instead of an emphasis on retribution or deterrence, for the first time rehabilitation was emphasized in American prisons (Banks 2005).

The rise of reformatories from the 1890s until the 1960s instituted a form of prison governance in the United States that David Garland (2001) has called "penal welfarism." Penal welfarism was largely based on two assumptions. First, there was an assumption that social reform, together with growing affluence, would eventually reduce the frequency of crime. Criminal behavior was viewed as a reflection of environmental factors, and it was believed that an alleviation of poverty could therefore reduce crime. The second assumption was that the state is responsible for the care of offenders as well as their punishment and control. Consequently, the treatment of criminals was individualized and largely based on an individual's capability of being rehabilitated, and a central role was given to professionals such as parole officers and social workers who worked together to help reintegrate former prisoners (Garland 2001).

Since the 1960s, this "rehabilitative model" has been gradually supplanted by a "crime control" model in which incapacitation and punishment have replaced reform and rehabilitation as the primary goals guiding the treatment of criminal offenders. There are several features that distinguish the new system from its predecessor. First, the new system aims to separate the criminal from society rather than reintegrate the criminal into society. Second, criminals are primarily seen as "deviants" or "delinquents" rather than as reflections of their social environments. Since prisoners are "deviants," any attempt at rehabilitation is seen as a waste of time and money. Third, the role of case workers and parole officers has been reduced, while the importance of victims has increased. As a result, the goals of rehabilitation and reintegration have been surpassed in priority by the goal of retribution (Garland 2001).

While the crime control model is the dominant model in the United States, features from other models remain. Many correctional departments at least provide lip service to the rehabilitation and individualized treatment associated with reformatories and penal welfarism. Features of penitentiaries still exist in American super-maximum security prisons. Although convict leasing has disappeared, the economic exploitation of prison inmates certainly has not. Even the religious impulses of the colonial era echo to today. Anyone who has entered an American jail or prison knows that religious programming, such as prayer groups and Bible studies, are some of the only programs available. The most popular prison treatments for substance abuse are based on the tenets of Alcoholics Anonymous. Alcoholics Anonymous is both largely religious in nature and largely ineffectual (Dodes and Dodes 2014).

While the United States has used many different types of prisons, and prisons have varied geographically and temporally, one feature of punishment has remained consistent: the disproportionate punishment of the vulnerable. Prison has remained a place to punish the marginalized, the sick, the poor, and racial minorities. The main purpose of American prisons, both historically and contemporarily, has been the social control and management of vulnerable populations.

Modern American Prisons—Punishing the Vulnerable

American prisons are not full of violent predators but of "nonviolent criminals and petty delinquents . . . drawn from the most vulnerable fractions of the working class" (Wacquant 2009, p. 131). Approximately 80 percent of inmates are too poor to afford a lawyer (Alexander 2010). Eighty-three percent of people currently in American jails remain there for no other reason than that they cannot afford to pay their bail (Hill 2016). It is important to note that inmates who are placed in jail because of an inability to pay bail *have not been convicted of a crime*. Jails are a form of pretrial detention. More than half of all prison and jail inmates have a mental health problem. Sixty-six percent of state prison inmates have a substance abuse problem. Only 19 percent of state prison inmates do not have a substance abuse or mental health issue (James and Glaze 2006).

Our prisons are full of the poor, the sick, and the marginalized because law enforcement activities target these groups. With the shift toward a crime control mentality in the 1960s and with a disintegration of other forms of social control (political marginalization, Jim Crow laws), law enforcement stepped in to manage vulnerable populations. This phenomenon is evident in not just the United States but worldwide. Didier Fassin (2013, p. 216) writes,

> Over recent decades, the general evolution of policing worldwide has been toward the harsh version of law enforcement. Or, more precisely, this harsh version has been almost systematically imposed as a form of government of the most precarious and marginalized groups, notably working-class communities and ethnic minorities. A key element in this process has been the spread of a securitarian ideology, backed up by discourses that fan public fears to justify more repressive policies, a rise in police numbers, and the escalating severity of penalties, regardless of whether there is an objective increase in crime and criminality, and often even when they are falling. The geographical segregation of the poorest groups, especially those of Third World immigrant origin, has considerably aided this shift, both by allowing police action to be focused on specific neighborhoods, and by rendering this reality invisible to the majority. But it has also been facilitated by changes in technology, with the move from foot to vehicle patrols, the development of more sophisticated and routinely carried weapons, and the computerization of services that results in the systemization and multiplication of files on individuals convicted, suspects and even victims.

This increasingly harsh form of policing has led to more frequent and negative interactions with the vulnerable. This move is driven not by crime reduction concerns but by the perceived need for social order. Police patrols have little to no effect on crime, either in terms of offenses recorded by law enforcement or from the point of view of residents' perception of crime. In fact, as early as 1983, social scientist Carl Klockars had written, "It makes about as much sense to have police patrol routinely in cars to fight crime as it does to have firemen patrol routinely in fire trucks to fight fire" (Fassin 2013, p. 59). Many scholars have argued that policing is more about enforcing order than stopping or solving crimes (Alexander 2010; Comaroff and Comaroff 2016; Fassin 2013; Wacquant 2009; Williams 2015).

While it is uncommon to hear that law enforcement is more about social order than solving crimes, it makes sense on further thought. Police patrols involve large amounts of time driving around without encountering any forms of criminal behavior. At the same time, it is relatively easy to avoid the police due to their distinctive clothing and vehicles. (The vehicles for the Michigan State Police tend to be painted a deep blue and have a large, flashing red button on the roof. Traffic police in many states tend to park in easily seen locations, such as highway cutouts.) Anyone who regularly exceeds the speed limit in their car knows that there are certain spots to avoid and certainly knows the difference between a police car and a civilian car. For the middle class and the upper class, it is relatively easy to avoid the police, because police do not regularly patrol middle- and upper-class neighborhoods.

Police do heavily patrol poor neighborhoods. These police patrols ensure "the reproduction of social order," reminding people of their place in relation to the state (Fassin 2013, p. 71). Didier Fassin (2013, p. 74) argues that "what is at stake is not so much the protection of public order as the maintaining of social order." Policing "has come to be dedicated primarily to the preservation of social order, focusing, above all else, on the containment of those who, putatively at least, pose an imminent threat to peace, property, public assets and polite society" (Comaroff and Comaroff 2016, p. 41). Those who are considered threatening are the poor, the marginalized, and the vulnerable. The poor and marginalized are seen as the perpetrators of crime rather than its primary victims (Comaroff and Comaroff 2016). The poor are considered "unruly, indolent, inherently violent and expendable" (Comaroff and Comaroff 2016, p. 41). Marc Lamont Hill (2016) has argued that the vulnerable are viewed as so disposable that to be poor and marginalized is to be "nobody."

There are also bureaucratic reasons for focusing on poor and vulnerable populations. (I would argue that more discrimination is caused by the need to bureaucratically process people than by overt bias.) Police have difficulty meeting targets, so they focus on tasks that are easy to accomplish and easy to resolve, such as low-level drug possession and immigration violations. Police focus on drug users rather than drug dealers and on street-level drug dealers rather than higher-level drug dealers. Higher-level drug dealers are harder to catch and may require weeks or months of investigation. On the other hand, drug users can be caught with mass stop and frisks (Fassin 2013). According to data from the Bureau of Justice Statistics, less than 2 percent of prison inmates were drug dealers higher than the street level.

Actual policing involves long periods of boredom punctuated by responses to calls. Whether on foot or in a car, most police work involves patrolling different neighborhoods and districts. Most of the time spent patrolling does not turn up evidence of criminal activity, hence the reliance on stop-and-frisk tactics and arrests for minor violations in order for police to make their numbers (Fassin 2013). Fassin (2013, p. 67) writes that

> a number of studies in the United States reveal that officers on patrol spend between 30 and 40 percent of their time responding to calls (on average five calls per team per hour in cities), only 7–10 percent of which are related in some way to offenses or crimes, and between 40 and 50 percent of their working day on random patrol and paperwork, with the rest of the time devoted to various tasks.

Focusing on the poor and marginalized keeps the poor under the supervision of the criminal justice system and serves to preserve existing inequalities. "When the police enforce the law, they do so unevenly, in ways that give disproportionate attention to the activities of poor people, people of color, and others near the bottom of the social pyramid. And when the police *violate* the law, these same people are their most frequent victims" (Williams 2015, p. 48, emphasis in original). Police can threaten or negatively interact with poor people, knowing that most people will stay silent. Those who do not stay silent can be charged with resisting arrest, which improves the police officer's numbers (Fassin 2013).

There are at least three reasons why the police focus on the vulnerable. First, many police officers have internalized American rhetoric about poverty and racial minorities; thus, many police officers genuinely view the vulnerable as threatening. Second, the vulnerable have fewer resources with which to resist the police or to win in a court of law. Finally, social constructions of the vulnerable reinforce group identities; when a poor person or a Latino/a person is caught with drugs or other contraband, it reinforces the connection between poverty or ethnicity and criminality. Of course, searching a vulnerable person and finding nothing does not cause most law enforcement officers to reevaluate their stereotypes.

Discriminatory treatment by police is matched by discriminatory treatment by prison guards and other staff. The vulnerable are subject to not only higher levels of arrest and incarceration but also to worse treatment inside prison. Prison staff have a significant level of discretion in their treatment of imprisoned individuals and the ability to pick which inmates they want to help or harm. Police officers and prison guards use group stereotypes to decide punishments. The next chapter provides an explanation for why prison guards choose some inmates to punish over others. The explanation stems largely from the inmates' vulnerability.

CHAPTER TWO

Discretion and Punishment

A lot of people let their badge go to their head.
—Correctional officer at Western Kentucky Correctional Center

Occasionally you have someone in mind.
—Correctional officer at Kentucky State Reformatory

In the summer of 2008, I was a fresh graduate from the masters of public administration program at the University of North Carolina at Charlotte. I was enthusiastic about beginning a career in public service; however, I graduated just in time for the Great Recession and the collapse of the Charlotte area's housing and job market. After a few interviews and some side jobs working at restaurants, I secured a relatively well paid (by my standards at least) job working for Mecklenburg County. I was hired as a detention officer for the Mecklenburg County Sheriff's Office.

My experience as a detention officer was brief but formative. After an intense period of training that included reporting for work at 6:45 a.m., getting pepper sprayed, and being regularly reprimanded for uniform code violations, I began working directly with inmates. With a considerable amount of nervousness and fear, I would enter units containing between 60 and 80 inmates. Initially, training officers were there to assist me; eventually, I was alone in a unit with 70 male inmates. It was quite the change from my career as a student!

Popular depictions of jails and prisons make it seem as though there is a continual war between inmates and guards. Although there are intense moments and instances of violence, the majority of an officer's shift is routine and boring. Filling out paperwork, answering inmate questions, reading lists of rules, searching for contraband, and attempting to keep the unit quiet and under control make up the bulk of an officer's day. There was one day when a weapon made from the metal part of a mop bucket was found in my unit. However, most days simply contained lists of tasks to complete. Check the fire extinguishers, note that the sergeant was in the unit for a tour, send three inmates to medical, confiscate surplus oranges from an inmate's cell. Monotony and routinization are more common than dramatic instances of violence, at least for any one officer.

American prisons are notoriously overcrowded, and this leads to high inmate-to-staff ratios. The federal prison system crams 169,840 inmates into facilities designed to hold 132,731. Alabama has 25,664 inmates in prisons designed to house 13,318. Ohio holds 46,151 inmates in space designed for 34,986. Twenty-eight states hold more inmates than their prisons were designed to hold, and a further 15 states are at over 90 percent capacity (Carson 2015). It is worth noting that many of these inmates are held in rooms converted from other uses, such as gymnasiums and libraries. When I worked for Mecklenburg County, most inmates slept in individual cells. However, when the cells were full, extra inmates slept on small portable cots. There was nothing separating those extra inmates from either each other or staff.

The actual number of staff supervising inmates may be surprising. A report by the Association of State Correctional Administrators (2010) found that the ratio of inmates to correctional officers ranged from a low of 3 to 1 in New York to a high of 21 to 1 in California. On average, American state prisons have a ratio of 6.4 inmates to every correctional officer. It is important to keep in mind that many correctional officers are not directly supervising large numbers of inmates; some are working security in towers or at entrances, some are held in reserve in case of an incident, and others may supervise a small number of inmates in the kitchen or medical bay. Ratios of 60, 70, even 100 inmates to 1 correctional officer are common.

Overcrowding and high inmate-to-staff ratios are common issues in American prisons. During interviews, a social service clinician told me, "I don't think the mission is to rehabilitate but to warehouse." Anyone who has seen photos of prison overcrowding in places like California can empathize with such a statement. It is impossible to provide specialized services to everyone in the current American prison system. The resources simply do not exist. We do not even have the resources to provide every inmate with a cell. This overcrowding leaves prison staff with high levels of discretion when deciding who to provide services to and who to punish.

Simply observing and keeping track of inmates is a daunting task. Further complicating matters is the plethora of rules and regulations governing guard and inmate behavior. For example, the Kentucky Department of Corrections has seven categories of inmate disciplinary infractions, listing a total of 101 possible offenses, ranging from littering and faking an illness to sexual assault and inciting a riot. Violations vary by state, and in some cases the "violation" is innocuous or even positive. The Idaho Department of Corrections has a ban on sharing resources or materials. Inmates who are caught bartering or sharing items more than once are sent to solitary confinement (Law 2012). This rule is particularly cruel when one considers that most prison inmates are economically disadvantaged.

The list of possible violations is extensive, and some common offenses, such as inmate disrespect, are open to interpretation. I have witnessed officers yelling at inmates for giving a "disrespectful look." Disrespect can involve an inmate rolling his or her eyes, snickering, talking back, or simply not paying attention. While this may seem minor, a guard can write up an inmate for talking back, and multiple write-ups can lead to placement in solitary confinement. Or an officer can provoke an inmate by invading the inmate's personal space, talking disrespectfully, or making vague threats. If the inmate responds to such provocation, the officer can have the inmate immediately placed in solitary confinement.

The two quotes at the beginning of this chapter highlight the dynamics of high inmate-to-staff ratios. One correctional officer, at Western Kentucky Correctional Complex, told me, "A lot of people let their badge go to their head." Prison guards have a lot of power and the ability to punish inmates selectively. Some guards will let that power fuel their ego, with predictably negative consequences for staff and inmates. Instances of bias do not need to be widespread in order to affect the culture of a prison. If some officers are believed to be disrespectful, that may lead to increased tensions between all inmates and all officers. There is also pressure on officers to defend bad colleagues, as opening the door for criticism is seen as undermining the power of all correctional officers.

A correctional officer at another prison, Kentucky State Penitentiary, told me that "occasionally you have someone in mind" for random searches. Typically you might thoroughly search four random cells in a 70-cell unit, but prison guards will often have "someone in mind" when looking for an inmate to punish. When I worked as a detention officer, I repeatedly heard officers say they were going to "get" so-and-so or to be "on the lookout" for so-and-so. In my experience at one jail system, the inmates officers said they would "get" were universally young, African American men. These sorts of actions are almost impossible to observe or prevent, except by other correctional officers. This is difficult given professional norms about defending colleagues.

While an officer has power over inmates, it is not absolute. For example, an officer could discipline 1 inmate for being disrespectful but cannot discipline 10 inmates for being disrespectful. Enforcement of the rules is necessarily selective due to the plethora of rules and the fact that inmates greatly outnumber prison staff. No officer can enforce all the rules all the time, because officers need inmates' acquiescence to rules. Inmates may undermine an officer who spends too much time enforcing petty rule violations. Consequently, inmate–staff interactions involve compromises by which officers overlook some forms of behavior in return for order (Philliber 1987; Poole and Regoli 1980). While I worked a unit, I would emphasize the rules that I felt were most important, such as collecting contraband and keeping the noise level down, while deemphasizing rules such as those related to wearing uniforms in a certain way. My enforcement of rules was largely based on what rules I preferred to enforce, an approach that is common among government bureaucrats.

The presence of high numbers of inmates means that officers cannot dedicate resources to learning about each individual inmate. Even if officers tried to get to know inmates individually, there is high turnover within prisons. Annually, 630,000 inmates leave prison and new inmates take their place (Mears et al. 2008). There are also high levels of turnover among the correctional staff. Around 20 percent of prison guards voluntarily quit every year (Udechukwu et al. 2007; Wright 1993), although in some Deep South states the turnover rate is as high as 50 percent (Hager 2015; Lommel 2004). In many cases, inmates are trying to learn about officers at the same time that officers are learning about inmates. Correctional officers often have to make decisions with a great deal of uncertainty about the inmates. Since all rules cannot be enforced all the time, it is necessary to decide who is worthy of help or of punishment.

Deciding Who to Help and Who to Punish

Although political actors provide the legal basis for prison treatment, and state correctional departments add rules and regulations, most of the day-to-day decision making is left to staff at individual prisons. Political actors may decide how much money to allocate toward building maximum security cells or decide what offenses warrant solitary confinement, but it is up to prison staff to decide which particular inmates to sanction. American prison inmates are the literal definition of a captive clientele, with few advocates and few formal rights within prisons. An inmate can appeal a punishment, but those appeals go through the prison bureaucracy and are rarely overturned (Calavita and Jenness 2013). Even if an officer is wrong, it is in the interest of the prison to support the officer rather than the inmate; otherwise the authority of other officers might be lessened. Prison staffs therefore exert wide discretion over inmate sanctions and other treatment.

This level of discretion is commonly left to frontline governmental workers, known as street-level bureaucrats. Police officers, prison guards, teachers, counselors, and caseworkers are examples of the types of government employees that citizens regularly encounter. The lower levels (i.e., nonmanagement employees) have the most frequent encounters with citizens. A student may have extensive contact with a college professor but rarely, if ever, meet with a dean. A warden may conduct tours once a week, but correctional officers are in the units full time every shift. Correctional officers are regularly in direct contact with prisoners. This face-to-face interaction is common among street-level bureaucrats, who have "considerable discretion in determining the nature, amount, and quality of benefits and sanctions provided by their agencies" (Lipsky 1980, p. xi).

This discretion is given because street-level bureaucrats work in difficult environments that cannot be reduced to step-by-step routines. A prison guard is almost always outnumbered, and it is impractical to define every aspect of the guard's daily routine. Discretion is also necessary because of the human dimensions of problems. Two inmates may exhibit the exact same behavior, but only one inmate may deserve punishment. This is not necessarily unfair; the inmates may have chosen the same behavior for different reasons, or the inmates may differ on other important characteristics. For example, one inmate may have broken a rule knowingly, while another broke the rule unknowingly. It may be appropriate to give a warning to the inmate who broke the rule unknowingly but to sanction a repeat offender. Or perhaps an inmate with a mental illness commits a rule infraction; that may be a reflection of the need for better mental health treatment rather than intransigence on the behalf of the mentally ill inmate.

Upward of 80 percent of formal disciplinary hearings result in guilty findings (Lovell and Jemelka 1996). Inmates also face high barriers to having disciplinary decisions or conditions of confinement changed by the court system. In 1995, President Clinton signed the Prison Litigation Reform Act, which severely limited prisoners' ability to legally challenge their conditions of confinement. The law forces prisoners to exhaust every administrative remedy before filing a lawsuit—administrative remedies that are controlled by the prison. It also requires prisoners to prove a lasting physical injury to collect for any mental or emotional harm (Law 2012). In some states, legal remedies are even more limited. For example, in Michigan, female inmates are not able to seek monetary damages for most sexual abuse, including rape. In California, any prisoner filing a grievance for sexual abuse must first speak to the perpetrator (Law 2012).

At the same time, staff are overwhelmed by the number of possible violations. In one study, 92 percent of inmates admitted to committing a major rule violation, but only 16 percent were officially disciplined for their violation (Poole and Regoli 1980). If every incident was formally punished, correctional officers would spend most of their time writing disciplinary reports. (You can imagine how happy their supervisors would be about this prospect.) It is impossible to enforce all rules, but at the same time some inmates must be sanctioned in order to maintain order and security. Given this difficulty, prison staff have wide discretion over which specific inmates are punished.

Correctional officers have similar reward and punishment powers as other frontline government workers (Liebling 2000). Officers influence access to programs and decide whether or not to punish an inmate. Officers sometimes have discretion to shut down an entire unit (known as locking down the unit). Even minor infractions can have major consequences, such as taking away an inmate's visitation privileges. At a basic level, an officer can decide whether to write up an infraction, issue a verbal warning, or ignore the infraction altogether. In my experience, there are as many different ways to run a unit as there are different ways to run a classroom. Due to overcrowding and staff shortages, most guards have considerable discretion in running their unit. Officers also often rely on the informal handling of problems, which can lead to discrimination without a paper trail.

Correctional officers experience many of the same temporal, cognitive, and financial resource constraints as other street-level bureaucrats (Brehm and Gates 1997; Lipsky 1980; Schaufeli and Peeters 2000). Working as a detention or correctional officer is tiring, stressful, and exhausting work. Even trying to visually track 70 people for 12 hours can be difficult, let alone dealing with problematic inmates or difficult incidents. Prison resources are notoriously limited. Not everyone can participate in programming, because programming is limited. For many reasons, not everyone can be punished; most rule violations go unnoticed, and those that are noticed cannot always be punished. If the solitary confinement unit is full, solitary confinement is no longer an available punishment. If the prison has few rewards, loss of rewards is not an available punishment.

To maintain control and order, it is necessary to sanction some inmates, but it is difficult to know which inmate to sanction if there are multiple rule violators. This leads to the difficult question of who should be sanctioned. A trial-and-error approach is unlikely to be successful (Simon et al. 1987). Some inmates are more physically dangerous than others, and a staff member who uses a trial-and-error approach may be assaulted. Moreover, a trial-and-error approach is cognitively unsatisfying. Most people do not go into government work, whether law enforcement or teaching or welfare, so that they can randomly assign treatment to their clients. A more realistic approach to decision making is discussed by Steven Maynard-Moody and Michael Musheno (2003).

Maynard-Moody and Musheno (2003) describe two coexisting narratives for street-level bureaucrats: a state-agent narrative and a citizen-agent narrative. Under the state-agent narrative, street-level bureaucrats are concerned with following rules, proper procedures, and professional norms. The state-agent narrative may be difficult for prison staff, given the plethora of procedures and possible violations and the threat of violence. Under the citizen-agent narrative, street-level bureaucrats are concerned with identifying clients who are worthy citizens and those who are not. Once a client's worth is determined, that dictates the treatment option (Maynard-Moody and Musheno 2003).

Clients who are deemed responsible for their own plight, such as those on general assistance welfare, are viewed more negatively than clients who are not responsible for their own condition, such as those who suffer from a disability (Barrilleaux and Bernick 2003). Extra efforts are made to help worthy clients, while extra efforts are made to punish unworthy clients (Maynard-Moody and Musheno 2003). Clients who are viewed as unmotivated or lazy, or as constant troublemakers, are also deemed unworthy (Maynard-Moody and Musheno 2003). Other forms of law enforcement rely heavily on the citizen-agent perspective. When police officers decide who to search, the decision is largely based on appearance rather than behavior (Epp, Maynard-Moody, and Haider-Markel 2014).

Similarly, Schneider and Ingram (1993) argue that the social construction of a group, which is the group's stereotypes and reputation, help determine the policy options for that group. Schneider and Ingram (1993, p. 336) write, "Public officials commonly inflict punishment on negatively constructed groups who have little or no power, because they need fear no electoral retaliation from the group itself and the general public approves of punishment for groups that it has constructed negatively." Correctional officers may have an incentive to punish those inmates who are stereotyped as more likely to break rules and/or to become violent. Even if a correctional officer tried to get to know each inmate individually, he or she would be influenced by rumors and gossip and other correctional officers' opinions about inmates.

Prison staff must make numerous decisions, and those decisions need to be made quickly. Psychologists distinguish between two systems of thought: one based on reasoning and the other on intuition. System 1 decision making is typically fast, automatic, and emotionally charged. System 2 decision making is slower, takes more effort, and is potentially more rule governed (Kahneman 2003, 2011). System 1 decision making is prevalent in other areas of criminal justice, such as the decision making of judges (Bradbury and Kellough 2011), federal probation officers (Kautt 2009), and police officers (Epp, Maynard-Moody, and Haider-Markel 2014). Correctional officers are likely to use system 1 thinking as well.

Instead of the controlled reasoning of system 2, system 1 thinking relies on the use of heuristics or rules of thumb to simplify decision making (Simon et al. 1987). One common heuristic is the idea of representativeness (Kautt 2009; Tversky and Kahneman 1974). Paula Kautt (2009, p. 195) writes that representativeness is "when equivalence is assumed from a surface or limited similarity (e.g. appearance, a certain number of common characteristics)."

Representativeness simplifies decision making because a person can make decisions based on group characteristics rather than obtaining information about every individual. A prison guard may have stereotypes about inmates based on age, gender, race, or criminal record. Rather than judge each inmate individually (which may be impractical if not impossible), the guard can judge inmates based on their representativeness. In that scenario, a guard does not need to get to know an inmate individually; instead, all African American, or female, or young, or old, or Latino/a, or mentally ill inmates behave the same way. Or all inmates charged with cannabis possession behave the same way. System 1 thinking emphasizes speed and efficiency at the expense of accuracy.

Do correctional officers make decisions based on rules, based on views of client worth, or based on some combination of the two? Do correctional officers distinguish between inmates, and are some inmates stereotyped as more difficult or dangerous than others? In order to find out, I conducted interviews at two prisons in the state of Kentucky. The next section details that fieldwork.

The Kentucky Interviews

Prisons can vary greatly. In the state of Kentucky alone, there are reformatories, a penitentiary, work camps, training centers, halfway houses, probation and parole services, rehabilitative programs, and severe punishments. Throughout the state are scattered 13 adult prison facilities. Each facility has a different composition of staff and inmates in terms of race, gender, security level, and special needs. Many of the inmates at Kentucky State Reformatory have severe health concerns, unlike the mostly physically healthy inmates at the state's minimum security facilities. The facilities also vary widely in terms of safety. Fights that would be rare at a minimum security facility are common at the penitentiary. I asked the sergeant who was giving me a tour of Kentucky State Penitentiary how often fights broke out. He replied, "Every day."

In September 2012, I conducted interviews and toured Western Kentucky Correctional Complex (WKCC). WKCC is located in rural Eddyville, Kentucky, a four-hour drive from Lexington. Eddyville is a tiny town of 2,300 residents, close to the Mississippi River. The closest city is Paducah. Correctional services are a major industry in the area, and WKCC is only a few miles from the state's only maximum security prison, Kentucky State Penitentiary, which I also toured. The differences between WKCC and Kentucky State Penitentiary are readily apparent and enough to support the conclusion that there is not a single, universal American prison system but rather thousands of different fiefdoms. The first time I drove toward Kentucky State

Penitentiary, the edifice was so intimidating that I turned my car around and returned to my hotel. WKCC, despite its razor wire and guard towers, was not nearly as frightening.

WKCC is a multiple security level facility housing approximately 700 inmates, mostly in dormitory-style minimum and medium security units, but the prison does have a disciplinary solitary confinement unit. WKCC has a large substance abuse treatment program with higher than average inmate participation (although at 53 inmates, the program is not universally available). The facility costs the state of Kentucky nearly $11 million a year.

In the same month, I visited and conducted interviews at Kentucky State Reformatory (KSR). KSR is located in LaGrange, Kentucky, about 30 miles northeast of Louisville. KSR is a medium security prison with an administrative segregation unit and is the second-largest prison in the state, with a capacity of over 2,000 inmates. The reformatory specializes in inmates with significant mental and/or physical health concerns. KSR costs the state around $32 million a year.

In the course of my research, I conducted interviews with a total of 23 staff members at two different prison facilities. I was lucky enough to have a wide variety of volunteers: correctional officers, treatment staff, supervisors, and senior-level wardens. I began by asking about their job in general and what their daily routine was like. When I asked whether some inmates were more difficult to deal with than others, 21 of the 23 staff members agreed they were. The vast majority of staff members were able to organize inmates into categories, with judgments about those groups' worth. It might be thought that all inmates are viewed universally, possibly as universally bad, but my interviews suggest that nearly all staff members were able to place inmates into different groups.

Next I asked whether certain groups of inmates were more difficult to deal with than others. It was an open-ended question, and a lot of thought seemed to go into each answer. Four of the respondents said that there were no patterns or significant differences. Seven of the staff members said that the mentally ill were more difficult to deal with, for reasons that may become clearer in chapter 4. Three staff members suggested that younger inmates were more difficult to deal with. Five staff members replied with a racial response or at least a response that suggested some racial tension. The more difficult inmates were described as "wannabe gangbangers," "urban," and inmates with a "drug and thug" culture. These coded descriptors are similar to what Jill McCorkle (2013) found in her study of a female prison. More explicitly, one white female officer replied that "black inmates" were harder to deal with, and one white male officer replied that "colored inmates" were harder to deal with. I heard a similar racially charged statement during my time as a detention officer when a white female officer referred to the inmates as "monkeys." During the interviews, I did not ask if African American (or Latino/a or white) inmates were harder to deal with than others. When one skeptical treatment staff member asked if I meant "racial categories," I replied that they were his categories and his definition.

I also asked whether staff thought inmates could be rehabilitated. Twelve of the 23 staff members agreed that most inmates could be rehabilitated. Six other staff members indicated that some proportion of inmates could be rehabilitated. Only two people flatly said no, although the remainder did not answer the question. Part of the answer depended on the specific occupation of the prison staff. Treatment workers, such as caseworkers and social service clinicians, were more positive in their views on rehabilitation. Unit administrators, employees with a mixture of security and treatment roles, were also broadly positive about the inmates' ability to be rehabilitated. Correctional officers were split exactly 50-50 on the question of rehabilitation. Half of all correctional officers agreed that most inmates at their facility could be rehabilitated, while half answered no or argued that a smaller percentage of inmates could be rehabilitated. This suggests a significant level of variation in how staff view inmates.

Some staff members reported a tension between security and rehabilitation. An inmate may act one way, and a treatment worker will attempt to deescalate; that same behavior may elicit force or a trip to the solitary confinement unit by the security staff. Treatment staff expressed a preference for increased rehabilitative services. On the other hand, some members of the security staff expressed a desire for increased punishments, fewer luxuries, and even an expansion of the prison or the prison's solitary confinement unit. Prison staffs are not monolithic; some express a preference for more rehabilitation and some for more punishment. When I worked for Mecklenburg County, a detention officer suggested that the best way to deal with younger inmates was to rough them up. This was said in a shift meeting and made most of the staff and all the supervisors uncomfortable. The broader point is that there is a wide range of beliefs on what needs to be done to improve American prisons.

An inmate's ability to be rehabilitated, in staff's view, hinges on two categories: a desire to change and an ability to change. Some inmates were viewed as committed to a criminal lifestyle and not wanting to change. These inmates are viewed as "core troublemakers." The estimate of core troublemakers varied from less than 10 percent to around 25 percent of the population. This is broadly in keeping with findings by the Prisoner Research Education Action Project (1976). Prison administrators suggest that between 10 and 20 percent of inmates need to be in prison (PREAP 1976), which of course means that 80–90 percent do not necessarily need to be in prison.

Still, this is not to say that a belief in rehabilitation is widespread among clinical staff and nonexistent among correctional officers. The true story is more complicated. Even treatment workers viewed some inmates as more capable of rehabilitation than others. A treatment worker told me that the inmates who want to change are more engaged in programming. Some of the inmates were resistant to change and were "stuck on stupid." Another treatment worker said that some inmates felt entitled and were incapable of changing. Other inmates were too mentally ill to be effectively rehabilitated. Jill McCorkel's (2013) work on a female prison's drug treatment suggests that treatment staff can be as harsh and disrespectful as the most hardened correctional officer.

While these findings are limited to a small number of prison staff members at two prisons in Kentucky, the findings are in line with the larger work on discretion and street-level bureaucrats. Still, the reader may think that any lessons drawn from the interviews are limited due to a relatively small sample size. Or perhaps there is something unique about prison staff in Kentucky that is not in effect in other states. While I don't necessarily think Kentucky prisons are significantly different from other prisons, I am sympathetic to the charge. This book relies on multiple sources of data, including the Kentucky interviews, quantitative analysis of the Bureau of Justice Statistics' Survey of Inmates in State Correctional Facilities, and perhaps most importantly, the scholarship of other social scientists. In addition to these sources, there is a separate nationally representative survey of correctional officers, called the Criminal Justice Drug Abuse Treatment Studies. This survey allows another way to test for variation in correctional officer views similar to the findings from the Kentucky interviews.

The Criminal Justice Drug Abuse Treatment Studies

The Criminal Justice Drug Abuse Treatment Studies (CJ-DATS) was conducted by the National Institute on Drug Abuse between 2002 and 2008. Five separate surveys were conducted, and I focus on the Survey of Correctional, Probation and Parole Staff. Frontline staff are examined because they play a significant role in deciding treatment and likely play the most important role in the prison disciplinary process. In enforcing rules, guards must define inmate actions as rule violations or not, decide whether or not to intervene, and select an appropriate punishment. Since punishment depends to a large degree on the definition of rule violations, guards may be said not only to interpret rules but also to make them (Howard et al. 1994; Poole and Regoli 1980). Upper-level staff do play a role, but the initial decision to punish comes from frontline staff. The vast majority of disciplinary proceedings result in guilty findings (Howard et al. 1994; Lovell and Jemelka 1996), suggesting that supervisors largely support frontline staff.

The CJ-DATS asked respondents about their views on inmates. Three measures are particularly important and are used as dependent variables: the survey respondent's support for rehabilitation, support for deterrence, and support for "just desserts" punishment. These measures match previous studies of correctional workers' views (Cullen, Fisher, and Applegate 2000; Applegate, Cullen, and Fisher 1997; Cullen et al. 1993). Support for rehabilitation measures the respondent's preferences for matching, providing, and increasing treatment for offenders. Support for deterrence measures the respondent's preferences for deterring future criminals by punishing current offenders. Support for "just desserts" punishment measures the respondent's preferences for punishing current offenders for their moral failings. "Just desserts" punishment can be thought of as retributive, moralistic, "eye for an eye" punishment.

The independent variables of interest focus largely on the demographic characteristics for the CJ-DATS respondents. I include dependent variables for race and ethnicity, gender, education, and age. More detailed information about the methodology for this analysis, along with full model estimations, are presented in the technical appendix. It is difficult to know how much technical information is desired by the reader, so I have decided to discuss the findings in the body of the book while presenting more technical details in the appendix.

Overall, I found that there is significant variation in how correctional staff view inmates. African American staff members have higher levels of support for rehabilitation and lower levels of support for just desserts punishment. Latino/a staff have lower levels of support for both deterrence and just desserts punishment. Those with higher levels of education, especially holders of bachelor's and master's degrees, have higher levels of support for rehabilitation and lower levels of support for deterrence and just desserts punishment. Older workers were less punitive, while female corrections workers were more punitive across all three measures. These sorts of differences in preferences are a common finding in the literature on street-level bureaucrats (Keiser and Soss 1998; Meier and Nicholson-Crotty 2006; Wilkins and Keiser 2006).

Correctional officers have different preferences for rehabilitation and punishment. Officers view some inmates as more difficult to deal with than others, and the categories that separate difficult from easy-to-deal-with inmates are not random. The nature of prison work, like other street-level bureaucracies, involves a lot of discretion. These elements all add up to the ability of a correctional officer to discriminate against some inmates. With 750,000 correctional employees, we have the possibility of 750,000 different preferences and biases. All these biases translate into systematic discrimination—against the poor, against the sick, against racial minorities, against immigrants, and against drug users.

Guards are unable to apply punishments or programs fairly due to a lack of time, money, and cognitive resources. Because of this, prison guards, like other street-level bureaucrats, rely on system 1 decision-making processes. System 1 decision making is prone to cognitive biases; if nothing else, guards are likely to be at least as biased as the general public. Bias and discretion are the necessary ingredients for discrimination. Even small biases among a multitude of prison guards can lead to widespread, systematic discrimination. While discrimination may be inevitable due to a lack of resources, and while cognitive limitations suggest that guards may be acting unconsciously, discrimination does disproportionately burden the vulnerable. The next seven chapters of this book will document those burdens.

CHAPTER THREE

Punishing the Poor

On January 11, 2016, in Grand Rapids, Michigan, teenager Djibril Niyomugabo was found unresponsive in a Kent County Correctional Facility jail cell. Only 18, he would die two days later in a Grand Rapids hospital, having committed suicide. The teenager was in jail on a charge of larceny for less than $200 and personal property damage between $200 and $1,000 (Avila 2016). Unable to post bail, Niyomugabo was placed in a jail cell. His parents, refugees who relocated to Michigan from Rwanda, lacked the necessary funds to post his bail (Avila 2016). A young man's life was cut short because he could neither handle the pressures of a jail cell nor afford a couple of hundred dollars for bail. We will never know if Djibril was guilty, because his case never went to trial. We will never know what Djibril could have been, because he lost his life in an American jail.

America's jails and prisons are filled with poor, vulnerable young men and women like Djibril Niyomugabo. The "war on crime" is largely a war on the poor. Eighty-three percent of people currently in American jails remain there for no other reason than that they cannot afford to pay their bail (Hill 2016). Not only are prisoners drawn largely from the ranks of the impoverished but also many "crimes" are related to poverty. Cities and states have increasingly criminalized homelessness, law enforcement deliberately targets low-income areas, and many "crimes" are a reflection of an inability to pay for state regulations (e.g., court fees, license fees, and car maintenance issues). These fees do not pose the same burdens for middle- and upper-class people.

Why focus on minor "crimes" such as an expired license or a broken taillight? Rather than an uncaring conspiracy against the poor, the focus on minor crimes is based on a popular, but deeply flawed, criminological theory. The focus on minor offenses is a central tenant of the "broken windows" theory of policing. Developed by political scientist James Q. Wilson and criminologist George L. Kelling, "broken windows" theorized that the fear of crime was related to disorderly neighborhoods and that disorder incentivized more serious crime. By concentrating on minor crimes, police could deter and prevent serious crimes.

In a 1982 article in the *Atlantic* magazine, Wilson and Kelling wrote,

> Many citizens, of course, are primarily frightened by crime, especially crime involving a sudden, violent attack by a stranger. This risk is very real, in Newark as in many large cities. But we tend to overlook another source of fear—the fear of being bothered by disorderly people. Not violent people, nor, necessarily, criminals, but disreputable or obstreperous or unpredictable people: panhandlers, drunks, addicts, rowdy teenagers, prostitutes, loiterers, the mentally disturbed. (pp. 1–2)

The last sentence of Wilson and Kelling's quote highlights that the vulnerable make up the population most often targeted by the police. Even Wilson and Kelling admitted that these people are "not violent people, nor, necessarily, criminals."

Wilson and Kelling (1982, pp. 2–3) continued,

> At the community level, disorder and crime are usually inextricably linked, in a kind of developmental sequence. Social psychologists and police officers tend to agree that if a window in a building is broken and is left unrepaired, all the rest of the windows will soon be broken. This is as true in nice neighborhoods as in rundown ones. Window-breaking does not necessarily occur on a large scale because some areas are inhabited by determined window-breakers whereas others are populated by window-lovers; rather, one unrepaired broken window is a signal that no one cares, and so breaking more windows costs nothing.

According to Wilson and Kelling, one broken window encourages more broken windows.

The "broken windows" theory became very popular in the decades after Wilson and Kelling's article. In fact, it is hard to overstate the impact and influence of that article. As of January 2018, it has been cited 5,419 times and has received wide academic exposure and influenced policing policy. New York City hired Kelling as a consultant and "broken windows" proponent William Bratton as first head of the transit police and then as police commissioner. Bratton focused police on subway fare jumpers, people drinking in public, the homeless, and the dreaded "squeegee men"—homeless residents who would attempt to put dirty water on passing cars unless the car's driver gave them money (Hill 2016). We live in a society where fraud, embezzlement, and recession-generating behavior are less threatening to the powers that be in New York City than subway fare jumpers or squeegee men. It is also a society where the homeless receive more scrutiny and punishment than police officers who kill citizens.

"Broken windows" policing was and is a major contributor to mass incarceration. It forced police to focus on minor, nuisance offenses rather than more substantial issues. This allowed for more contact between the police and the vulnerable and a deterioration in the relationship between the police and poor communities. Similar forces are at work in American prisons; most rules regulate nonharmful or minimally harmful behaviors. For example, most searches for contraband turn up items like excess food, clothing, and personal items. I spent a good deal of my time as a detention officer confiscating surplus oranges from inmate cells. It is possible for an inmate to make alcohol from surplus oranges. It is also possible for an inmate to use an orange as a snack to stave off hunger, or to eat an orange rather than overpay for unhealthy snacks from the prison commissary. The larger point is that "broken windows" policing applied an academic and theoretical cover for an increasingly intrusive form of law enforcement, both inside and outside of prisons.

Alex Vitale (2017, p. 7) writes, "Broken-windows policing is at root a deeply conservative attempt to shift the burden of responsibility for declining living conditions onto the poor themselves and to argue that the solution to all social ills is increasingly aggressive, invasive, and restrictive forms of policing that involve more arrests, more harassment, and ultimately more violence." Broken windows policing is self-reinforcing; arresting people disrupts an individual's and a neighborhood's economic capital, which leads to higher unemployment, increased forms of petty public disorder, and a subsequent increase of broken windows policing to combat high unemployment and petty public disorder.

In New York City, 7.3 million citations were issued between 2001 and 2013 for things like cannabis possession, public urination, littering, and public consumption of alcohol. In 2011, there were 50,000 arrests for cannabis possession alone. In 2013, one precinct issued summonses to nearly one in five residents. The New York Police Department had a strategy of underreporting serious crime statistics (in order to maintain the narrative that serious crime was down) while at the same time enforcing a quota system requiring officers to complete a predetermined number of nuisance arrests. One officer fulfilled his quota by ticketing subway riders who occupied more than one space (Hill 2016). An additional consequence is that policing becomes a numbers game, and increasing citations can lead to increasing budgets, which lead to increasing citations and even more revenue.

One manifestation of "broken windows" policing is the policy known as "stop and frisk." Between 2002 and 2015, over 5 million people were subject to "stop and frisk" (NYCLU 2016). At the height of the program, in 2011,

685,724 New Yorkers were subjected to "stop and frisk." According to the NYPD's own internal reports, nearly 90 percent of those stopped and frisked were completely innocent (NYCLU 2016). It is widely acknowledged that the program disproportionately targeted the poor and racial minorities. Residents described a police presence so heavy that it felt like a siege. They suffered from sexual harassment, humiliation, and physical violence at the hands of NYPD officers during the program (Center for Constitutional Rights 2012). "Stop and frisk" was declared unconstitutional in 2013, although similar programs still exist. The increased harassment of citizens did not have a beneficial impact on crime rates. Crime rates and the "stop and frisk" policy were uncorrelated (Bump 2016).

The 2012 report by the Center for Constitutional Rights featured interviews with New York City residents and their opinions on why they were stopped. Multiple interviewees mentioned being stopped for being poor. The following quotes were representative of the report's findings: "I live in the Bronx, and the Bronx is like one of the . . . poorest counties in the nation, so I feel like that itself is a target" (p. 14). "If you have a status in society, I think they kind of, like, let you off the hook. But if they think you're, like, lower class or poor, working poor, forget about it. It's a wrap. They know that you're not going to have [any] resources to, like, fight anything" (p. 14).

"Stop and frisk"–style tactics are not unique to New York City. When Baltimore publicly adopted zero tolerance policing in the early 2000s, it resulted in the arrest of one in six people and a federal lawsuit filed by the ACLU. In Ferguson, Missouri, police "routinely conducted stops that had little relation to public safety and a questionable basis in law" often issuing multiple citations for the same violation. It was not unusual for towns in St. Louis county to cite residents for loud music, unkempt property, disruptive behavior and "saggy pants" (Hill 2016, pp. 22–23). Similarly, Charles Epp, Steven Maynard-Moody, and Donald Haider-Markel (2014) argue that the most important factor in investigative police stops is not how people drive but how they look. Drivers of less expensive, less well-maintained cars were especially targeted.

In her seminal book, *The New Jim Crow*, Michelle Alexander describes how the rights of citizens have diminished while the legal protections for police officers have increased dramatically. Supreme Court decisions have enabled the police to search and seize people basically anywhere and for any reason. "It is no longer necessary for the police to have any reason to believe that people are engaged in criminal activity or actually dangerous to stop and search them. As long as you give 'consent,' the police can stop, interrogate and search you for any reason or no reason at all" (Alexander 2010, p. 64). Given that the police are armed and in many cases physically intimidating, it is not surprising that most people consent to police orders.

Police officers cast a wide net in modern crime enforcement. Alexander (2010, p. 71) found that the Drug Enforcement Agency provided "drug courier" profiles to help police identify potential violators of drug crimes. The list of what constitutes suspicious behavior would be comical were it not for the serious consequences such profiles have had for the vulnerable. The profile can include "traveling with luggage, traveling without luggage, driving an expensive car, driving a car that needs repairs, driving with out-of-state license plates, driving a rental car, driving with 'mismatched occupants,' acting too calm, acting too nervous, dressing casually, wearing expensive clothing or jewelry, being one of the first to deplane, being one of the last to deplane, deplaning in the middle, paying for a ticket in cash, using large-denomination currency, using small-denomination currency, traveling alone and traveling with a companion." Even strict adherence to laws is considered suspicious. The Florida Highway Patrol drug courier profile cautioned troopers to be suspicious of "scrupulous obedience to traffic laws" (Alexander 2010, p. 71).

I would ask the reader to pause and consider the fact that using these profiles, literally anyone can be targeted.

Police have discretion on which neighborhoods and which individuals inside those neighborhoods to target. The poor are disproportionately targeted because their poverty makes them vulnerable. Many rich and powerful people commit "crimes" at higher rates than the poor. For example, cannabis use is higher among adolescents of higher socioeconomic status (Patrick et al. 2012). Employed Americans use illegal drugs at higher rates than do unemployed Americans (Substance Abuse and Mental Health Services Administration 2012). Poverty does not equate to crime, while wealth equates to innocence, despite popular rhetoric.

There is a system of justice for the wealthy and powerful and a much harsher system for the vulnerable. Djibril Niyomugabo was vulnerable and poor. If his father had been wealthy rather than a refugee from Rwanda, Djibril might be alive today.

Why Punish the Poor?

The poor are a weak and isolated political target, unable to push back as others could. When attacked, the poor are rarely able to defend themselves in the policy process" (Soss, Fording, and Schram 2011). The poor are not only less capable of resisting the state but also viewed negatively in American society. Poor women are denigrated as lazy and licentious. Poor men are viewed as a labor source at best and as "social dynamite" at worst (Soss, Fording, and Schram 2011). Every society has to find a way to manage the poor; the most common strategies are either generous safety nets or repressive security forces. It is clear which path the modern United States has emphasized.

The dominant ideology in the United States currently is sometimes referred to as "neoliberal paternalism." The neoliberal part reflects a belief in market efficiency and views people as clients rather than citizens and as individuals rather than members of groups. Neoliberalism defines social problems as matters of personal choice. The default assumption is that the problems of the person are the products of individual choice best resolved through individual solutions (Soss, Fording, and Schram 2011). This ideology is dominant in both major political parties. Republicans will point to the need for personal responsibility or accountability. Democrats will echo many of the same points. Even Democrats who support rehabilitation are implicitly arguing that the vulnerable are broken or inferior. A focus on rehabilitation ignores the presence of discrimination. Job training programs do not protect against racial profiling. Life skills classes do not protect against discriminatory police patrols. Overall, the neoliberal emphasis states that the problems of the poor are individual and not structural. Both political parties largely view the poor as responsible for their own predicaments.

The paternalism part reflects a belief that government knows better than people what those people need. This paternalism is reflected in the plethora of government codes and regulations. The Heritage Foundation estimates that there are more than 4,500 offenses in the federal criminal code and 300,000 more regulations that carry criminal consequences (Hill 2016). Congress creates an average of 56 new federal crimes a year. Crimes can be as trivial as the lack of a buckled seatbelt, jaywalking, having a dog off its leash, failure to move promptly in a park, or having feet on a subway seat (Ferguson 2014). The paternalism can be a ban on trans fats or big gulp sodas, speed limits, gun control laws, or, more devastatingly, the criminalization of poverty.

Under paternalism, government agents believe that it is necessary to step in and tell the poor what to do. Since government actors believe they know better than the poor, government actors are morally obligated to intervene. "Government must step in as a disciplinary authority, and must do so for the poor's own good" (Soss, Fording, and Schram 2011, p. 26). The American government, at all levels, simply does not trust the poor or even middle-class Americans to police themselves. Ironically, the same government that does not trust the poor has more faith in capitalism, the wealthy, and free markets (Comaroff and Comaroff 2016).

In his brilliant 2009 book *Punishing the Poor*, Loic Wacquant describes the natural consequences of the neoliberal paternalist ideology. A government based on generosity and welfare has been gradually replaced by a police and penal state. "As the social safety net of the charitable state unraveled, the dragnet of the punitive state was called upon to replace it" (Wacquant 2009, p. 58). This can be seen distinctly in the change in funding for welfare programs compared to that for prisons in the last 40 years. If our funding reflects our priorities, it is clear that we have prioritized incarceration while minimizing welfare payments.

We can compare welfare spending using funding for Aid to Families with Dependent Children (AFDC) prior to 1994 and based on Temporary Assistance to Needy Families (TANF) after 1994. State corrections spending is also available from the Bureau of Justice Statistics expenditure data. In 1980, welfare spending was over $30 billion, while corrections spending was around $10 billion. By 1995, corrections spending began to surpass welfare spending. By 2010, we were spending over $10 billion more on corrections than on welfare. In the span of 30 years, we completely flipped our spending priorities.

These numbers point to a clear trend; as welfare spending decreased, state prison spending increased. This finding echoes a broad literature that finds increasing state punitiveness toward the poor (Garland 2001; Soss, Fording, and Schram 2011; Wacquant 2009). Between 1994 and 2008, the number of AFDC/TANF recipients in the United States declined by about 72 percent. The real value of AFDC benefits declined by 42 percent between 1970 and 1996 (Soss, Fording, and Schram 2011). In 1980, the United States spent 58 percent more on AFDC than on jails and prisons; by 1995, U.S. spending on jails and prisons exceeded investments in AFDC as well as food stamps (Wacquant 2009).The vulnerable poor are punished twice: first by losing access to welfare benefits and second by increased incarceration.

However, this trend underestimates the true shift away from welfare generosity and toward a system of mass incarceration. It is not possible to include longitudinal estimates of local jail and Federal Bureau of Prisons spending. I have estimated the total amount of yearly correctional spending by assuming that the spending ratio in 2011 is representative of earlier year spending. In 2011, state correctional spending accounted for roughly 63 percent of overall correctional spending. By adding federal and local jail spending to the equation, the shift from welfare to prison becomes even more stark.

In 1980, welfare spending was more than twice the rate of total correctional spending. By 2010, the pattern was reversed, with total correctional spending at more than twice the rate of welfare spending. In 2010, there was over $50 billion in total correctional spending but only slightly more than $20 billion in welfare spending. Increasing numbers of poor people became managed by prisons rather than through a generous welfare safety net. Wacquant (2009, p. 284) has referred to this as "punitive containment of the poor." Prison has become a holding pen for the vulnerable poor—when there are not enough housing opportunities, the homeless can be placed in jail; when there is extreme poverty, the poor can be placed in prison. Wacquant argues that American prisons are not full of violent predators but of nonviolent criminals and petty delinquents drawn from the most vulnerable sections of the working class.

Some might argue that the poor are in fact incarcerated at higher rates but due to the fact that the poor commit crime at higher rates. Surely, most people in prison are guilty of the crime they committed. This is inaccurate in at least two respects: the poor do not necessarily commit "crimes" at higher rates, and we are not entirely sure what a "crime" is anyway. White-collar crime is not taken as seriously as public intoxication or trespassing. Even violent "crime" is in the eye of the beholder. Not every killing constitutes a murder, which is cold comfort to the families of Trayvon Martin, Walter Scott, Michael Brown, Philando Castile, or the 90 percent of drone attack victims overseas who were not the intended target (Fang 2015).

In reality, most poor people are targeted precisely because of their vulnerability. And their vulnerability is punished multiple times after an arrest.

The Crime of Being Poor

In Ferguson, Missouri, 16,000 out of the town's 20,000 people had some form of outstanding arrest warrant, nearly all related to a missed payment or court appearance on a traffic fine or other minor municipal code violation (Hill 2016). Police departments have an economic incentive to ticket poor people with a variety of fines for low-level offenses. In Ferguson, fines and fees accounted for nearly a quarter of the police department's operating revenue (Hill 2016). The poor are more likely to be fined simply because they have fewer resources to comply with government regulations. Small fines and offenses can add up to millions of dollars for police departments and cities as well as the arrest and incarceration of vulnerable Americans.

This focus on petty offenses is not new. After the Civil War, the South's economy was in shambles, and there was heavy demand for cheap labor. In the late 1860s, every Southern state except Arkansas and Tennessee passed laws outlawing vagrancy, which effectively allowed law enforcement to seize unemployed people. An 1865 Mississippi law required African Americans to enter into labor contracts by January 1 of every year or risk arrest. The arrest records of many counties in the South reveal the petty infractions that constituted "crime," including changing employers without permission, vagrancy, riding freight cars without a ticket, and engaging in sexual activity or loud talk with white women. The timing and scale of surges in arrests was correlated with the demand for cheap labor (Blackmon 2008).

Currently, 150 years later, the poor are still heavily targeted by law enforcement. Many inmates are placed in jail based on minor and in many cases ambiguous charges. Inmates are swept up because of trespassing, failure to signal, cannabis possession, "disorderly conduct," or simply because the police do not like a certain individual. After being arrested on a minor charge, the vast majority of inmates must stay in jail because they cannot afford to post bail. In New York City, more than half of inmates remain in jail until trial because they cannot afford bail of $2,500 or less. Grand Rapids teenager Djibril Niyomugabo pled not guilty to two misdemeanor charges but could not afford the $200 bail required to leave jail (Roelofs 2016). Once in jail, the vulnerable face a system designed to punish rather than determine objective levels of guilt or innocence.

The standard view of the American criminal justice system is wildly inaccurate:

> Full-blown trials of guilt or innocence rarely occur; many people never meet with an attorney; witnesses are routinely paid and coerced by the government; police regularly stop and search people for no reason whatsoever; penalties for many crimes are so severe that many innocent people plead guilty, accepting plea bargains to avoid harsh mandatory sentences; and children, even as young as fourteen, are sent to adult prisons. Rules of law and procedure, such as "guilty beyond a reasonable doubt" or "probable cause" or "reasonable suspicion" can easily be found in court cases and law-school textbooks but are much harder to find in real life. (Alexander 2010, p. 59)

Conditions of detention in big-city jails are so punishing that the majority of inmates rush to plead guilty and negotiate a reduced sentence. "For the vast majority of the urban poor sent behind bars, a trial has become a judicial oddity they encounter only on television shows such as 'Law and Order'" (Wacquant 2009, p. 123). Even misdemeanors are pled out. One public defender in Georgia handled 1,493 cases in four years; of those, 14 went to trial. It is estimated that 97 percent of federal cases and 94 percent of state cases end in some kind of plea deal. "As Supreme Court justice Anthony Kennedy acknowledged in his *Lafler v Cooper* majority opinion in 2012, 'Ours is a system of pleas, not a system of trials'" (Hill 2016, p. 72).

Another misconception is that poor people can afford public defenders. Public defenders are not actually free. Two-thirds of states allow judges to require defendants to pay for a court-appointed public defender. Fees for a public defender range from $450 to actual costs (Harris 2016). States establish their own policies for indigent defense; four states do so without any funding or oversight. "Thousands of persons are processed through

America's courts every year either with no lawyer at all or with a lawyer who does not have the time, resources, or in some cases the inclination to provide effective representation." As a result "defendants plead guilty, even if they are innocent, without really understanding their legal rights or what is occurring" (Hill 2016, p. 86). Approximately 80 percent of inmates are too poor to afford a lawyer (Alexander 2010).

Even if a poor person can afford a public defender, that public defender is likely to be of low quality and, in some cases, ethically compromised. Sixty-four percent of U.S. counties use a "flat-fee system" where a judge provides a contract to private attorneys to represent every defendant that comes before them. Because of their relatively low pay rates, flat-fee systems tend to attract less experienced lawyers. Within a flat-fee system, attorneys are paid the same amount regardless of the complexity or severity of the case. The financial costs of representation, such as hiring investigators and expert witnesses and requesting records, subtract from the attorney's profits. "Essentially, it is in the best interest of the flat-fee defense attorney to do as little work as possible" (Hill 2016, p. 91). These attorneys are also incentivized to please judges in order to get future contracts.

While public defenders are compromised, lawyers for the state have significant advantages. Prosecutors have enormous power and are able to convince most defendants to accept a plea deal. Prosecutors offer a brutal bargain; Robert Ferguson (2014, p. 112) describes the process:

> Bargaining often means "an exploding offer," one that disappears if it is not accepted quickly, and it applies to separate defendants at different times in order to break down solidarity among codefendants. A prosecutor says "take the bargain now, or the offer is dead or goes to your codefendant." For strategic reasons, defendants are threatened with trials even when the prosecutor has no intention of seeking one.

It is difficult for even the innocent to risk a jury trial and many years of prison time.

As if being disproportionately targeted and being unable to launch a credible legal defense were not enough, the criminal justice system also includes monetary sanctions on poor defendants. Monetary sanctions are nothing new. Douglas Blackmon (2008) writes of a man named Green Cottenham who was arrested for vagrancy in 1908. Unable to pay the fees assessed on every prisoner, including fees to the sheriff, the deputy, the court clerk, and witnesses, Cottenham's sentence was extended to nearly a year of hard labor (Blackmon 2008). Today, the majority of people convicted of misdemeanor and felony crimes in the United States receive some type of monetary sanction. State statutes allow judges to sentence people involved in the criminal justice system to fines, fees, restitution, and surcharges (Harris 2016). These monetary sanctions vary by state and county, but all place an extra burden on poor defendants.

In Pennsylvania, there are 2,629 types of monetary sanctions, 90 percent of which are fees and court costs. In Louisiana, even if someone is found not guilty, that person has to pay $100 to have the record of their arrest removed from their legal record. In a study of 11 states, it was found that in each state an average of $178 million was owed in court costs. In Washington state, poor defendants are hit with a fee for requesting a jury of $125 to $250 depending on the size of the jury, warrant costs of $100, court costs of $200, and an annual $100 collection surcharge. In some states, inmates are charged between $50 and $100 a day for "rent." States can also charge interest on monetary sanctions; Washington state charges 12 percent, Georgia charges 7 percent, and Florida charges just under 5 percent. Illinois allows judges to assess a 15 percent penalty on monetary sanctions in addition to a 30 percent collection fee. Arizona charges a $35 fee and a 19 percent collection fee for delinquent payments on monetary sanctions (Harris 2016).

In 2014, a total of $740,716,759 was owed on monetary sanction accounts in Alexander County, Washington. The average arrear was $4,713. Eight percent of the adult population was in legal debt to the county (Harris 2016). Similarly, a study by Joyce Arditti and April Few (2006) found that 92 percent of incarcerated mothers reported that they currently had fines due to the criminal justice system (on average $4,718). It is difficult for many people to have to pay a nearly $5,000 fee, but it is especially difficult for the poor. "As the poor become ever more trapped, in a cycle of poverty and debt fueled by the LFOs [legal financial obligations, another term for monetary sanctions] imposed by the criminal justice system, people with financial means are able to escape the burden of legal debt and at least begin to plot a path to successful reintegration and community reentry" (Harris 2016, p. 53).

Further complicating community reentry is that many states restrict political rights as long as someone owes a monetary sanction. Debtors cannot regain certain rights lost on conviction, such as the right to vote, carry a weapon, serve on juries, or run for elected office until their account is paid in full. Seventeen states prohibit legal debtors from voting until their debts are paid in full. Thirteen additional states make voting dependent on regular debt payments. Forty-four states and the District of Columbia allow judges to incarcerate people for unpaid monetary sanctions (Harris 2016).

These harsh penalties trap the vulnerable but are beneficial to the state. Monetary sanctions and the enforcement of minor fees generates revenue, and punishing the poor makes them more easily exploitable by the labor market. Prisoners are a source of cheap, easily controlled labor. Once people leave prison, they are often on parole, which usually comes with job requirements, and parolees are typically pressured to take any job available. Aggressive policing and incarceration make any legal job more appealing (Soss, Fording, and Schram 2011). Using prisoners or parolees as a labor force depresses the incomes of other low-wage workers.

The scale of prison labor is staggering. In Texas, about 10,000 inmates work in the system's agriculture jobs, producing almost $50 million worth of edible crops, livestock, and cotton. About 8,000 inmates work in the prison industries program, producing $100 million worth of products (Wacquant 2009). Inmates are employed to make license plates, grow vegetables, paint public buildings, pick up litter on the road, and tend municipal graveyards (Brown and Severson 2011). A sheriff in Massachusetts recently offered to supply free inmate labor to help build additions to the United States–Mexico border wall (Edwards 2017). Inmates provide labor for multiple U.S. private companies, including Whole Foods Market, IBM, Motorola, Compaq, Texas Instruments, Honeywell, Microsoft, Boeing, Nordstrom, McDonald's, Wendy's, Walmart, Starbucks, Sprint, Verizon, Victoria's Secret, Fidelity Investment Services, J.C. Penney, Kmart, American Airlines, and Avis Rent A Car (Davis 1998; Riley 2014). This exploitation is part of a long tradition dating back to the old convict leasing system in the South (Blackmon 2008).

Prison labor is appealing to companies because there are no prison unions and prisoners do not have the ability to strike. Prison labor offers fewer issues with the types of language barriers that occur when companies offshore jobs. In addition, companies using prison labor do not have to pay benefits like health insurance, unemployment insurance, or workers' compensation (Davis 1998). Despite often dangerous conditions, it is very difficult for inmates to organize, and that lack of bargaining power makes inmates a reliable workforce. However, the main benefit to using inmate labor, both for private companies and for various governments, is that inmates work for incredibly low wages.

Today, inmates who work maintenance jobs in the federal prison system make between 12 and 40 cents an hour. The wage for those working in federal prison industries programs is between 23 cents and $1.15 an hour. A prison camp in Nevada paid 13 cents per hour. The average minimum wage per day paid to state prisoners is 93 cents. The maximum wage per day paid to state prisoners is $4.73 (Prison Policy Initiative 2017). Even in cases where inmates provide dangerous, critical services, wages are minimal. Thirty-four hundred inmates serve as firefighters in California, battling the state's frequent wildfires. The inmates are paid $2 a day and then $1 per hour for each hour of active firefighting. Over 2,000 inmates were involved in active firefighting in July 2018. The program cannot even claim to be providing valuable skills and job experience; most fire departments in California require firefighters to be licensed emergency medical technicians (EMTs), and most EMT certifying boards deny applicants with a criminal history (Hess 2018).

Prison labor has also been used in disaster cleanup. In April 2010, a British Petroleum (BP) drilling rig exploded in the Gulf of Mexico, killing 11 people and spilling about 205 million barrels of oil into the Gulf (Jones 2011). The BP oil spill damaged more than 1,300 miles of coastline (Milman 2018). The company hired prisoners for its cleanup operations because "it could work those men an average of seventy-two hours a week and pay them little to nothing. It also could get away with providing flimsy coveralls and gloves as protection from extensive exposure to crude oil and chemical dispersants—all of which damage every system in the body, as well as cell structures and DNA" (Thompson 2012, p. 42). The oil spill did not damage BP's long-term profitability. By 2012, BP was pulling in $25 billion in annual profits (MacAlister 2012).

It is not just inmates who are involved in firefighting and disaster relief who must risk their lives for low compensation; many prison factory jobs are performed in terrible working conditions. Heather Ann Thompson (2012, p. 43) describes conditions at a federal prison where female prisoners recycled computer parts by smashing the computers with hammers. The prisons "were engulfed in thick clouds of cadmium and lead dust that covered surfaces throughout the prison and coated the windshields of cars parked outside. Yet none of the prisoners or staff were supplied with masks, gloves, coveralls, or other personal protective equipment and when they asked about possible risks to their health they were told not to worry about it." The federal prison industries corporation UNICOR has concealed actual working conditions by cleaning up production lines before inspectors arrived (Thompson 2012).

Given the frequent use of monetary sanctions, and the incredibly low wages that most inmates work for, it is impossible for most inmates to pay off their debts, and interest rates cause those debts to rise. The wages that are earned are soon consumed by a series of fees and overcharges. Inmates who work in the high-security facility of Fort Madison, Iowa, receive wages ranging from $10 to $60 per month. Inmates must pay $5 each month for "rent." A visit to the prison dentist costs $3. Their earnings are subject to further deductions, such as restitution and court costs. In addition, personal hygiene supplies, stamps, paper, and extra food have to be purchased from the prison commissary at inflated prices (Wacquant 2009). Due to fees and inflated prices, inmates are often dependent on money sent from outside friends and family members. Even then, the state takes a cut. California inmates face a restitution fine of 22 percent of all the sums they receive in custody, whatever their source.

Commissary serves as a lifeline for inmates in many prisons. The largest demand is for food items. The quality of food in many prisons is poor and the portions are small. Commissary food helps to supplement the inadequate and insufficient food at most prisons. Meals are often served at poorly spaced times. At Delaney Hall immigration detention facility, meals are served at 6:45 a.m., 12:00 p.m., and 5:00 p.m. with no food offered in between (Conlon and Hiemstra 2014). When I worked for Mecklenburg County, we served inmates breakfast at around 4:00 a.m. Many inmates did not want to get up that early for a mediocre to worse breakfast.

Table 3.1 lists select items from the Mecklenburg County (North Carolina) jail's commissary list, with a corresponding price for the same products at the Walmart website. When equivalent items were not available, I based the price comparison on per-unit costs. Some items, for example the indigent stationery item listed on the commissary list, are also not comparable. Still, it is possible to see broad patterns in pricing.

The vast majority of items for sale at the Mecklenburg County commissary are significantly more expensive than those same items at Walmart. Some items, especially clothing and medicine, are two to three times as expensive at the commissary as in the outside world. It is also worth noting

Table 3.1 Select commissary item price comparison

Item	Mecklenburg County	Walmart
20 oz. Mountain Dew	1.59	1.72
6 oz. lemonade mix	1.49	0.79
Baby Ruth candy bar	1.19	1.25
Eraser pencil cap	0.19	0.04
Greeting card with stamp	1.59	1.09
Manila envelope with 2 stamps	1.79	1.14
Playing cards	2.39	0.59
Medium sports bra	10.25	3.5
Women's underwear, size 8	3	1.41
Canvas shoes	5.75	2.99
Men's undershirt	4.25	2.81
Socks	2.5	0.99
English/Spanish dictionary	3	3.99
Deodorant	2.5	1.98
Soap, Dove 2.6 oz.	3.23	2.73
Colgate regular toothpaste	2.5	1.65
Advil 2-pack	0.89	0.12
Toothbrush	0.89	0.88
Indigent stationery	0.99	not available
3 oz. generic bar soap	0	not available

that anyone who deposits money into an inmate's commissary account (which is necessary, given low inmate wages) has to pay a significant convenience fee. Mecklenburg County has contracted out its commissary processing service to TouchPay Payment Services. TouchPay does not have a list of fees on its website; however, after signing up for an account, I was able to see the convenience fees for various amounts. Donations to inmate accounts range from $10 to $300. The minimum convenience fee is $6.35 for a $10 donation, and the maximum is $16.50 for a $300 donation. It is worth remembering that most people are in jail because they cannot pay bail; therefore, it is unlikely that their family members can easily afford the TouchPay convenience fees.

Even the process of contacting family members can be a burden for inmates. As can be seen from the commissary list, inmates are overcharged for stamps and envelopes. Calling home also involves significant charges. A 15-minute phone call can cost $3.15. This was actually a vast improvement. Prior to 2014, inmates could be charged as much as $70 for a 15-minute phone call. New FCC rules under President Obama imposed a limit of 25 cents per minute for debit calling and 21 cents per minute for collect calling. These regulations are in the process of being overturned. As of June 2017, a federal court has overturned the Obama-era regulation, and FCC chairperson Ajit Pai has said the agency will not defend the new rules (Kang 2017). If the prices return to pre-2014 levels, inmates will have a much harder time maintaining regular contact with their family members. These issues will be brought up again in chapter 8, which discusses the pains of incarceration that extend to the inmate's family.

Nationally, the earned annual income of two-thirds of jail inmates was under $12,000 for the year prior to their arrest. A study of New York parolees in 2004 found that 49 percent were unemployed, 81 percent needed services for drug abuse, and 15 percent had only a grade-school education. Thirty to 36 percent of jail and state prison inmates did not have a job prior to their conviction. Another 26 percent were working part time. Of those working before arrest, 23 percent reported monthly earnings of less than $600. Half reported a monthly income of $1,200 or less (Harris 2016). By most measures, prisoners are an exceedingly vulnerable population.

Although it seems unbelievable, inmates who were making between $600 and $1,200 a month prior to their arrest are the relatively affluent ones. Many inmates are destitute and have experienced homelessness. Compared to other Americans, inmates suffered high rates of homelessness before their time in prison. In a study of people staying at homeless shelters in New York City, it was found that 23 percent had been incarcerated in the previous two years (Metraux and Culhane 2006). Shelter use is also correlated with increased incarcerations (Metraux and Culhand 2004). Another study found that around 9 percent of inmates experienced homelessness in the year prior to their arrest, a rate four to six times that of the general population (Greenberg and Rosenheck 2008).

In many American cities, homelessness is literally criminalized. Due to a lack of shelter and a lack of access to bathrooms, the homeless are forced to sleep and urinate in public. Many cities have passed bans on sleeping in public, sleeping in cars, lying down in public, and camping in public. In addition, many cities have passed bans on loitering, asking for money, or sharing free food (Vitale 2017). Even attempting to help the homeless is criminalized in some cities. In 2014, a 90-year-old man named Arnold Abbott and two South Florida ministers, Rev. Dwayne Blackand and Rev. Mark Sims, were arrested for handing out food to the homeless in a Fort Lauderdale, Florida, park. Violation of the ordinance risks up to 60 days in jail and a $500 fine (Chasmar 2014).

In order to examine the treatment of the poor in American prisons, I have relied on data from the Bureau of Justice Statistics *Survey of Inmates in State and Federal Correctional Facilities, 2004* (hereafter referred to as 2004 Survey). The 2004 Survey involved personal interviews in both state and federal prisons that provided information about the inmate's criminal offense, personal history, demographics, precarceral life, participation in treatment programs, and punishment inside prison. A detailed explanation of the 2004 Survey analysis and full model estimations are included in the technical appendix of this book. An updated version of the data, which covered inmates surveyed in 2016, is scheduled to be released by the Bureau of Justice Statistics in 2019. Once the new data set is released, I will post the results from a similar analysis on my website, www.punishingthevulnerable.com. The website also contains original content related to this book and larger issues surrounding vulnerable populations in American prisons.

The 2004 Survey contains several variables that serve as proxies for poverty. Slightly less than 4 percent of all inmates are in prison for a public offense, such as disorderly conduct or loitering. While a small percentage, in absolute numbers that comes to nearly 87,000 inmates (using 2015 prison and jail population estimates). The number of people in prison or jail for public offenses exceeds the capacity for the University of Oklahoma or the Florida State University football stadium. Public offenses are not the only minor crimes for which the poor are disproportionately punished. Over 12 percent of inmates are in prison for property offenses (nearly 270,000 inmates in absolute numbers). The combined inmate population in jail and prison for property or public offenses is greater than the populations of Lexington, Kentucky; St. Louis, Missouri; and Pittsburgh, Pennsylvania.

Using the 2004 Survey, I was able to estimate whether treatment in prison varies based on economic resources. The 2004 Survey contains information about whether an inmate was working full time or part time before being incarcerated, had a court-appointed attorney, had ever been on public assistance, and had ever experienced homelessness. Approximately 57 percent of inmates were working full time prior to their arrest, and another 9 percent were working at least part time. Consistent with findings by Michelle Alexander and Marc Lamont Hill, the majority (72 percent) of inmates were too poor to afford legal representation and had to rely on a court-appointed lawyer. Around 19 percent of inmates received public assistance, and nearly 9 percent had experienced homelessness.

Overall, American prisons are full of economically disadvantaged men and women. The vast majority are unable to pay for adequate legal representation and of those who had a court-assigned lawyer, on average they only spoke to their attorney a total of three times. As mentioned earlier in this chapter, American public defenders face daunting caseloads and are in some cases dependent on trial judges for work, which can lead to ethical dilemmas. A majority of inmates are members of the working poor, and a significant minority are even more economically marginalized. The most economically marginalized suffer from a lack of services and increased punishment in prison.

I include five different dependent variables related to prison treatment (see the appendix for more details). While the 2004 Survey presents a wealth of information, and these dependent variables are certainly not the only outcomes of interest, I think that the five dependent variables offer a nice array of treatment variables. I include dependent variables for whether the inmate has been visited in the past month, for whether the inmate has received mental health medication, whether the inmate was subject to police use of force, and finally two disciplinary measures—whether the inmate was written up and whether the inmate was placed in solitary confinement. Incorporating the police use of force variable is admittedly speculative; however, it is my view that an inmate subject to police use of force during arrest is more likely to be subject to similar use of force by prison staff. The 2004 Survey does not include a variable for uses of force during incarceration, and it is likely that some inmates would feel uncomfortable reporting use of force by prison guards. Table 3.2 highlights model estimations for the impact of poverty on treatment inside prisons. Full model estimates, with all explanatory and control variables, are contained in the appendix.

Inmates who are relatively more economically advantaged receive better treatment inside prison. Inmates working full time prior to their incarceration were more likely to be visited by their families and were less subject to disciplinary punishments (both being written up and being placed in solitary confinement). Those inmates who were relatively more economically disadvantaged received worse treatment inside prison. Those with a court-appointed attorney were less likely to be visited by family members and were

Table 3.2 Poverty and treatment

	Visit in the Last Month	Received Mental Health Medication	Police Use of Force	Writeups	Solitary Confinement
Court-appointed attorney	−0.171*** (.009)	0.004 (.006)	−0.012 (.008)	0.018** (.009)	0.006 (.007)
Experienced homelessness	−0.045*** (.013)	−0.010 (.009)	0.025** (.013)	0.026* (.014)	0.018* (.010)
Worked full time	0.023*** (.008)	−0.012** (.006)	−0.010 (.008)	−0.049*** (.009)	−0.017*** (.006)
Worked part time	0.021 (.014)	−0.013 (.009)	−0.013 (.013)	−0.002 (.015)	0.009 (.011)
Number of observations	14,037	14,037	14,037	14,037	14,037

*p<.1, **p<.05, ***p<.01

more likely to be written up. Those who had previously experienced homelessness are perhaps the most economically vulnerable. Those inmates were less likely to be visited by family members, were more likely to be written up, were more likely to be placed in solitary confinement, and were more likely to report being subject to a police use of force.

Relatively little research has focused on treatment inside prisons. While we know that the poor are more likely to be placed in prison, there has been little differentiation between levels of poverty, and there has been little focus on prison conditions. Relatively more marginalized inmates do seem to have a worse experience in prison, including increased punishment and fewer visits from family members. Chapter 8 will discuss in more detail the effect of prison on families, but it is likely that most poor inmates are not visited by their families because their families cannot afford to visit them. A majority of inmates (79 percent) were living with family members prior to their incarceration, and roughly 82 percent of inmates had phone contact with their family members, while less than a third (29 percent) received a visit from their families. Only 5 percent of inmates are incarcerated less than 50 miles from their homes. Fully 85 percent are incarcerated more than 100 miles from home. Prison has a disproportionate impact on the poor and on poor families.

Suggestions for Reform

There are many complicated causal mechanisms that lead the poor and impoverished into prison. Some reforms are relatively straightforward, while others will require a wholesale change in law enforcement culture and in American political participation. However, it should be pointed out that advocating for policies that lessen discrimination against the poor are less controversial than advocating for policies that lessen discrimination based on race. A prison reform movement based on poverty issues may be fruitful and may be less likely to be dismissed in the same way that some people dismiss the Black Lives Matter and other race-focused movements. Given the complex realities of intersectionality and the disproportionate poverty rates among racial minorities, it may be possible to lessen racial discrimination by lessening economic discrimination.

I recommend the following:

1. Eliminate cash bail.
2. Eliminate monetary sanctions or at least base those sanctions on a sliding scale.
3. Decriminalize poverty-related crimes, such as minor traffic fines, loitering, vagrancy, and so on, and decriminalize survival-related crimes, such as prostitution and small-scale theft.
4. Inmates should be incarcerated in the prison closest to their home.
5. Efforts should be made to address the economic challenges that inmates face on their release from prison.

While relatively straightforward, many of these changes would have a monumental impact. For example, 83 percent of jail inmates are incarcerated because they cannot afford their cash bail. This system incentivizes people to plead guilty to crimes they may not have committed in order to get released from prison. These guilty pleas can have serious consequences in future interactions with the court system. In addition, many of these recommendations should not be politically controversial. The fact that some states require payment for a jury trial or for a public defender seems unjust and likely unpopular. Finally, many poverty- and survival-related crimes are relatively minor in nature and pale in comparison to the cost of incarceration. To spend thousands of dollars on incarcerating someone who loitered or stole a small amount of money seems, at the very least, inefficient.

Readers might object that these recommendations do not change the root causes of poverty, or the root causes of crime, or a political and law enforcement culture that targets the economically disadvantaged. This is certainly true. However, the psychologist Karl Weick (1984) recommends focusing on small public policy wins that can motivate further reforms. The advantage to focusing on small wins is that it leaves people less psychologically aroused and more able to concentrate, take in new information, and consider new options. Ending cash bail or decriminalizing loitering may not change the political culture in the United States, but it will help end the jail-to-prison pipeline. For more information about prison reforms and about prison reform organizations that work on issues of economic discrimination, visit this book's website at www.punishingthevulnerable.com.

CHAPTER FOUR

Punishing the Sick

While the poor are disproportionately punished in American prisons, income is not the only element of vulnerability. People with poor health, both physical and mental, are swept up into our massive carceral system. It is estimated that 20 to 26 percent of all persons infected with HIV/AIDS in the United States, 29 to 43 percent of those detected with hepatitis C, and 40 percent of those struck by tuberculosis had passed through a correctional facility in 1997 (Wacquant 2009). Mental health issues are also prevalent in jails and prisons. The Bureau of Justice Statistics reports that more than half of all prison and jail inmates have a mental health problem. In 2005, this included 705,600 inmates in state prisons, 78,800 in federal facilities, and 479,900 in local jails.

In 2011–2012, half of state, federal, and jail inmates reported having a chronic health condition. Chronic conditions include cancer, high blood pressure, stroke-related problems, arthritis, asthma, and cirrhosis of the liver. Twenty-one percent of prisoners and 14 percent of jail inmates reported having an infectious disease, including tuberculosis, hepatitis B and C, and other sexually transmitted diseases. About 1 percent of prisoners and jail inmates who had been tested for HIV reported being HIV-positive. Seventy-four percent of prisoners and 62 percent of jail inmates were overweight, obese, or morbidly obese (Maruschak, Berzofsky, and Unangst 2015).

In many ways, prisons have filled some of the gaps caused by the inadequacy of America's mental and physical health care systems. As our health care system increasingly fails to meet the needs of the physically and mentally ill, many people end up placed in prison. Unfortunately, the health care systems in American prisons range from inadequate to horrific. Modern American prisons are not designed to provide health care or rehabilitation; instead, they are designed to segregate inmates from broader society and to address security concerns within the prison. In many cases, prisons are given an unfair and impossible mandate: to deal with a population with significant physical and mental health issues without adequate resources. Many inmates are not healthy enough to work or participate broadly in American society. Health care is another aspect of vulnerability for American inmates.

American prisoners do not just have significant health problems; they have significantly worse health than the general population. Rather than a group of healthy super predators, inmates are sicker than the general public. Table 4.1 gives a breakdown of the prevalence of various health conditions among inmates versus the general public, along with a rate of difference. All statistics are taken from the Bureau of Justice Statistics (James and Glaze 2006; Maruschak, Berzofsky, and Unangst 2015) and the Centers for Disease Control (CDC 2015a, 2015b, 2016a, 2016b). Statistics about cancer rates were not available for the general public. In addition, the Bureau of Justice differentiates between inmates who have a mental health problem, those who have a substance dependence, and those who have both. The CDC data is only broken down into any mental health problem or a substance dependence problem. The three variables with missing data for the general public are reported as "not available" in Table 4.1.

For every major health condition, inmates have a higher prevalence of occurrence than the general public. Inmates have nearly twice the rate of high blood pressure and hypertension issues as the general public. Inmates have around three times as many heart-related problems, stroke-related problems, and occurrences of HIV/AIDS. Five times as many inmates suffer from mental health problems, and six times as many suffer from major depression. Instances of cirrhosis of the liver, hepatitis, and tuberculosis are 9 to 12 times the rate of those diseases in the general public. The vast majority of state prisoners have a substance abuse issue and/or a mental health issue. In fact, only 19.5 percent of state inmates *do not* have a mental health and/or substance abuse issue.

Prison health care is notoriously insufficient and is often cause for court orders mandating changes in conditions. In 2005, 239 prisons were under court orders for overcrowding and insufficient health care (Stephan 2008). After years of lawsuits, the state of California's prison system was taken into receivership by the federal court system in 2006. In 2006, a federal monitor reported that on average an inmate was dying every week from preventable causes. The state was found to have violated the ban on cruel and unusual punishment through overcrowded facilities and inadequate health care. Folsom State Prison was returned to the state's control in 2015, but the state's other 33 prisons remain in federal receivership (St. John 2015).

Inadequate health care extends far beyond California. For inmates with a chronic medical condition, 20 percent of state inmates and 68 percent of jail inmates had not received a medical examination since their incarceration. Approximately 30 percent of state inmates and 40 percent of jail inmates

Table 4.1 Prevalence of health conditions

Health Condition	Inmate Population	General Public	Difference
Cancer	3.5	Not Available	Not Available
High blood pressure/ hypertension	30.2	18.1	1.7
Stroke-related problems	1.8	0.7	2.6
Diabetes/high blood sugar	9	6.5	1.4
Heart-related problems	9.8	2.9	3.4
Asthma	14.9	10.2	1.5
Cirrhosis of the liver	1.8	0.2	9.0
Tuberculosis	6	0.5	12.0
Hepatitis	10.9	1.1	9.9
Sexually transmitted diseases	6	3.4	1.8
HIV/AIDS	1.3	0.4	3.3
Major depression	49	7.9	6.2
Psychotic disorder symptoms	15.3	3.1	4.9
Any mental health problem	56.2	10.6	5.3
Substance dependence only	24.4	9.3	2.6
Substance dependence or mental health issue	41.7	not available	not available
No substance dependence or mental health issue	19.5	not available	not available

stopped taking a prescription medication on incarceration. Following a serious injury, 12 percent of state inmates were not seen by medical personnel (Wilper et al. 2009). A concern for cost reduction often leads to inadequate and unethical health care. One immigration detention facility gave adult detainees with hepatitis B pediatric doses of medicine because the pediatric doses were cheaper (Dow 2004). Health care tends to be inadequate in most facilities, whether public or private prisons. Many public prisons contract out to private health care providers and even those that do not are still cost conscious. Neoliberal priorities dominate health care in America, both inside and outside prisons.

Women's health care in particular is lacking. Around 4 percent of female inmates enter state prisons while pregnant. Only 8 states provide prenatal exams, only 19 provide proper prenatal nutrition, and only 17 provide screenings and treatments for high-risk pregnancies. Pregnant women are often shackled during labor, reliant on the discretion of a guard who can decide whether or not to remove the restraints. If the guard fails to remove restraints, women are forced to give birth with their legs shackled (Law 2012). Most women who give birth in prison have to turn their baby over to a family member. If there is not a family member available, the infant becomes a ward of the state (Palsha 2016). As we will see in chapter 8, despite paternalistic demands that people take better care of their children, criminal justice policies often result in the separation of mothers and fathers from their children.

Other areas of women's health care are inadequate. Treatment for breast cancer is virtually nonexistent, with some women waiting years for screenings. Screenings for prisoners are especially important because female prisoners frequently enter prison after years of poverty, poor nutrition, inadequate health care, and substance abuse issues (Law 2012). Many inmates have chronic illnesses that have been untreated or poorly managed for years. We send deeply unhealthy people to prisons that lack the capacity to provide adequate health care to inmates. Prisons exacerbate and in some cases cause illnesses. Medical neglect and incompetence has led to preventable deaths (Law 2012).

Medical care is also provided in insensitive and hostile settings. AIDS is the leading cause of death among American prisoners, and staff often ostracize inmates believed to be HIV-positive. At one Michigan prison, a woman was told she had HIV within audible range of other inmates. The nurses at the prison said they could not help because they did not have experience with HIV. After waiting months to see a specialist, the inmate was prescribed a multivitamin to boost her immune system. Those vitamins had to be purchased from the prison commissary at inflated prices (Law 2012). I experienced a similar insensitivity when I worked as a detention officer and was informally taught code words to identify inmates with HIV.

Medical treatment for transgender prisoners also ranges from inadequate to nonexistent. Nineteen states reported that they have no policies on transgender inmates. Florida explicitly states that any inmate who was receiving hormonal treatment prior to incarceration will not receive hormones while incarcerated. For states with a policy, there is considerable variation in evaluation, medical care, and housing for transgender inmates. No state allows for gender reassignment surgery (Brown and McDuffie 2009). At least four transgender inmates have resorted to "life-threatening surgical self-treatments," known as autocastration (Brown 2010).

Prisons have a long history of providing inadequate health care to inmates. While both physical and mental health treatment is inadequate, more literature has focused on mental health issues than physical health issues. Given a lack of adequate mental health care among the general population of Americans, mentally ill people often come into contact with law enforcement—first with police and then with jail/prison guards. People with mental health issues are usually viewed as especially dangerous rather than as especially vulnerable.

This oversimplification has led to heavy reliance on arrest for police officers and heavy reliance on solitary confinement for prison guards. Once, while working as a detention officer, I had a mentally ill, irate inmate who was difficult to talk to. I made a phone call to a nearby hallway station and asked if they could send someone to talk to the person. In response, the hallway station called over the radio, which led to several other detention officers rushing into the unit and hauling the man away to solitary confinement. I still feel guilty that my inability to communicate with this man led to his placement in a tiny cell by himself. Even if I had been able to talk to the inmate, it probably would have taken some time to get the inmate to calm down. In the meantime, I was responsible for the supervision of 60 other inmates. While I can blame myself for the situation, the truth is that the inmate should have been in a specialized mental health care facility or at the very least a facility with better treatment than we had available.

There is a close connection between the size of a country's prison population and the population kept in mental hospitals. Lionel Penrose (1939) wrote that there are people in every society whose behavior is so undesirable that they require segregation from the rest of society. Generally, there are two ways to segregate the socially undesirable: either to place the person in a mental institution or to wait until the person commits a crime and then incarcerate that person. Penrose (1939, p. 3) noted the connection between these two institutions, stating that "as a general rule, if the prison services are extensive, the asylum population is relatively small and the reverse also tends to be true." Since the 1950s, the United States has gone from having an extensive population in state mental health hospitals and a relatively small prison population to a country with an extensive prison population and a relatively small population in state mental health hospitals.

In 1955, there were 560,000 resident patients in American state and county mental hospitals. These hospitals provided almost all inpatient mental health care in the United States (Frank and Glied 2006). Deinstitutionalization led to a dramatic decrease in the number and capacity of public mental health facilities. By 2005, 95 percent of the hospital beds available in 1955 were gone (Fisher, Geller, and Pandiani 2009). While private inpatient and outpatient facilities have absorbed some of the mentally ill who would have previously ended up in a state mental hospital, many of the mentally ill are now held by the criminal justice system. In fact, patients with serious mental illnesses are three times as likely to be held in a prison or jail rather than in a hospital (Torrey 1995).

People with mental health disorders and co-occurring substance-related problems are more likely to be incarcerated and to serve longer sentences (McNiel, Binder, and Robinson 2005). In the past, many of these people would be sent to long-term inpatient care at a state mental health hospital. In the state mental hospitals, people were institutionalized to the point of passivity and generally followed orders. When those patients were placed back into the community, they tended to remain there and to accept treatment. Today, most of the severely mentally ill have not spent large parts of their lives in hospitals and are not passive. The current generation of severely mentally ill people are more likely to go off their medications and encounter the criminal justice system, leading to inappropriate incarceration (Lamb and Bachrach 2001).

The closing of state mental hospitals and reductions in psychiatric beds is a significant factor for the placement of mentally ill people in jails and prisons rather than in the community or in hospitals. As socially disruptive people are excluded from psychiatric facilities, the criminal justice system has become the system that "can't say no" (Lamb and Weinberger 1998). Jails and prisons have become de facto mental health hospitals (Lamb and Weinberger 1998; McNiel, Binder, and Robinson 2005). Unfortunately, jails and prisons lack the resources to treat every inmate with a mental illness. The result is a large gap between the level of need and the level of treatment. Only a third of state prisoners, a fourth of federal prisoners, and less than an eighth of local jail inmates with a mental illness were treated since admission (James and Glaze 2006).

In 2011, the Supreme Court ruled that California's prison system failed to deliver minimal care to prisoners with serious medical and mental health problems and that lack of care produced "needless suffering and death" (Liptak 2011, p. A1). There are about 33,000 mentally ill prisoners in California, and inadequate treatment has led to a suicide rate that is 48 percent higher than the national average. About 70 percent of the suicides could have been prevented with proper care. A federal district court judge in Sacramento wrote, "Systemic failures persist in the form of inadequate suicide prevention measures, excessive administrative segregation of the mentally ill, lack of timely access to adequate care, insufficient treatment space and access to beds, and unmet staffing needs" (New York Times Editorial Board 2013).

Prison staff are underequipped to deal with mental illness and are consequently overwhelmed. Prison security staff receive minimal training on how to recognize and deal with people with mental illnesses. During my field interviews, 7 of 23 staff members said that mentally ill inmates were the most difficult group of inmates to deal with. The standard response to a belligerent inmate is to place him or her in a solitary confinement cell. While professional mental health counselors have multiple tools and strategies, for most prison guards the only realistic tool is solitary confinement. To get a sense of the tragic lunacy of modern American corrections, consider this: we put mentally ill inmates in solitary confinement, a practice that is proven to cause and/or exacerbate mental illness.

Solitary confinement is one of the harshest punishments in modern prisons. Inmates in solitary confinement are placed alone in a cell for 22 to 24 hours a day (American Friends Service Committee, n.d.). Cells can be as small as six feet by nine feet, smaller than an average apartment bathroom. In fact, about 19 solitary confinement cells fit in the average one-bedroom apartment (Lopez 2015). Contact with other human beings is severely limited, phone calls are infrequent, and any family visit is noncontact. Reading material and personal property is restricted, and access to rehabilitative programming is extremely limited (American Friends Service Committee, n.d.).

Large-scale use of solitary confinement is an American invention, dating back to the 1820s, with the opening of Eastern State Penitentiary in Philadelphia (Banks 2005). Designed to isolate inmates and provide an opportunity for penitence and self-reflection, penitentiaries fell out of favor due to concerns about mental illness and cruelty. Famed English writer and social critic Charles Dickens described Eastern State Penitentiary in 1842 as a system that is "rigid, strict and hopeless solitary confinement. I believe it, in its effects, to be cruel and wrong" (Davis 2003, p. 48). Following a more punitive turn in criminal justice (Garland 2001), modern solitary confinement expanded rapidly from the late 1980s until the present with the building of supermax facilities.

In theory, solitary confinement is a way to manage hostile and aggressive inmates, but it is also a way to manage inmates who the staff view as difficult. For example, many inmates are unsatisfied with the quality of their healthcare, but prison staff have learned how to limit complaints. Prison officials have punished inmates seeking medical attention by upending their cells and confiscating medications. Prisoners have faced retaliation for demanding medical treatment. Staff at the Central California Women's Facility placed the entire facility on lockdown after inmates filed grievances about their conditions (Law 2012).

Solitary confinement can be used to stop other serious inmate complaints, especially related to sexual assault. Women who are sexually assaulted face retaliation if they speak out. Guards have planted drugs in the cells of women who reported sexual assaults. When a sexual relationship between a prisoner and guard is discovered, the prisoner is usually placed in solitary confinement while the guard is not punished (Law 2012). In 2015, 24 detention officers in the Baltimore, Maryland, jail were convicted of smuggling drugs into the jail and having improper sexual relationships with inmates, which resulted in multiple pregnancies (Jedra 2015).

Sexual assaults by staff are common. A Department of Justice investigation of two women's prisons in Michigan found that "nearly every woman . . . interviewed reported various sexually aggressive acts of guards" (Law 2012, p. 60). This included rape, sexual assault, mistreatment of inmates impregnated by guards, abusive searches, and surveillance during medical appointments. In both men's and women's prisons, prisoners are more likely to experience sexual violence at the hands of prison staff than from fellow prisoners (Law 2012). As we will see again in chapter 6, limiting complaints and grievances by inmates is often a motivation behind the use of solitary confinement (rather than security concerns). Inmates are subjected to high levels of sexual violence and are then severely punished if they report those abuses.

Solitary confinement is used to discipline a variety of offenses and nonoffenses. Prisoners can be in solitary confinement for serious infractions, such as fighting with another inmate, to minor offenses, such as talking back to a guard or getting caught with contraband (American Friends Service Committee, n.d.). It is worthwhile to note that contraband includes many items that would be legal in the free world, such as cigarettes, pornography, extra sheets and bedding, or having more than the allotted amount of an otherwise legal item. I spent most of my time during cell searches taking surplus oranges away from inmates.

Inmates can also be placed in solitary confinement in the absence of a rule violation. Prisons have used solitary confinement as a tool to manage gangs, isolating inmates simply for talking to suspected gang members. While gang violence is a serious problem, the threat of gangs has also been used as a political pretext. Prisons have used solitary confinement as retribution for political activism (American Friends Service Committee, n.d.). Sometimes political activism is equated with gang involvement. In California, evidence of gang involvement has included having writings by Mumia Abu-Jamal or the Black Panther Party; having pictures of Assata Shakur, Malcolm X, George Jackson, and Nat Turner; using indigenous Mexican languages; and using the image of the huelga bird, the symbol of the United Farm Workers. Other evidence of gang activity included possession of Machiavelli's *The Prince* and Sun Tzu's *The Art of War*. Writing about prisoner rights is also considered evidence of gang affiliation (Bauer 2012). I would like to point out that such standards would validate multiple members of my university political science department as gang members.

Although it was designed to house only "the worst of the worst," between 80,000 and 100,000 inmates are currently in solitary confinement (Hardman 2015). California supermax facilities alone hold more than 3,300 inmates (Reiter 2012). In the 2004 Survey, 15 percent of inmates report being placed in solitary confinement at some point in their incarceration. As mentioned above, a solitary confinement cell is as small as six by nine feet, or 54 square feet. If 100,000 people are in solitary confinement, those cells take up approximately 5,400,000 square feet, which sounds larger than it is; the space is roughly equivalent to 124 acres, which is roughly equivalent to the footprint of the Pontiac Silverdome (where the Detroit Lions used to play football) or two copies of the Palace of Auburn Hills (where the Detroit

Pistons used to play basketball). For a nonsports equivalent, every solitary confinement cell in America would fit in the Mall of America. One final comparison: one of former presidential candidate Mitt Romney's four homes is large enough to fit 161 solitary confinement cells.

Solitary confinement has become a common punishment in American jails and prisons. It is also an expensive habit. The Federal Bureau of Prisons spends approximately $75,000 per solitary confinement per year—three times more than incarceration in a regular prison unit (Johnson and Chappell 2014). Using the federal rate difference, if every inmate in solitary confinement was placed in a regular prison cell, the nation would save $4 billion to $5 billion a year. In the state of Illinois, it costs $92,000 per solitary confinement per year—again, a figure two to three times higher than the cost of keeping an inmate in a regular prison cell (Solitary Watch 2011). While there are not standardized measures, many states spend two to three times more on solitary confinement than on general population units (Solitary Watch 2011; Mears 2006). Assuming that solitary confinement units are twice as expensive as general population units, which is a conservative assumption, the United States would still save between $2.8 billion and $3.5 billion a year if solitary confinement was eliminated. Mears (2006) found that most states did not conduct benefit-cost analyses of supermax prisons prior to or after investing in them.

Any benefit-cost analysis has to also consider the considerable harm that solitary confinement causes inmates. The extreme psychological trauma caused by solitary confinement amounts to torture. United Nations special rapporteur on torture Juan E. Méndez has labeled the use of solitary confinement as torture and has called for solitary confinement to be used only in extraordinary circumstances, and even then for a maximum of 15 days (UN News Centre 2011). The head of the Catholic Church, Pope Francis, has also called the practice of solitary confinement torture (Gavula 2014). Groups such as the American Civil Liberties Union, Human Rights Watch, the American Friends Service Committee, Critical Resistance, and the National Religious Campaign Against Torture have all called for the end of solitary confinement. Those organizations are unlikely to find President Donald Trump's administration to be friendly. In addition to "tough on crime" statements more generally, President Trump has repeatedly said that he believes torture "absolutely works" (Klapper, Butler, and Reichmann 2017).

Solitary confinement has the potential to aggravate existing mental illness and to create new mental illness, including perceptual distortions, panic attacks, paranoia, obsessive and aggressive thoughts, and problems with impulse control (Grassian 2006). Isolated inmates develop unhealthy coping mechanisms, including drug use and antisocial behavior, which can also cause or aggravate mental illnesses (Nurse, Woodcock, and Ormsby 2003). Harsh prison conditions are linked to increased recidivism (Chen and

Shapiro 2007; Drago, Galbiati, and Vertova 2008) and to maladaptive social skills and networks (Lerman 2014). Most inmates will eventually be released, and solitary confinement can have a significant impact on their future chances of success. In California alone, hundreds of inmates are released directly from supermax prisons onto parole, having spent at most 90 days outside of solitary confinement prior to being released (Reiter 2012).

The 2004 Survey includes information about prison inmates' physical and mental health. Earlier in this chapter, I discussed the prevalence of physical health problems among prison inmates. I do not include physical health variables in my model estimations because of a lack of physical health expertise and for conceptual clarity. In addition, there is a broad literature, cited in this chapter, on the link between mental health and prisoner treatment, while I have not included an equivalent literature linking physical health and prisoner treatment. I would encourage public health scholars to delve more deeply into some of the physical health variables included in the 2004 Survey in order to explore statistical patterns. As it is, there is a great deal of information to include even though I have limited myself to mental health variables.

As discussed previously, inmates commonly face mental health and substance abuse issues. Fifty-seven percent of inmates in the 2004 Survey sample reported receiving, at some point, treatment for drug or alcohol issues. Nearly 17 percent are on mental health medications or have experienced mental health counseling. Fifteen percent of prisoners have reported attempting suicide, a serious expression of mental anguish. In fact, more inmates have reported attempting suicide than have received mental health counseling. There is a large gap between the level of need and the level of treatment, which exacerbates vulnerabilities.

While not strictly a mental health variable, many prisoners have faced instances of physical and sexual violence, which may cause or intensify mental health issues. Thirteen percent of inmates were sexually assaulted before their incarceration, and 48 percent were physically assaulted prior to incarceration. It is possible that inmates who were previously sexually or physically victimized outside of prison will also be victimized inside prison. Those two statistics, 13 percent being victims of sexual assault and 48 percent being victims of physical assault, help point out the flaws in the "super predator" narrative. If inmates were "super predators," why are so many physically and sexually abused?

The 2004 Survey includes data on specific mental health conditions. Twenty-one percent of inmates report being diagnosed with depression, 11 percent report being diagnosed with manic depression/bipolar disorder, around 5 percent with schizophrenia, and 6 percent with personality disorders (such as antisocial or borderline personality disorders). As will be seen shortly, it is not necessarily that every inmate with a mental health issue is treated a certain way but that certain specific mental health issues are associated with negative prisoner treatment. This may help identify which mentally ill prisoners are most harmed by prison treatment.

Table 4.2 presents findings of interest related to mental health and treatment inside prison. Full model estimations are available in the appendix.

In one way, prisons are working well with mentally ill inmates. Inmates who were sexually assaulted before prison, who attempted suicide, or who have a diagnosed mental health issue (depression, manic depression/bipolar disorder, schizophrenia, and personality disorders) report receiving mental health medications at a statistically significant higher rate than other inmates. However, the relatively good news ends there. Inmates who were sexually assaulted, and those with depression, manic depression/bipolar disorder, and/or a personality disorder, were more likely to be subjected to police use of force (and, I speculate, would be more likely to be subjected to use of force by prison staff). Inmates who were sexually assaulted, who have attempted suicide, and who suffer from a depression and/or a personality disorder were

Table 4.2 Mental health and treatment in prison

	Visit in the Last Month	Received Mental Health Medication	Police Use of Force	Writeups	Solitary Confinement
Sexual assault before prison	-0.022* (.013)	0.026*** (.008)	0.031*** (.012)	0.049*** (.013)	0.013 (.010)
Depression	0.014 (.011)	0.349*** (.008)	0.025** (.011)	0.053*** (.012)	-0.002 (.009)
Manic depression, bipolar	-0.022 (.012)	0.133*** (.009)	0.031** (.014)	-0.003 (.015)	0.017 (.011)
Schizophrenia	-0.049*** (.019)	0.204*** (.013)	0.000 (.018)	-0.015 (.020)	0.015 (.015)
Personality disorder	-0.024 (.017)	0.065*** (.011)	0.049*** (.016)	0.065*** (.018)	0.041*** (.013)
Suicide attempt	-0.004 (.012)	0.115*** (.008)	-0.012 (.011)	0.042*** (.013)	0.027*** (.009)
Number of observations	14,037	14,037	14,037	14,037	14,037

*p<.10, **p<.05, ***p<.01

more likely to be written up by correctional staff. Those with a personality disorder and a previous suicide attempt were more likely to be placed in solitary confinement. Inmates with personality disorders may be particularly difficult to deal with, leading to their increased placement in solitary confinement. Inmates are also sometimes placed in solitary confinement as a form of suicide watch; although it is known that solitary confinement exacerbates mental health issues.

One difficulty in writing this book is in the interconnectedness of many of these problems. The third chapter began with a story about Djibril Niyomugabo, a Grand Rapids, Michigan, teenager who took his own life while in jail. Djibril was unable to pay his relatively small cash bail. Was Djibril's death caused by the cash bail system or was it due to inadequate mental health care? How many prisoners attempt suicide due to the very conditions of their imprisonment? We know that solitary confinement is associated with increased mental health issues, but it also may drive some inmates to attempt to take their own lives. In fact, the percentages of inmates who attempted suicide and the number of inmates in solitary confinement are within 0.004 percent of each other. Both numbers are slightly below 15 percent (which in absolute numbers, using 2015 prison population estimates, is around 324,000 inmates). We may not know the exact causes, but we can get a small glimpse into the extent of the problem. And while the 2004 Survey asked about suicide attempts and not their larger context (i.e., whether the attempt occurred in prison or outside of prison), it still points to the vulnerability of many American prison inmates.

My analysis of the 2004 Survey data is largely in line with the broader findings about the mental and physical health challenges that inmates face. Prisons are filled with inmates with serious mental and physical health issues. The prison environment itself can lead to increases in infections, sexual assaults, improper medical care, and mental health issues. Stigmatization of former inmates can also lead to physical and mental illnesses (Freudenberg 2002). One study in Washington state found that the mortality rate for former inmates is 3.5 times higher than the mortality rate of state residents of equivalent age, sex, and race (Binswanger et al. 2007). Goals of rehabilitation or treatment have fallen by the wayside, as vulnerable, unhealthy people enter prison and are in many cases sicker and more vulnerable when they reenter the community.

Suggestions for Reform

Physical and mental health issues are difficult to address without massive social spending. In some cases, the high percentage of inmate health problems is a reflection of society's failure to provide adequate health care to its citizens. There are fundamental issues in the provision of mental and physical health care in the United States that are beyond the scope of this chapter. Thus, my recommendations are somewhat modest in comparison with the large-scale social change that is likely necessary to address fundamental health inequalities. I would also suggest that, similar to issues of poverty, a focus on health issues may be less controversial than the current emphasis on issues of racial justice. A health-based framing, especially regarding mental health, may elicit less resistance to reform. A social construction of prisoners as mentally ill is at the very least more positive than a social construction of prisoners as "super predators."

I recommend the following:

1. Prisons should identify which specific mental health issues are most associated with prisoner–staff conflicts. Staff should receive training on how to deescalate such situations and to better understand why a mentally ill inmate may be acting in a certain way.
2. The use of solitary confinement should be abolished.
3. If prisons cannot adequately provide for the physical and mental health needs of their inmates, those inmates should be sent to alternative custodial settings.

CHAPTER FIVE

Punishing Race

Perhaps the most well-documented aspect of mass incarceration in the United States has been its disproportionate impact on racial minorities. One of the most consistent predictors of state imprisonment rates has been the size of the state's minority (especially African American) population (e.g., Beckett and Western 2001; Greenberg and West 2001; Jacobs and Helms 1996 Smith 2004; Sorensen and Stemen 2002). This relationship is usually attributed to some combination of racial threat theory (Blalock 1967; Key 1949) and the use of a "law and order" strategy by conservatives to drive a wedge between African American and white voters in the South (Beckett 1997; Beckett and Sasson 2000; Jacobs and Carmichael 2001). The relationship is quite strong and robust to alternative measures of imprisonment. Later in this chapter, I will explain that racial discrimination continues inside prison walls, with African American, American Indian, and Latino/a inmates all receiving harsher punishments and less access to rehabilitative treatment.

Despite progress toward greater racial equality, many Americans still hold negative stereotypes about African Americans. Those negative stereotypes have a long tradition in the United States. White Americans have long viewed criminal behavior as an inherent characteristic of African Americans, a reputation that extends back to the enslavement of Africans in the United States (Welch 2007). In the 1890s, some social scientists argued that crime in African American communities was a sign of racial inferiority, while similar criminality in white communities was a result of poverty and structural problems. Due to supposed racial inferiority, scholars wrote that African Americans were incapable of controlling their sexual impulses, working together for a common purpose, or delaying gratification (Muhammad 2010). Sadly, these views are not completely a vestige of the past. Current media portrayals disproportionately associate African Americans with crime stories, and politicians have used stereotypes of African American criminality, such as the Willie Horton ads, to attract voters (Garland 2001; Western 2006).

Research has shown that African Americans are stereotyped as more aggressive, hostile, and criminal (Devine and Elliot 1995). It is unnecessary for someone to be explicitly racist in order for that person to respond to stereotype-consistent cues. Research by Jennifer Eberhardt and her colleagues (2004) illustrates how such cues may affect policy decisions. In one study, Eberhardt and colleagues subliminally primed participants with African American male faces, white male faces, or no faces at all. Then participants were presented with objects on a computer screen that was severely degraded and became less degraded in small increments. Some of the objects were crime related (a gun or a knife), and some were unrelated to crime (a camera or a book). Participants were asked to write down what they thought the object was. Participants who were given a white face prime took longer to identify a crime-related object, while participants who were given an African American face prime identified a crime-related object much quicker.

African Americans are judged more harshly than white Americans on issues of crime. In a set of survey experiments, when the race of a suspect varied, white respondents were more likely to view African Americans as guilty of crimes, to envision that African Americans would commit more crimes in the future, and to suggest harsher punishments for African Americans (Hurwitz and Peffley 1997; Peffley, Hurwitz, and Sniderman 1997). Experimental studies with juvenile probation and police officers found that an African American prime led to preferences for harsher punishments (Graham and Lowery 2004). Perceptions are not necessarily accurate. For example, the percentage of young black men in a neighborhood is associated with higher perceptions of crime, even after controlling for crime rates and other neighborhood characteristics (Quillian and Pager 2001).

These stereotypes about crime are likely shared by street-level bureaucrats working in the criminal justice system. Official training films by the Drug Enforcement Agency (DEA) specifically identified African Americans and Latino/a Americans as more likely to carry drugs. This DEA training reached around 27,000 state and local police officers, many of whom went on to train others. The New York City Police Department also trained its officers to implicitly and sometimes explicitly consider the race of a driver when deciding who to stop and search (Epp, Maynard-Moody, and Haider-Markel 2014). Experimental evidence suggests that police officers were significantly more likely than nonofficers to perceive evidence of guilt and deceptiveness in African Americans' actions compared to similar actions of white Americans (Epp, Maynard-Moody, and Haider-Markel 2014).

As long as there is explicit racism in the United States, it is likely that some law enforcement officers will share those views. Law enforcement officers are drawn from the general public and are likely to share the biases of the public. I have heard racial slurs spoken hundreds of times by white Southerners when I lived in North Carolina, Kentucky, and Florida. I myself knew racial slurs for African American people as early as elementary school. There are certainly still expressions of open racial prejudice, as the recent white supremacist march in Charlottesville, Virginia, attests to. However, even someone who is not explicitly racist may still respond to stereotypes. Even if explicit racists are a small minority, a much larger group of Americans is aware of racial stereotypes. Those stereotypes are automatically activated (Kahneman 2011).

Automatically activated stereotypes can lead to unconscious biases. Researchers using the Implicit Association Test have gained some insight into people's unconscious biases. The Implicit Association Test asks respondents to categorize a series of words into groups. Two of the groups are racial categories, while the other groups are pleasant or unpleasant categories (Greenwald, McGhee, and Schwartz 1998). Faster matching of African American and unpleasant categories versus matching of African American and pleasant categories is defined as an implicit bias against African Americans (Greenwald, McGhee, and Schwartz 1998; Jolls and Sunstein 2006). Implicit bias is extremely widespread: "most people tend to prefer white to African American, young to old, and heterosexual to gay" (Jolls and Sunstein 2006, p. 4).

Negative stereotypes and different historical experiences have led to a large racial divide that affects support for a variety of criminal justice policies. African Americans are more likely to perceive unfairness in the criminal justice system and have lower levels of support for punitive measures (Engel 2005; Peffley and Hurwitz 2010). African Americans are more likely than white Americans to distrust police and the court system (Henderson et al. 1997; Unnever, Cullen, and Johnson 2008a). African Americans are significantly opposed to the death penalty, while white Americans are largely in favor (Bobo and Johnson 2004; Unnever, Cullen, and Johnson 2008a). African Americans, unlike white Americans, are more likely to view incarceration as a result of racial discrimination than personal failings (Unnever 2008). Americans with racial resentments against African Americans are less likely to support structural changes to reduce crime (Unnever, Cullen, and Johnson 2008b). African Americans are less likely than white Americans to support major criminal justice initiatives such as the war on drugs (Bobo and Johnson 2004). A broad and diverse literature documents the ways in which the preferences and experiences of African American and white Americans differ.

Given that prison guards are drawn from the general public, guards are likely to share many of the same stereotypes as Americans in general. Stereotypes may be an important heuristic for prison staff. Negative stereotypes of

African Americans as more criminal may lead to closer supervision of African American inmates. If African Americans are watched more closely, they will receive a higher percentage of incident reports; alternatively, African American inmates might react to fulfill the negative expectations of staff (Howard et al. 1994; Poole and Regoli 1980). Poole and Regoli (1980) offer a possible explanation of the process, which is worth quoting:

> Perceptions of inmate behavior based on racial stereotypes may foster a more oppressive disciplinary posture among guards in their response to blacks. The greater visibility of black inmates may also evoke greater attention to and concern for their actions; i.e., their behavior may be viewed more suspiciously. The black inmate is then more likely to be scrutinized and therefore to be observed in any rule violations, which will in turn reinforce the prior stereotypic expectations. Similarly, if black inmates perceive that they are being differentially treated (e.g., subject to stricter rule enforcement), they may react more defiantly or with greater hostility toward guards. (Poole and Regoli 1980, p. 933)

There is convincing evidence that African Americans are subjected to disproportionate punishment in the implementation of criminal justice policy. African Americans are more likely than white Americans to come into contact with police or other law enforcement officers (Alexander 2010), and those interactions are more punitive for African Americans. For example, there is substantial evidence of racial discrimination in traffic stops, the most common interaction between police and the public (see Bradbury and Kellough 2011; Close and Mason 2006, 2007; Theobald and Haider-Markel 2009). Charles Epp, Steven Maynard-Moody, and Donald Haider-Markel (2014) argue that the most important factor in investigative police stops is not how people drive but how they look, with African Americans 2.2 times more likely to be stopped than other drivers. African Americans are more likely to report unfair treatment by the police (Peffley and Hurwitz 2010), and police are more likely to punish African American suspects (Close and Mason 2006, 2007; Ridgeway 2006).

The disparate treatment in interactions with the police is matched by disparate treatment in incarceration. African Americans are incarcerated at higher rates (Human Rights Watch 2009; Mauer and King 2007; Weaver and Lerman 2010; Western 2006). African Americans receive substantially longer sentences than white Americans for similar crimes (Blair, Judd, and Chapleau 2004; Everett and Wojtkiewicz 2002; Mustard 2001; Steffensmeier, Ulmer, and Kramer 1998). Treatment differences continue inside prison. African Americans are subject to higher rates of punishment (Olson 2016) and are provided with inferior health care while incarcerated (Nicholson-Crotty and Nicholson-Crotty 2004).

In 2007, the incarceration rate for white Americans was 412 per 100,000 residents, compared to 2,290 for African Americans. Over 2 percent of all African Americans were incarcerated in 2007, compared to less than 1 percent for the white and Latino/a populations (Mauer and King 2007). Eleven percent of African American men aged 25 to 29 are incarcerated, and a third are under some type of correctional supervision (Weaver and Lerman 2010). Bruce Western estimates that the cumulative lifetime risk of incarceration for African American males is 20 percent, versus 3 percent for white males. African American males are more likely to be incarcerated than to receive a bachelor's degree or serve in the military (Western 2006). Empirically, one of the largest drivers of state incarceration rates is the size of the state's minority population (e.g., Beckett and Western 2001; Greenberg and West 2001; Jacobs and Helms 1996; Smith 2004; Sorensen and Stemen 2002). In part due to the statistical realities of disparate treatment, African Americans are more likely to perceive unfairness in the criminal justice system and have lower levels of support for punitive measures (Engel 2005; Peffley and Hurwitz 2010).

Higher levels of punishment for African Americans would not be as much of a cause for concern if African Americans committed crimes at higher rates. However, differences in incarceration rates cannot be completely explained by differences in criminal activity (Alexander 2010; Yates and Fording 2005; Western 2006). African Americans do have higher rates of violent crime and violent crime victimization, which could lead to higher incarceration rates. However, that may be due to higher levels of social disorganization in primarily African American communities. Peterson and Krivo (2005) performed a meta-analysis of articles on race and violent crime. They found zero significant differences in criminal violence between neighborhoods of varying racial composition when the neighborhoods were similarly disadvantaged. Peterson and Krivo (2005) also found that disadvantaged neighborhoods exhibit more tolerance for crime and deviance, but there is no evidence of a unique African American subculture of violence. One consistent finding in the meta-analysis was that structural disadvantage contributes significantly to violence for both black and white Americans, and the findings were resilient to the exact operationalization of social disorganization (i.e., poverty, income, family disruption, unemployment) (Peterson and Krivo 2005), echoing a 120-year-old debate on race versus structural factors (Muhammad 2010).

American society has long associated race with criminality. Joe Soss, Richard Fording, and Sanford Schram (2008; see also Schram et al. 2009) have developed a racial classification model for when racial heuristics will be relevant. They argue that policy actors rely on social classifications and group reputations to determine what action to take. The degree to which racial classifications will be used is dependent on three factors: the prevailing cultural stereotypes of racial groups, the extent to which policy actors hold relevant group stereotypes, and the presence of stereotype-consistent cues. Criminal justice policy in general, and prisons in particular, have long been associated with race-based stereotypes. It is likely that prison staff use race-based stereotypes as heuristics.

Correctional staff are likely to punish members of groups that are negatively stereotyped. Since staff cannot punish or help everyone, they must punish those viewed as most problematic and help those considered most capable of success. No one wants to waste time helping someone who won't respond to the help or punishing someone who is not threatening. There is a widespread belief that African Americans and Latino/a Americans are more prone to crime. The existence of this stereotype has been documented in numerous studies (Hurwitz and Peffley 1997; Muhammad 2010). Quillian and Pager (2001, p. 722) write, "The stereotype of blacks as criminals is widely known and is deeply embedded in the collective consciousness of Americans, irrespective of the level of prejudice or personal beliefs." Even people who are not racist or are antiracist are often aware of the popular stereotypes about different groups. Even if someone is not racist, knowledge of racist stereotypes may bias his or her decision making.

During interviews, I asked which inmates were more difficult to deal with than others. Five of 23 (22 percent) staff members replied with a racial response or at least a response that suggested some racial tension. The more difficult inmates were described as "wannabe gangbangers," "urban," and inmates with a "drug and thug" culture. More explicitly, one white female officer replied that "black inmates" were harder to deal with, and one white male officer replied that "colored inmates" were harder to deal with. It is possible that social desirability bias kept some interviewees from giving a racialized response. I also never asked pointed questions about race, allowing staff members to come up with their own categories. It is impossible to know how widespread racial antipathy is among American prison staff. However, given evidence of racial discrimination in other areas of American public policy, especially in the criminal justice system, it is likely that the use of race-based stereotypes and heuristics among American prison staff is significant.

Does race inform treatment inside prison? One objection may be that disproportionate punishment is actually a reflection of disproportionate rule violations. Some might theorize that African American and Latino/a inmates are more likely to commit violations (which itself seems to suggest belief in the stereotype that African Americans and Latino/a are more prone to criminality). If that is the case, there is not necessarily an issue with punishing African American and Latino/a inmates more harshly. Due to this concern, all statistical models using the 2004 Survey include multiple controls for the inmate's criminal history.

If African American or Latino/a inmates were likely to behave differently in prison, this might be reflected in the types of offense they were incarcerated for. There is little support for this hypothesis. Remarkably, the percentage of violent offenders in state prisons was exactly the same for all racial categories. Violent behavior should be the greatest concern for prison order, and there are not racial differences in violent offenses. To the extent that there are racial differences in offense characteristics, African American and Latino/a inmates were significantly more likely to be convicted for drug offenses. This is likely not a huge cause for concern, because different racial groups use drugs at approximately the same rates (Alexander 2010).

Previous research suggests that there are not significant racial differences in prison rule violations (Cao, Zhao, and Van Dine 1997; Finn 1995; Hewitt, Poole, and Regoli 1984). Poole and Regoli (1980) found that African American and white inmates were equally likely to engage in rule-breaking activity but that African American inmates were more likely to be officially reported for rule infractions. Similarly, African American male inmates were not involved in more violent misconduct than were white inmates (Berg and DeLisi 2006). Rather than a difference in offending, there is evidence that patterns of rule enforcement were systematically biased against African American inmates (Poole and Regoli 1980). Correctional officers have been charged with filing racially biased disciplinary reports (Jiang and Fisher-Giorlando 2002). In at least one prison, African Americans were charged in a disproportionate number of disciplinary reports (Howard et al. 1994).

Race seems to be an important heuristic for determining punishment inside prison. From the previously cited literature, we know that race is an important factor in other areas of criminal justice policy. From the CJ-DATS survey and the Kentucky interviews, we know that correctional staff place inmates in categories and that staff vary in their views on punishment and rehabilitation. We know that police officers respond to race-based heuristics. The question that remains is whether prison staff also, whether consciously and/or unconsciously, use race-based heuristics to determine punishment. We can gain some insight from an analysis of the 2004 Survey.

African American inmates make up about 43 percent of the 2004 Survey sample. Around 17 percent of inmates are Latino/a. The 2004 Survey also has categories for Asian American, American Indian, Hawaiian Pacific, and "other race" inmates. The sample size for those four categories is somewhat small. While there is some limited evidence that American Indian inmates have a more negative prison experience, there were not any statistically significant results for Asian, Hawaiian Pacific, or "other race" inmates. Thus, this analysis focuses primarily on African American and Latino/a inmates. In each analysis, white inmates are the reference category, so the treatment of African American and Latino/a inmates is in comparison to the treatment of white inmates. Table 5.1 presents the impact of prisoner race on treatment inside prisons.

Table 5.1 Race and treatment inside prison

	Visit in the Last Month	Received Mental Health Medication	Police Use of Force	Writeups	Solitary Confinement
African American	-0.064***	-0.027***	0.048***	0.056***	0.030***
	(.009)	(.006)	(.008)	(.010)	(.007)
Latino/a	-0.008	-0.027***	0.029***	-0.014	0.020**
	(.012)	(.008)	(.012)	(.013)	(.009)
American Indian	0.003	-0.009	0.048***	0.031*	-0.001
	(.017)	(.011)	(.016)	(.018)	(.013)
Number of observations	14,037	14,037	14,037	14,037	14,037

*p<.10, **p<.05, ***p<.01

The results for African Americans and Latino/as strongly suggest negative treatment in prison. African American inmates were less likely to be visited, less likely to receive mental health medications, more likely to be subject to police use of force, more likely to be written up, and more likely to be placed in solitary confinement. Latino/a inmates were less likely to receive mental health medications, more likely to be subject to police use of force, and more likely to be placed in solitary confinement. While not significant for the other dependent variables, American Indian inmates were more likely to be subject to police use of force and more likely to be written up.

Broadly, the findings point to significant racial discrimination in the treatment of American prison inmates. While this is perhaps not surprising, it is of critical importance. If inmates are more likely to be punished with solitary confinement, that may lead to mental health illnesses and other maladaptive social behavior. If inmates are more likely to be subject to use of force (assuming that police use of force is an adequate proxy for use of force in prison), inmates will be more likely to be exposed to disciplinary proceedings and physical injuries. If inmates are less likely to receive mental health medication or less likely to receive visits from their family, those inmates may have a more difficult time in prison and in society once they are released. All these variables are affected by the inmate's race.

The appendix describes, in detail, the various model estimations. The 2004 Survey is quite comprehensive, and I could have included other examples of negative treatment based on race and ethnicity. The five dependent variables that I have chosen provide a broad overview of different forms of treatment that prisoners face. I do not think it is particularly good science to run every possible permutation of a statistical model in search of those magical asterisks that we have agreed represent "statistical significance." I am also conscious of the need for readability, which is probably reduced when there is excessive exposition on methods. However, I will point out two broad points on race-based analyses of the 2004 Survey: first, the findings are robust, with nearly every analysis finding statistically significant, negative results for African American and to a lesser extent Latino/a and American Indian inmates; second, these findings exist even after controlling for socioeconomic variables, criminal history, and fixed effects at the prison level. The findings related to race are robust statistically and are in line with a very broad and deep literature on racial discrimination in criminal justice policy.

Suggestions for Reform

Issues of racial discrimination are difficult to solve, especially in an area as rife with racial stereotyping as American criminal justice policy. It is difficult to know how to implement changes, especially given the unique physical characteristics of American prisons. In an article for the journal *Administration and Society* (Wade-Olson 2016), I argued that having a more diverse prison staff can help limit racial discrimination in the use of solitary confinement. It was an article based on the idea of representative bureaucracy, which states that a diverse bureaucracy is necessary to represent the interests of a diverse clientele. I do think that hiring more African American and Latino/a staff would help but that such a step would have serious practical limitations. Prisons tend to be located away from urban centers for reasons of security and rural investment, while African Americans and Latino/as tend to be concentrated in urban centers. It would be difficult, for example, for an African American person from Flint or Detroit to relocate to the Upper Peninsula in order to work at a rural Michigan prison. Trying to solve racial discrimination with a representative bureaucracy approach is unlikely to be sufficient.

Charges of racial discrimination have also made prison policy reforms more difficult. Racism is presented as a moral failing, and the solution is elusive—maybe fewer racist cops or racist prison guards or racist politicians. At its worst, it is an elitist approach that looks down on what academics view as mostly conservative, mostly white law enforcement officers. This is an oversimplification that ignores the widespread variation in views that prison staff have. Insisting that prison guards are racist may not necessarily lead to buy-in from those same officers. While almost all Americans will say that racial discrimination is wrong, race relations are still one of, if not the most divisive issues in contemporary American politics.

In some ways, my recommendations involve me punting on the larger issue. This may be interpreted as timid or, perhaps more generously, as practical. I did grow up as a Carolina Panthers fan, and that football team once used the franchise tag on their punter. When your offense sputters against intense opposition, it is sometimes practical to punt and wait for a better opportunity. I cannot think of many things that Americans are more defensive about than race relations. Maybe punting is cowardly, but continuing to blame prison guards for being immoral racists seems like running into a wall. If prison guards are explicitly racist, they are unlikely to change. If prison guards are implicitly racist, it may be best to not charge them with moral failings, which will invoke hostility. Instead, it may help to view racism as a cognitive heuristic that developed over hundreds of years of American history and that is persistent even though it is discredited.

I recommend the following:

1. Frame race-based stereotypes as resulting from cognitive limitations. Training or retraining of prison staff should begin with this framework. Not only is it less provocative and thus less likely to cause resistance among prison staff but it is also more in line with psychological theories of human decision making.
2. Explore prison reform through a lens of intersectionality. Many policies that would benefit economically disadvantaged inmates, or inmates with drug charges, or inmates with mental health issues will also disproportionately benefit African American, American Indian, and Latino/a inmates.
3. Treatment decisions affecting inmates should be made by a diverse prison staff. This diversity should include gender and racial diversity as well as treatment staff and supervisors. From my interviews and the CJ-DATS data, it is clear that older and better-educated staff members are less punitive in their views. It will also be necessary to include, for lack of a better phrasing, both pro-inmate and pro-staff advocates.

CHAPTER SIX

Punishing Immigrants

> Felons, not families. Criminals, not children. Gang members, not a mom who's working hard to provide for her kids.
>
> —President Barack Obama, 2014

> What we are going to do is get the people that are criminal and have criminal records, gang members, drug dealers.
>
> —President-Elect Donald Trump, 2016

The above quotes represent the views of the last two presidents on who should be subject to detention and deportation. The quotes sound reasonable and generous but are in fact misleading. Any immigrant in the country illegally has technically committed a crime, and both presidential administrations have deported immigrants whose only crime was immigration based. The distinction between criminal and noncriminal undocumented immigrants is a false dichotomy; the federal government does not acknowledge any noncriminal undocumented immigrants. In addition, the "criminal" category includes people who committed traffic violations or petty crimes like shoplifting. Immigrants are held to a different standard than are American citizens; crimes that would lead to a fine or ticket for an American citizen can lead to a prison sentence and deportation for an immigrant.

Anti-immigrant sentiment is common in both political parties. President Trump is well known for sensationalistic anti-Mexican rhetoric. This rhetoric, chosen for domestic consumption, has serious implications internationally. At the very least, it makes it difficult for American tourists. While traveling in Colombia, I was asked why Donald Trump hates Mexicans; while traveling in Kenya, I was asked why Donald Trump wants to "deport all the Africans." Harsh immigration rhetoric helps define who gets to take part in the American experience and who will be marginalized. While we focus on Trump's rhetoric, President Obama was derisively known as the "deporter in chief" after overseeing the deportation of more than 2.4 million people (Shoichet and Kessler 2016). The differences between the two presidents are in some ways more rhetorical than substantive.

As seen with the past two presidents, immigration policy is surprisingly harsh and bipartisan. Some of the harshest reforms to immigration law took place under President Bill Clinton. It is not surprising that both political parties have made anti-immigrant statements and policies—immigrants cannot vote and do not have the same political resources that American citizens have. Immigration policy has become harsher in much the same way that war on crime policies in general have become harsher. There is likely a feedback loop for both immigration and broader crime policy—harsh treatment garners votes and other political benefits for politicians, incentivizing other politicians to ratchet up their own harshness.

During the third 2016 presidential debate between Trump and Democrat Hillary Clinton, Clinton emphasized her support for increased border security and stated that resources should be directed toward "getting rid of any violent person. Anybody who should be deported, we should deport them" (Moore 2016, p. 1). This logic is somewhat circular and places an emphasis on deportation. President Trump's anti-immigrant preferences and Hillary Clinton's basic support for detention and deportation point to a broad consensus on punishing immigrants. Although the Democratic position may be less sensationalistic, both parties have framed immigration in terms of security and detention rather than human rights or economic opportunity. Liberal Democratic support for immigration may be in part driven by opposition to President Trump in the same way that liberal Democratic opposition to the Iraq War was driven in part by opposition to President George W. Bush. Antiwar Democrats largely stopped protesting once President Obama was elected (Heaney and Rojas 2011).

Concerns over immigration and crime are not new. Some of the first immigration restrictions took place in the 1920s in response to public fears of a link between crime and immigration. Immigrants from Southern and Eastern Europe were vilified for "their alleged alcohol and drug abuse as well as for their putative criminality. The assumed link was clear and crude: Immigration caused crime" (Hagan, Levi, and Dinovitzer 2008, p. 96). This assumed link is still popular in spite of a lack of empirical evidence. Immigrants commit fewer crimes than do native-born Americans, and across a variety of studies, the correlation between immigration and crime is either weak or negative (Hagan, Levi, and Dinovitzer 2008; Kubrin, Zatz, and Martinez 2012; Lee and Martinez 2009). Immigrants who live in neighborhoods with high percentages of immigrants are especially law abiding (Martinez, Rosenfeld, and Mares 2009; Martinez, Stowell, and Lee 2010).

Guided more by political motivations and moral panic than empirical data, U.S. politicians have emphasized security and law and order, which has had a negative effect on vulnerable immigrant populations. The emphasis on border security has led to increasing exploitation of vulnerable migrants. A massive border patrol force and a heavily militarized United States–Mexico border has led migrants to attempt border crossings in dangerous, isolated areas of the Southwest desert. The United States' policies on the drug war and the deportation of gang members has destabilized Central America, leading to mass migration from Central American countries to the United States through Mexico.

Many migrants travel through Mexico on top of freight trains, as Oscar Martinez (2013) describes in his book *The Beast*. Along the way, migrants face kidnappings, sexual assaults, extortion attempts, exploitative smugglers, corrupt officials, and the very real risk of being killed or maimed by the train itself (Martinez 2013). If migrants make it to northern Mexico, they then face dangerous physical obstacles and thousands of border patrol agents. It is worth noting that these burdens are only faced by poor migrants. Wealthier migrants can afford tourist visas (which they can then overstay) or counterfeit travel documents. Wealthier migrants can come to the United States on planes, while the poor have a much longer and more difficult journey.

Our narratives about immigration describe immigrants as folk devils rather than as a vulnerable population. Millions of people are forced to flee political instability, economic disorder, and violence, some of which was partially caused by the United States. During their journey to the United States, these people risk their lives and face sexual assaults and economic exploitation. Once they arrive, they face further difficulties with poorly paid jobs, little economic or political power, and few social services. Due to their willingness to work for low pay in industries like agriculture, construction, cleaning, and childcare services, the American standard of living is raised. In spite of their struggles and lack of financial resources, when they arrive in the United States, they statistically commit fewer crimes than America-born citizens. Despite the economic benefits and sheer bravery that many immigrants bring, we have decided to scapegoat, ostracize, and incarcerate this population.

Once in the United States, undocumented immigrants are subject to arrest. For those who are arrested by law enforcement officers inside the United States, the experience can quickly become Kafkaesque (Welch 2002). Immigrants are frequently transferred between different prison facilities, often without notifying attorneys or family members. Immigration detainees face inadequate resources and brutality (Welch 2002). After years of bipartisan moral panic over immigration, immigration charges have surpassed drug violations as the leading charge that sends people to prison. Immigration prosecution now drives incarceration rates (Macias-Rojas 2016). This may also give pause to those who think mass incarceration can be stopped simply with the reform of drug laws. Prisons are a bureaucracy, and bureaucracies are self-interested. More prisoners can lead to a higher budget, and in the case of immigration detainees, there is significant financial compensation to prisons from the federal government.

The mass enforcement of immigration laws is a recent invention, and even the idea that immigration in the United States should be regulated is a relatively new idea. In order to understand contemporary immigration policy, it is important to consider the policy's historical evolution. It is a history, like many others in America, in which the vulnerable are targeted and exploited.

A Brief History of American Immigration Enforcement

The massive growth of the United States from a handful of weak British colonies to the world's economic superpower has been driven in part by immigrant labor. The usual platitude of American politicians, including the 2016 Democratic presidential candidate Hillary Clinton, has been that the United States is a "nation of immigrants." This oversimplification ignores several historical tragedies, including the genocide of indigenous peoples and the forced migration of African slaves. However, the cliché does have some merit; for a country with vast physical expanses and a low population, immigration has allowed for spectacular growth.

Immigration enforcement was minimal until the 1920s. The earliest attempts were bans on Chinese immigration in 1882, but prior to the 1920s, exclusion laws did not extend to immigrants from Europe or the Western Hemisphere. There was some screening for people with physical or mental deficiencies, but most (European) immigrants were let into the country. Between 1908 and 1920, the Immigration Service deported an average of 2,000 or 3,000 immigrants per year, at a time when approximately 1 million immigrants entered the United States every year. While a low number of European immigrants were deported, there were effectively no restrictions on Latin American immigrants (Ngai 2004).

As the country's population grew and most areas of the country became settled, there was no longer as much need for massive influxes of cheap labor. The first immigration restrictions took place once labor shortages were less of a concern. The Johnson-Reed Immigration Act of 1924 placed the first numerical limits on immigration and established a quota system based on nationality and race (Ngai 2004). The numerical restrictions mostly affected Europeans. Nearly all Asians were already excluded, and even after the Johnson-Reed Immigration Act, there were no numerical restrictions on countries from the Western Hemisphere (Ngai 2004).

Already, we can see that there was not one immigration policy but at least three: numerical restrictions for Europeans, exclusion for Asians, and no restrictions for immigrants from Latin America. Border security was virtually nonexistent, and from the late 19th century until World War I, migration across the United States–Mexico border had an "informal, unregulated character" (Ngai 2004, p. 55). During that time, there was great demand for Mexican migrant labor, and there were not the same racial concerns about Mexicans as there were for Asians. For example, the 1848 Treaty of Hidalgo considered Mexicans as "white" for governmental purposes (Rodriguez 2007).

Mae Ngai (2004, p. 169) explains the relationship between Mexican immigration and the development of the Southwest United States:

> From the turn of the century to World War I, labor flowed more or less freely from Mexico into the United States. Mexican workers provided the human labor power for the region's agricultural revolution and laid the infrastructure for the modern Southwest's economy: they laid railroad tracks that connected the region to the national market, cleared ranch lands for farming, and dug irrigation canals.

Moral panics about Latino/a immigration ignore the significant contributions that Latin Americans have made to the economic growth of the United States. We have already seen a similar dynamic where the labor contributions of leased African American convicts went unacknowledged.

For decades, Mexican immigrants provided useful labor to the United States. The need for temporary, migratory workers was created in part by American companies. U.S. aid and investment "directly uprooted Mexican peasants, recruited them into a migrant labor stream, and initiated the social and cultural changes that led them to leave their homes and work for cash in distant lands" (Chomsky 2014, p. 52). However, economic insecurities during the Great Depression of the 1930s led to efforts to deport Mexican immigrants (Ngai 2004). This treatment of Mexicans fits the larger pattern of our fluctuations between welcoming and restricting immigrants. Our openness to immigration has largely depended on economic conditions.

World War II brought about significant labor shortages, which led to the United States and Mexico signing a bilateral agreement establishing the Bracero guest worker program. The Bracero program created a large, migratory workforce (Ngai 2004). Between 1942 and 1964, 4.8 million contracts were signed by U.S. farmers and Mexican workers. The Mexican workers were known as Braceros because they worked with their *brazos*, or arms ("The Bracero Program" 2003). The Bracero program was a gift to Southern and Southwestern agriculturalists, some of whom actively recruited a migratory workforce. The second gift to agriculturalists was increased deportation of non-Bracero workers (Ngai 2004).

A major anti-immigrant campaign, named after a racial slur for Mexicans, took place on the United States–Mexico border in 1954. Seven hundred and fifty immigration officers were involved. The campaign apprehended 3,000 undocumented workers a day and 170,000 during the first three months. The Immigration and Naturalization Service apprehended 801,069 Mexican migrants from 1953 to 1955 (Ngai 2004). Southern and Southwestern agriculturalists had the best of both worlds: the Bracero program provided labor when it was needed, while deportation allowed for the removal of surplus labor and made it easier to manage non-Bracero migrant labor. The threat of deportation remains a useful way for employers to limit the political and economic power of their undocumented workforce.

Once agriculture became more mechanized, the dependence on migrant labor decreased, lessening the appeal of the Bracero program for American agriculturalists.

> American agribusiness found itself far less dependent upon imported contract labor. Cotton, the chief crop drawing braceros in Texas, Arizona, and parts of California, was mechanized by the early 1960s. The mechanization of sugar beets reduced demand for braceros in other western states. In California, where the majority of braceros were employed after 1961, growers felt increasingly inconvenienced by the Labor Department's tougher enforcement practices and anticipated the mechanization of tomato-harvesting, which was finally achieved in 1965. (Ngai 2004, p. 166)

Other than economic considerations, the main factor deciding openness or punitiveness toward immigrants is the social construction of the immigrant group in question. As stated previously, Chinese immigrants were excluded as early as 1882. Concerns about Asian immigration were not limited to the Chinese. After the Spanish-American War in 1898, the United States gained colonies in Asia and Latin America, including the Philippines. Large numbers of Filipino migrants freely entered the United States and engaged in migrant farm labor. Americans on the West Coast had negative views of Filipinos. Filipino men were viewed as sexually threatening, leading to anti-Filipino riots in California (Ngai 2004). One consequence of American imperialism was the uncertain status of American possessions like the Philippines and Puerto Rico. American policy makers wanted the economic benefits of those territories without necessarily allowing for the integration of their populations.

Other examples of defining immigrants and ethnic groups as dangerous "others" took place during World War II. German Americans were pressured to stop speaking German and to stop certain religious practices in order to prove their loyalty as Americans. Japanese Americans were infamously interned in concentration camps. "Presuming all Japanese in America to be racially inclined to disloyalty, the United States removed 120,000 Japanese Americans—two-thirds of them citizens—from their homes on the Pacific

Coast and interned them in ten concentration camps in the interior" (Ngai 2004, p. 175). The concerns over the linguistic and cultural assimilation of Latin Americans is an echo of earlier concerns about German and Japanese Americans.

After World War II, and with the success of the civil rights movement, there was a move to make immigration policy less biased and racist. In 1976, Congress imposed country quotas of 20,000 migrants on Western Hemisphere countries (Ngai 2004). Although this change placed Mexico and other Latin American countries on the same playing field as other countries, this nominal equality was impractical and ultimately harmful. With the strict quotas on immigration from Mexico, Mexican immigrants were given a new social construction. "The imposition of a 20,000 annual quota on Mexico recast Mexican migration as 'illegal'" (Ngai 2004, p. 261). The rhetoric of "illegality" has helped provide a cover for anti-immigrant activism. Anti-Latino/a, antirefugee, and racist ideologies can be recast as a simple demand for following the rules and abiding by laws.

Nativism and distrust of certain immigrant groups has a long history in the United States and predates President Trump's provocative statements regarding Mexicans and Muslims by about 170 years. The American or Know-Nothing Party, founded in 1849, was vehemently anti-Catholic and anti-immigrant. Anti-Catholic feelings rose again in the 1890s (when nativists were worried about Italians and Slavs) and in 1917 (when Florida governor Sidney Catts claimed Catholics were storing weapons in a Tampa church and there were concerns of "a papal invasion, followed by the construction of a new Vatican in Palm Beach") (*Economist* 2015b, p. 1). During the 1920s and 1930s, there was an equivalent moral panic over Jewish people. One of the more prominent anti-Semitic supporters of the day was industrialist Henry Ford, who placed reproductions of a fraudulent, anti-Semitic propaganda piece called "Protocols of the Elders of Zion" in Ford car dealership sales rooms (*Economist* 2015b).

The hysteria over Catholics, Germans, Italians, Jews, and the Japanese highlights the moral panic aspect that governs historical and modern immigration policy. Different religious and ethnic groups are seen as dangerous or incapable of assimilating. The bogeyman of Catholicism is replaced by the bogeyman of Islam, but the features remain consistent. Concerns about the laziness of Italians or the inability of Germans to speak English transform into concerns about Latino/as' ability to assimilate. As late as 2009, a respected political scientist argued in *Foreign Policy* that "demographically, socially, and culturally, the *reconquista* (re-conquest) of the Southwest United States by Mexican immigrants is well underway" (Huntington 2009, p. 13). Our moral panic emphasizes the language of warfare and invasion rather than discussing the contributions of and challenges faced by Latino/a immigrants. We also ignore the broader lesson of moral panics; if our hysterias over Japanese or Jewish Americans were unfounded, our modern hysteria over Latino/as and Muslims is also likely to be unfounded.

Moral Panics and Immigration

Multiple scholars have explicitly argued that the United States is in a moral panic over immigrants. "The public, angry over social and economic unrest, justifies scapegoating unpopular groups such as immigrants, who have already been criminalized, pathologized, and marginalized, because they are an easy target" (Welch 2002, p. 21). "The construction of unauthorized immigrants as bearers of crime is creating a moral panic about immigration control" (Kubrin, Zatz, and Martinez 2012, p. 44). Loic Wacquant (1999, p. 219) has declared that immigrants have become a "suitable enemy" who are "at once symbol of and target for all social anxieties." When societies face great social change or periods of anxiety, it is easier for politicians to blame outsiders than to address change and to acknowledge that those in power may be responsible for the country's problems.

This moral panic and criminalization of immigration is not limited to the United States. Disproportionate incarceration is common in Europe as well. In Germany, the Roma are incarcerated at 20 times the rate of native citizens, while Moroccans are incarcerated at eight times the rate and Turks at three to four times the rate of native citizens. In France, the share of foreigners in prison is 29 percent, although foreigners only represent 6 percent of the population. In England, West Indian, Guyanese, and African immigrants are disproportionately incarcerated (Wacquant 1999). Didier Fassin's (2013) ethnography of French police officers features the sort of racial profiling and anti-immigrant biases that have been documented in studies on American policing.

Australia has a particularly brutal policy for refugees seeking entrance by traveling on boat. The Australian Navy has the power to intercept refugees at sea and transport those refugees to detention camps on two Pacific Island nations, Nauru and Papua New Guinea. In the camps, refugees live in shipping containers, the lights do not work, there are no windows, and the heat is oppressive. Women and children complain of sexual abuse. The average stay at the camps is 450 days, though almost one-quarter of refugees spend more than two years in the camps. Multiple refugees have committed suicide in protest of their conditions (Phippen 2016). Harsh treatment of immigrants is common in many countries, even those that are broadly considered to be more liberal than the United States.

Punishing immigrants satisfies certain moral needs (Leerkes and Broeders 2010). Punishing immigrants helps manage social unrest related to unwanted migration. "Immigration detention communicates the message that the State is still in control over the geographical (and social) borders that citizens want to maintain" (Leerkes and Broeders 2010, p. 843). For politicians, anti-immigrant sentiment can bring votes and attention (Chomsky 2014). Immigration detention is a form of denunciation; it "expresses the value that there should be borders demarcating the divide between who belongs to the society and who does not" (Leerkes and Broeders 2010, p. 843). Politicians can appear tough and at the same time remind their supporters that the supporters are good citizens while immigrants are a dangerous other.

After the 1993 bombing of the World Trade Center and again following the September 11, 2001, attack, Congress passed tough new immigration laws. In 1996, Congress passed both the Illegal Immigration Reform and Responsibility Act (IIRIRA) and the Anti-Terrorism and Effective Death Penalty Act, which granted the Immigration and Naturalization Service authority to seek out and deport immigrants deemed a threat to national security (Kubrin, Zatz, and Martinez 2012). IIRIRA greatly expanded the grounds for criminal removal by including minor offenses like petty theft, driving under the influence, and minor drug offenses (Macias-Rojas 2016). In addition to the IIRIRA, President Clinton signaled his commitment to border enforcement by launching major border patrol operations, including Operation Gatekeeper in California, Operation Hold-the-Line in Texas, and Operation Safeguard in Arizona (Vitale 2017). The Democratic Party has played a major role in shaping harsh immigration policy, much like other forms of law-and-order politics. At the very least, punitiveness is a bipartisan accomplishment.

Laws like the IIRIRA increased the numbers of immigration officers and detention centers for immigrants. This has served to greatly increase the numbers of vulnerable immigrants sent to prison. In 1992, immigration-related charges accounted for 5 percent of federal convictions. By 2012, this had increased to 30 percent. In 1992, noncitizens accounted for 22 percent of federal prisoners; by 2012, they made up 46 percent. In 2008, 11 percent of those detained in California prisons were immigrants facing deportation (Escobar 2016). By 2016, Immigration and Customs Enforcement had a detention capacity of 34,000 beds and a mandate from Congress to keep the beds full (Macias-Rojas 2016). Increased immigration detention is one of the most significant trends in American correctional policy in the past 25 years.

Many of those detained have significant roots in the United States. Of the 12 million undocumented immigrants in the United States, 86 percent have been in the country for more than seven years (Chomsky 2014). Over half of the 16 million Latino/a children in the United States have at least one immigrant parent. A majority of Latino/as worry about deportation (Kubrin, Zatz, and Martinez 2012). Undocumented immigrants are often denied custody of their children (Escobar 2016). In 2011, over 46,000 parents of U.S. citizen children were deported. Over 5,000 U.S. children live in foster care because their parents are either in immigration detention or were deported (Chomsky

2014). Official government rhetoric, which emphasizes the importance of family, is undone by the state's own policies.

Many undocumented immigrants are themselves children or teenagers. In 2012, more than 14,000 youth, mostly from Central America, were taken into custody. High levels of violence and economic stagnation have driven thousands from their homes in Central America to the United States. The United States is responsible for a good deal of the unrest. Central America's political and economic crises have been exacerbated by U.S. military involvement and trade policies that "virtually guarantee that children will continue to try to escape" (Chomsky 2014, p. 157). Children, some of whom travel the dangerous migrant road through Mexico that Oscar Martinez (2013) so vividly describes in *The Beast*, flee violence and poverty in their home countries only to end up in an American prison.

Even if they are not arrested, migrants face a perilous journey to the United States. Since severe immigration enforcement began in the 1990s, thousands have died trying to cross the deserts of Arizona and New Mexico. In some years, as many as 500 people have died of heat, exposure, and dehydration. The journey through the desert may last days, cost thousands of dollars, and necessitate reliance on smugglers known as "coyotes," some of whom have kidnapped, raped, or killed their clients. Migrants are sometimes forced by the coyotes to carry drugs and often lack adequate water (Vitale 2017).

Not all undocumented immigrants are equally likely to be placed in prison. Even the categories of who is authorized and unauthorized is politicized and reflects government preferences. During the 1980s, when Central America was ravaged by civil wars, the Reagan administration denied asylum to Salvadoran and Guatemalan asylum seekers whose governments the United States supported while granting asylum to Nicaraguans and Cubans, whose governments the United States opposed (Welch 2002). Similar to other aspects of law enforcement, the determining factor in deportation and incarceration is what group someone belongs to rather than what that person did.

The politicization and unequal enforcement of immigration laws has serious consequences. Since the decision of which asylum seekers should be deported is in part affected by politics rather than strictly based on safety concerns, the United States has deported immigrants to dangerous countries. For example, migrants deported from the United States to El Salvador have faced random strip searches and imprisonment (Kubrin, Zatz, and Martinez 2012). The United States has also deported immigrants to Somalia, despite that country's lack of a viable central government (Hassan 2017).

Deciding who is worthy of sanctuary and who is deserving of arrest and incarceration filters down to street-level immigration enforcement officers. Patrisia Macias-Rojas (2016, p. 18) writes, "Frontline Border Patrol agents have been given tremendous power to decide whom to stop, question, and arrest, as well as whom to criminally prosecute, detain, or deport due to prior criminal history." Rather than treating all undocumented immigrants as equally worthy of arrest and incarceration, Border Patrol agents are likely making decisions based on stereotypes and group reputations. Indeed, support for targeting some immigrants over others is apparent in the quotes from both President Trump and President Obama at the beginning of this chapter.

Those deemed worthy of arrest and incarceration tend to be from minority ethnic groups or minority religions. Mexican nationals make up 58 percent of the undocumented population but 70 percent of the deported (Chomsky 2014). While immigrants from four Latin American countries made up 72 percent of the unauthorized immigrant population in 2012, they constituted 95 percent of removals (Escobar 2016). A portion of the remaining 5 percent are made up of Nigerian and Somali immigrants, who have also been disproportionately targeted (Dow 2004). Undocumented immigrants arrested for criminal offenses, immigration violations, or suspected terrorism are largely drawn from minority communities (Bosworth and Kaufman 2011).

After the September 11, 2001, terrorist attacks, American law enforcement has frequently targeted Muslim communities (Dow 2004). The Department of Justice has detained 1,128 immigrants, mostly Muslim and Arab men, as potential security threats. The Immigration and Naturalization Service rounded up 6,000 Arab and Muslim immigrants with outstanding deportation orders and detained another 2,747 Arab and Muslim immigrants under a special registration program (Macias-Rojas 2016). People of Middle Eastern descent have been increasingly targeted by immigration officers since 2001 (Bosworth and Kaufman 2011). This targeting has not had an effect on terrorism, which is thankfully a rare event. For the vast majority of detained Muslim and Arab immigrants, their only "crime" was an immigration violation (Dow 2004).

When immigrants are incarcerated, they have far fewer legal protections than American citizens, placing them in a vulnerable position.

> The U.S. immigration complex does not offer detainees the same degree of legal protections that the American criminal justice system offers citizen criminal offenders. There is neither automatic judicial oversight of immigration detention centers, nor independent review of ICE decisions to detain arriving asylum seekers. Unlike many prisoners, non-U.S. citizens detained by ICE are practically denied the chance at judicial review of their detention. (Bosworth and Kaufman 2011, p. B109)

Immigrant detainees have few rights and often lack the means to find out what rights they do have (Chomsky 2014). Noncitizens are often subjected to disparate treatment in bail and sentencing because of their immigration status (Kubrin, Zatz, and Martinez 2012). Immigration detainees have less access to services than do U.S. citizens (Chomsky 2014). Immigration hearings are quick and routinized; large groups of immigrants are processed in extremely short trials. Eighty-four percent of immigration detainees do not have a lawyer during court proceedings. Eighty-one percent of convicted immigrants receive a prison sentence (Macias-Rojas 2016). Due to language difficulties, immigrants often do not know what they are pleading guilty to. Due to a lack of legal representation, immigrants often do not know the full implications of their guilty plea.

Criminal charges are also counted differently in the immigration system than in the regular court system. Permanent residents are deported for minor crimes such as public intoxication (Kubrin, Zatz, and Martinez 2012). Offenses like driving without a license or disorderly conduct are counted as aggravated felonies in the immigration system (Macias-Rojas 2016). Aggravated felonies is a category that includes murder, rape, terrorism, and kidnapping (Welch 2002). The moral panic over immigration has gone so far that people with strong ties to the country, but who happen to lack citizenship, are placed under the same designation as murderers and terrorists. One need not be a bleeding-heart liberal to suggest that driving without a license isn't as bad as murder or terrorism.

Once incarcerated, immigrants face tremendous difficulties. Immigration detainees are frequently transferred between jails without warning (Bosworth and Kaufman 2011). Politically active immigrants are transferred to multiple different facilities to limit their influence. Despite this, there are frequent hunger strikes in immigration prisons. Immigrants complain of meaningless grievance procedures, arbitrary use of solitary confinement, verbal harassment, humiliation, and physical abuse. There is also a lack of an appeals process for custody reviews (Bosworth and Kaufman 2011).

The United States' lack of transparency and heavy-handed treatment of immigrants has serious consequences for American communities. The recent increases in immigration enforcement are matched by an increasing distrust of the U.S. justice system by immigrant communities. Latino/a confidence in the criminal justice system has declined as policies fuse criminal and immigration laws.

Aviva Chomsky (2014, p. 162) writes that we should look beyond immigration statistics and at the real human cost of harsh immigration laws:

> Beyond the statistics are the stories: a crying baby taken from her mother's arms and handed to social workers as the mother is handcuffed and taken away, her parental rights terminated by a U.S. judge; teenage children watching as parents are dragged from the family home; immigrant parents disappearing into a maze-like detention system where they are routinely

> locked up hundreds of miles from their homes, separated from their families for months and denied contact with the welfare agencies deciding their children's fate.

Chomsky (2014, p. 162) continues:

> When parents disappear into the immigration system like this, they run the risk of losing custody of their children. Courts may terminate parental rights after parents are deported or detained. In the criminal justice system, prisoners have guaranteed certain rights and access to services. Immigrant detainees, though, fall into a sort of constitutional and legal netherworld. Due to their vulnerability, immigrants have little ability to fight back against incarceration and deportation, the consequence of which is often the dissolution of previously strong families.

Immigration, which used to be a primarily federal issue, has now devolved to the local level. President Trump has issued an executive order withdrawing funding from so-called sanctuary cities—cities that do not comply with federal immigration requirements. The executive order is currently under judicial review, but if confirmed, it would take billions of dollars in funding away from cities like New York and Los Angeles (Yee 2017). The executive order would place cities in a difficult position: to go against local opinion and enforce harsh immigration laws or to lose federal funding. Even if the executive order is not upheld, it sends a signal to immigrant communities in the same way that President Trump's more famous travel ban sent a signal to Muslim communities.

The increasing linkage between immigration and crime puts local law enforcement in a difficult position. Tolerating undocumented immigrants is seen as tolerating crime and insecurity (Kubrin, Zatz, and Martinez 2012). The United States–Mexico border is an especially dramatic example. As the border becomes heavily militarized, border residents are placed under heavy surveillance. "Smuggling" can mean giving someone a ride. This naturally breeds a feeling of insecurity and distrust among border residents. As local law enforcement becomes more involved in enforcing federal laws, the opposite occurs as well. Federal immigration officers not only arrest and deport immigrants but also become involved in local crime control (Macias-Rojas 2016).

The enforcement of immigration laws is therefore subject to both moral and fiscal pressures. Tough-on-crime rhetoric incentivizes harsh law enforcement measures. Federal immigration officers are required to fill the 34,000 detention beds that Congress has appropriated funding for (Macias-Rojas 2016). Local law enforcement can receive extra funding if they participate in immigration enforcement, and cities risk losing funding if "sanctuary cities" are defunded. Still, there is a more direct link that helps explain why immigration prosecution is the fastest-growing driver of incarceration rates. Detaining immigrants can mean big money for local jails and prisons.

The federal government pays an average daily rate of $164 for each day an immigrant is held in detention (Conlon and Hiemstra 2014). While costs vary by state and security level, the average cost for a state prison is $91 per inmate per day. New York has the most expensive costs, at $190 per inmate per day, and Alabama has the lowest costs at $40 per inmate per day (Vera Institute of Justice 2017). The federal government estimates an average of $87 per day per inmate (Bureau of Prisons 2016). (Quick note: The Vera Institute reports expenditures as annual costs. For ease of comparison, I have adjusted this to daily rates.) Almost any jail or prison that can detain immigrants can charge the federal government at a rate much higher than the actual costs of incarceration. Immigrants are likely to be even cheaper than the average inmate, because they have fewer security concerns and less access to prison programs.

Detainees in immigration prisons are even more exploitable than regular prisoners. Undocumented immigrants are paid $1 to $3 a day to work through the detainee voluntary work program. Work includes maintenance, landscaping, laundry services, cooking, and cleaning (Hennessy-Fiske 2015). In some cases, immigrants "volunteer" to work for free, with the knowledge that if they do not work for free, they will be placed in solitary confinement. The GEO Group, a private prison company, allegedly forced more than 50,000 immigrants to work without pay or for $1 a day between 2004 and 2014 (Pauly 2017). The irony, of course, is that many immigrants are in jail or prison for coming to the United States to work without authorization. Working in the free world is penalized by working for free in the prison world.

In many ways, it shouldn't be surprising; much of American immigration policy is determined by economic concerns. When there is not enough work in developing countries, those forces pull migration to low-wage sectors of the U.S. economy (Chomsky 2014). Consumers benefit from low-cost goods and services. Employers benefit from low-wage labor and, by virtue of deportability, an easily coerced and controlled workforce (Chomsky 2014). Immigrants often benefit from the system as well. Rational people would not risk their lives to travel to the United States if opportunities in their home country were as appealing as opportunities in the United States. Then again, not all immigrants benefit. Some are more likely to be scapegoated than others and are more likely to be sent to prison.

Imagine leaving your home country, one that was potentially destabilized by U.S. foreign policy. You want to get to America, but you are not granted permanent resident status or even a tourist visa. So you begin a journey of thousands of miles. Maybe you ride a container ship from China or you ride on the top of a freight train through Mexico. Maybe you have to pay thousands of precious dollars to a smuggler. After you arrive in the United States, you put down roots, find a job, start a family, become part of the community.

One day, you're stopped by a local sheriff or the police or Immigration and Customs Enforcement. You were driving without a license, but in your state it is illegal for undocumented immigrants to have drivers licenses. You're sent to a prison where you are forced to work for free or for cheap wages. You may have difficulty communicating in English, and you almost certainly cannot afford a lawyer. After being transferred to multiple facilities whose main concern is revenue, you finally go before an immigration judge. The judge asks you a handful of questions and then orders your deportation. You are going to be separated from whatever friends, family, and community you have in the United States. You are going to be sent to a country that you may not have been to in decades. And if you come back to the United States and are caught again, you face a much longer prison sentence due to your previous guilty plea.

There are many elements of this story that seem criminal or immoral, but to me most of the immorality seems to be on the part of government policy makers.

U.S. immigration punishes millions of vulnerable immigrants. They are punished not for being undocumented—if that were the case, we would expect all undocumented immigrants to be equally likely to be arrested and incarcerated—but because they are easier to exploit, they are from negatively stereotyped groups, and they lack the resources necessary to mount a legal defense. Immigration laws fundamentally punish people for an accident of birth. The determination is not just whether the person was born inside the imaginary line denoting the United States; an immigrant from Somalia or El Salvador is treated very differently than an immigrant from Cuba.

The 2004 Survey has a very small number of noncitizens in its sample. Therefore, it was not possible to run an analysis on whether immigrants are treated differently in prison than are U.S. citizens. The 2016 version of the survey may have more information; if so, I will post an updated analysis onto this book's website (www.punishingthevulnerable.com). Until then, I have to rely largely on other scholars' work on conditions in immigration detention facilities. I would encourage other scholars to continue to explore those conditions.

Suggestions for Reform

I will begin with the caveat that many of the issues surrounding immigration policy have complex, multicausal relationships. Broader immigration reform is vital, but it is beyond the scope of this book. The recommendations that I have are relatively limited and are restricted to dealing with inmates.

I recommend the following:

1. Information about the location of immigration detainees should be given to their family members. Moving detainees between facilities should be limited and should not be used for purposes of retaliation.
2. Immigration detainees who do not have legal counsel should be provided with legal counsel.
3. Alternatives to incarceration should be considered for any immigrant who is not a flight risk or charged with a serious violent crime.
4. Prisons should be reimbursed at cost rather than reimbursed at the federal government's rate. This will disincentivize the building of prison or jail capacity purely to hold immigration detainees.

CHAPTER SEVEN

Punishing Drug Use

On July 6, 2016, Officer Jeronimo Yanez conducted a traffic stop in the Minneapolis, Minnesota, suburb of Falcon Heights. Yanez pulled over an African American man named Philando Castile for having a broken taillight. Police video recorded Castile announcing that he had a legal firearm on him. A few seconds later, Yanez fired seven shots from his weapon, hitting Castile five times and killing the 32-year-old cafeteria worker. Castile's girlfriend recorded the immediate aftermath of the shooting and posted the video online. The story would garner national attention (Karnowski and Forliti 2017).

Officer Yanez told investigators that the smell of cannabis in Castile's car made him fearful of his safety.

> I thought I was gonna die. And I thought if he's, if he has the, the guts and the audacity to smoke marijuana in front of the five year old girl and risk her lungs and risk her life by giving her secondhand smoke and the front passenger doing the same thing then what, what care does he give about me. And, I let off the rounds and then after the rounds were off, the little girl was screaming. (Ingraham 2017, p. 1)

Officer Yanez is not the only police officer to explain their use of force due to a suspect using cannabis. In 2016, Charlotte-Mecklenburg (North Carolina) police officers confronted an African American man, Keith Lamont Scott, in his car after observing Scott smoke cannabis. Scott also had a firearm in his car. In the Scott case, the police department stated, "Due to the combination of illegal drugs and the gun Mr. Scott had in his possession, officers decided to take enforcement action for public safety concerns" (Ingraham 2017, p. 1).

In both cases, police officers were not punished. The police officer who killed Keith Lamont Scott was never charged with a crime. Officer Yanez was charged but acquitted. The two police officers justified their decisions to use force on the basis of a behavior, in this case drug use. But it is difficult if not impossible to separate identity and behavior. Both Castile and Scott were lower-income African Americans and as such were more vulnerable than other drug users would have been in a similar situation. While news of disparate treatment in policing makes national headlines, disparate treatment against drug users in prison is not as well known. This chapter focuses on how drug use, dependence, and abuse make some prisoners more vulnerable to punishment.

Humans have a long history of experimentation with and use of different plant substances. All the naturally occurring narcotics, stimulants, relaxants, and hallucinogens were discovered and utilized thousands of years ago (McKenna 1999). Drugs have been used for religious and recreational purposes, to boost creativity and productivity, to provide an escape from daily life, and to provide enhanced spiritual experiences and increased connectedness to the universe. Drug use in the United States is widespread. For example, 43 percent of American adults report having used cannabis, the most popular illegal drug, at some point in their lives. About one in eight Americans are current users of the plant (McCarthy 2016).

The history of drug enforcement in the United States is long and fascinating. While it is beyond the scope of this book to offer a comprehensive account, it is worth noting that drug enforcement has focused largely on punishing vulnerable populations.

The first nonalcoholic drug ban was passed in 1875 in San Francisco, California. The law banned smoking opium, largely as a result of hysteria regarding Chinese immigrants (Fisher 2014). After the banning of opium in San Francisco, antinarcotics laws spread at the state, and later the federal, level. Three closely related events intensified the war on drugs—the Harrison Narcotics Tax Act of 1914, alcohol prohibition from 1920 to 1933, and finally the Marihuana Tax Act of 1937. The Harrison Narcotics Tax Act banned the sale of opium and coca. The antinarcotics bill was "fueled by a fusion of regional moral panics and the State Department's campaign for domestic legislation to bolster the government's nascent efforts to build an antinarcotics prohibition regime" (McGirr 2016, p. 20). Both the antinarcotics movement and the antialcohol movement were motivated by multiple concerns, including consumer safety, immigration, racial animus, and evangelical Protestant values.

Much like the current war on drugs, the war on alcohol disproportionately targeted the vulnerable. The rich were largely exempt from the pains of prohibition. Alcohol purchased before the official start date was not subject to seizure. The rich could, and did, buy large supplies of liquor to store throughout Prohibition. The rich could also afford to buy alcohol from pharmacists, to pay bribes, and to purchase high-quality smuggled alcohol.

Prohibition enforcement was largely relegated to poor neighborhoods. Organized crime placed speakeasies, dance halls, and jazz clubs in poor neighborhoods to avoid scrutiny. When pressure was placed on the police to make arrests, they arrested working-class people in poor neighborhoods rather than directly go after organized crime (McGirr 2016).

The protection given to the rich was also extended to organized crime. In some cases, police partnered with organized crime and protected bootlegging operations. Organized crime gangs could afford to bribe police officers and politicians and could even pay for insurance to mitigate the consequences of police raids. This led police to focus on small liquor operations, because they were easier to catch. The police engaged in selective enforcement, disproportionately targeting poor immigrants, African Americans, Mexicans, and poor white Americans. Marginal violators were disproportionately targeted because they lacked the funds for bribery and protection payoffs (McGirr 2016).

McGirr (2016, p. 98) writes,

> Outside of a few celebrated federal operations against criminal gangs in Detroit or the high-profile efforts to put "public enemies" like Al Capone behind bars, enforcement mostly captured and prosecuted small-scale violators marginal to the overall industry. Those of modest means, whether white, black, Latino, rural or urban, male or female, suffered not only from the high price of liquor, its poor and even poisonous quality, and the rise of gangland violence and vice in their neighborhoods, but also from the capricious and in some places terrorizing levels of enforcement.

Many of the themes of criminal justice policy today became evident during Prohibition. States used monetary sanctions, and an inability to pay a fine or court costs could lead to prison sentences that involved hard labor. Police were given financial incentives, such as special fees for stills captured and violators prosecuted (incentivizing mass arrests). Police violence was rampant. At least a thousand people were killed during Prohibition enforcement. Prohibition led to harsh sentencing and the erosion of legal protections. Penalties included mandatory minimums and life sentences for repeat offenders. Police applied the law unequally and obtained questionable search warrants. Finally, Prohibition led to the kinds of prison overcrowding that we experience today. Leavenworth housed 3,770 prisoners in a facility designed for 2,000. Pennsylvania's Eastern Penitentiary placed three or four inmates in cells designed for one person (McGirr 2016).

After the end of Prohibition, many of the antialcohol crusaders moved to the antinarcotics movement. Indeed, the two movements were tightly linked. One of the most famous antinarcotics advocates, Harry Anslinger, was a former prohibition agent. Anslinger famously wrote articles linking cannabis and violent crime—violent crime in which the perpetrators were almost always Latino/as or African Americans and the victims almost always white. Newspapers at the time, especially those owned by racist publisher William Randolph Hearst, linked cannabis with Mexican migrant labor (Booth 2005). It was not primarily drug use that was punished but drug use by vulnerable and marginalized populations.

Explicitly racist appeals have become less palatable; however, race baiting and race-based drug policy did not end with Anslinger. Politicians and bureaucrats are now more likely to use coded appeals (Haney-Lopez 2015), but the results remain similar. A quote from John Ehrlichman, President Richard Nixon's domestic policy chief, has recently gone viral on social media:

> The Nixon campaign in 1968, and the Nixon White House after that, had two enemies: the antiwar left and black people. You understand what I'm saying? We knew we couldn't make it illegal to be either against the war or black, but by getting the public to associate the hippies with marijuana and blacks with heroin, and then criminalizing both heavily, we could disrupt those communities. We could arrest their leaders, raid their homes, break up their meetings, and vilify them night after night on the evening news. Did we know we were lying about the drugs? Of course we did. (LoBianco, 2016, p. 1)

The violence and racial profiling inherent in both Prohibition and the drug war are not the only commonalities. Much as the rich and privileged had ways to avoid prosecution during Prohibition, the privileged today have ways of avoiding arrests and incarceration. Perhaps the best recent example of an institutionalized, legal double standard is related to medical cannabis. Although cannabis bought on the street or from a medical cannabis dispensary is at least roughly equivalent, the penalties for street-bought cannabis are severe, while medical cannabis is legal in over 20 states.

To take one example, medical cannabis was legalized in Michigan in 2008. Around 2 percent of Michigan residents have a medical cannabis card and are allowed to purchase cannabis legally from state-licensed dispensaries. Nearly 220,000 Michigan residents had a medical cannabis card as of September 30, 2016 (Mack 2017a). Around the same time, in 2015, police in Michigan made nearly 24,000 arrests involving nonmedical cannabis (Mack 2017b). What makes a medical card holder different from a non-card holder? While these groups are theoretically distinguished by a medical condition, card holders must also pay doctor's fees to qualify for the card and a $60 annual fee to the state of Michigan. To be set up as a new patient in Michigan can cost over $200. The medical condition requirement is potentially open to fraud, as some Michigan doctors are advertised as being cannabis friendly.

The medical condition requirements are also quite vague. For example, one condition that qualifies a patient to receive medical cannabis is "chronic pain," which can mean repeated headaches or back pain (which cannot be objectively verified).

A similar dynamic is at work when it comes to selling cannabis. In order to legally sell cannabis, a dispensary has to pay a one-time $6,000 application fee to the state, municipality fees of up to $5,000, and annual fees to the state (Mack 2017c). This effectively crowds out and criminalizes small-scale cannabis sellers while protecting larger growers. In spite of selling similar products, one group is penalized by the state of Michigan while the other is able to operate legally. Research on California's medical cannabis program found that medical cannabis patients were on average younger, better educated, and more likely to be employed. Three-fourths of patients were male, and three-fifths were white. Women, Latino/as, and Asian Americans were underrepresented as patients. Most patients requested medical cannabis to deal with pain-, anxiety-, or insomnia-related issues. The authors also write that "it seems likely that at least some MM (medical marijuana) patients use MM dispensaries as sources of supply for nonmedical use" (Reinarman et al. 2011, p. 133).

Michigan is not the only state with this dynamic. The Marijuana Policy Project estimates that there are 2.3 million medical cannabis patients in the United States. The contrast between medical cannabis patients and those who buy cannabis on the street is illustrative of the larger dynamics of privilege. Medical patients are able to buy cannabis in secure locations with knowledgeable staff, clear pricing, and dosage information. Medical cannabis is carefully labeled and regulated. It is even possible to comparison shop for medical cannabis, for the cost-conscious medical cannabis patient. The website WeedMaps functions as a sort of Yelp for cannabis. The site contains a database with over 3,000 medical cannabis dispensaries and contains review and pricing information for over 950 strains of cannabis. The site attracts roughly 2 million monthly visitors and has annual revenue of $18 million (Grant 2013; Kincaid 2009). A similar site, Leafly.com, provides ratings of cannabis delivery services.

For the relatively privileged drug user, it is possible to order cannabis from a legal service or to browse specials on the WeedMaps or Leafly apps. Less affluent cannabis users have to resort to traditional, illicit markets. In those markets, there is less competition, less standardization, less variety, less quality control, and more risk. It is primarily vulnerable drug users who face punishment for their cannabis consumption. Over a third of the people arrested for cannabis use in Michigan in 2015 were African American, despite being only 14 percent of the state's population. This is largely in line with findings for the country as a whole. Although white Americans constitute the large majority of drug offenders, African Americans constituted

53 percent of all persons who entered prison due to a drug conviction (Human Rights Watch 2008). Fully three-quarters of people incarcerated on drug offenses are African American or Latino/a.

This discrepancy is more a result of differential enforcement than differential drug use. For instance, all racial groups have similar rates of drug use and drug dealing (Alexander 2010; SAMSHA 2010). There are some suggestions that young white Americans use harder drugs (cocaine and heroin) at higher rates than other racial groups (Alexander 2010). White Americans also have two to three times as many drug-related emergency-room visits than do African Americans (Western 2006). Still, the current literature suggests that rates of drug use among different racial groups are similar if not identical.

Michelle Alexander (2010) argues that African Americans and Latino/as are arrested disproportionately for drug crimes for two reasons: First, police invest more energy and effort in arresting people in inner cities and on the streets, circumstances that disproportionately target drug transactions involving African Americans and Latino/as. Second, racial profiling in police stops disproportionately affects African Americans and Latino/as (Alexander 2010). Vulnerability may work in different ways. Police may focus on negative stereotypes associated with vulnerability; the vulnerable are easy to arrest because more of their activity, both legal and illegal, takes place in public; and the vulnerable lack the resources necessary to launch a successful legal defense.

The punishment for violating drug laws consistently falls on the vulnerable. It is not an accident that police focused on poor African Americans in both the Prohibition and more recent cannabis-related examples at the beginning of this chapter. Officially race- or class-neutral laws can mask discriminatory enforcement. The government can claim it is not opposed to African Americans or immigrants but is opposed to alcohol, or claim that it is not opposed to the counterculture or antiwar protesters but is opposed to cannabis and psychedelics. In practice, the enforcement of laws disproportionately affects the vulnerable. Race-and class-neutral laws are also a cover in the sense that they obscure police brutality and the messy realities of prohibition enforcement. Vulnerable drug users are disproportionately sent to prison, and while there, they are disproportionately punished.

Punishing Drug Users in Prison

Relatively privileged drug users escape punishment, while vulnerable drug users are placed behind bars. Drug users in prison are marked by two separate vulnerabilities. First, as this book has described, prisoners have characteristics of vulnerability such as race, poverty, and poor physical and/or mental health. Second, drug users in prison are statistically more likely to have problematic drug use. Drug users in prison have much higher rates of drug abuse and drug dependence. Because of this, many drug users in prison are in serious need of drug treatment.

The fourth edition of the *Diagnostic and Statistical Manual of Mental Disorders* establishes criteria for the medical designations of drug dependence and drug abuse. In the general population, approximately 5 percent of people over the age of 18 have a drug dependence and/or abuse issue. Among state prison inmates, that number is 58 percent, and for sentenced jail inmates it is 63 percent (Bronson et al. 2017). Therefore, the rate of drug dependence and/or abuse is about 12 times higher for prisoners than for the general population.

Drug dependence is defined as having three or more of the following symptoms:

- tolerance
- withdrawal symptoms or taking drugs to relieve withdrawal
- taking drugs in larger amounts for longer periods than intended
- a persistent desire or unsuccessful attempts to cut down or control drug use
- spending a lot of time obtaining, using, or recovering from the effects of drugs
- a reduction in or absence from social, occupational, or recreational activities
- continued use despite adverse consequences (Bronson et al. 2017)

Drug users who end up in prison are less successful at managing their drug use. They may try to quit but not succeed; they may need to keep using drugs in order to avoid withdrawal symptoms; they may spend more time recovering from the effects of drugs. In short, many of the drug users who end up in prison are not capable of regulating their own drug use. They are punished, in effect, for being unable to control their drug use.

The *Diagnostic and Statistical Manual of Mental Disorders* defines drug abuse as having one or more of the following criteria:

- recurrent drug use resulting in a failure to fulfill major role obligations
- recurrent drug use that is physically hazardous
- recurrent drug-related legal problems
- continued drug use despite having persistent or recurrent drug-related social problems (Bronson et al. 2017)

The type of drug user that ends up in prison is more likely to abuse drugs, and this abuse at some point is less than voluntary. Again, we are disproportionately punishing people for being unable to control their drug use. A relatively privileged drug user is not subject to the same level of scrutiny.

Drug use does not affect all people equally; prison inmates have much higher drug abuse and dependence rates than does the general population. In addition, drug abuse and dependence do not affect all people equally. The vulnerable are less able to afford or have access to treatment. In contrast, I work as an assistant professor at the University of Michigan, Flint. The university runs a faculty and staff assistance program that offers confidential, no-cost services for individuals with alcohol or other drug-related problems. I can also easily search for counseling services and rehabilitation programs that accept my health insurance. I have a spouse who works in health care, I have a job with flexible scheduling to allow for appointments, and, if necessary, I could pay for drug treatment out of pocket. I have intellectual, financial, and social capital that many of the vulnerable simply do not. If I did not have those tools, I might find myself in a precarious position, especially since I have a family history of substance abuse issues.

In contrast to the treatment options of relatively affluent Americans, prison inmates have access to minimal treatments. Modern American prisons are simply not designed to offer large-scale rehabilitative services for those with substance abuse issues. Of those inmates with a drug dependency or abuse issue, only 28 percent have participated in any form of drug treatment. Roughly 15 percent of inmates with drug dependency or abuse issues have received professional counseling or placement in a specialized drug treatment unit. Most of those treated participate in either self-help/peer counseling or educational programs (Bronson et al. 2017). Many self-help or peer counseling programs are based on the Alcoholics Anonymous or Narcotics Anonymous programs, which have limited efficacy (Dodes and Dodes 2014).

The 2004 Survey provides some evidence related to the treatment of drug users in prison. A large percentage of inmates are in prison due to drug-related charges. Approximately 20 percent of inmates are in prison for drug possession, and another 7 percent were street-level dealers. Less than 2 percent of inmates were drug dealers above the street level. This is not surprising, given the relative ease of arresting low-level drug users and dealers, both historically and currently. The Prison Policy Initiative (2017 estimates that a total of 453,000 people are in local jails, state prisons, and federal prisons for drug possession or dealing. All told, it costs over $14 billion a year to incarcerate drug users and dealers, very few of whom are above the street level.

Many inmates who did not have a drug-related charge still suffered from drug-related issues. Fully a third of inmates were under the influence of drugs or alcohol when they were arrested. Given that alcohol and drug use can affect decision making, it is likely that at least some inmates would not have committed their crime were they not under the influence. Fifty-seven percent of inmates in the 2004 Survey sample were treated for drug addiction at some point. Many drug users in prison are unable to control their addictions, unlike more privileged drug users who may not have an addiction or who may have the resources to fight their addiction. Overall, inmates are frequently in prison due to drug-related issues, were often under the influence of drugs or alcohol when committing their crime, and are a population that suffers tremendously from drug abuse and dependence but that has limited access to quality treatment.

A harsh drug war has been a key component of mass incarceration. The numbers are truly staggering. Roughly 453,000 people are incarcerated due to drug possession or drug selling. Around 430,000 inmates were under the influence of drugs when they were arrested. Over 770,000 state prison inmates have abused and/or are dependent on drugs. While the drug war is not the only cause of mass incarceration, drug use and drug law enforcement have affected the prison population in myriad ways. Vulnerable drug users fill the nation's jails and prisons, while relatively privileged drug users are able to consume substances with little fear of incarceration.

Unsurprisingly, inmates report using drugs at exceptionally high rates. Around 19 percent of inmates report using heroin, around 24 percent report using methamphetamine, 42 percent report using cocaine, and slightly over three-fourths of inmates report using cannabis. As stated previously, most of these inmates have experienced problematic drug use and many have been in treatment. Rather than being hedonists or evil people, many inmates are vulnerable, drug addicted, and/or drug dependent. As always, inmates have intersectional identities; it is likely that issues with drug addiction and dependence are related in multiple ways to other vulnerabilities, such as race, poverty, and mental health. Table 7.1 presents the estimations for the treatment of drug users inside prison.

Inmates who have used drugs are subject to harsh discipline in prison. Model estimations indicate that inmates who have used drugs are more likely

Table 7.1 Drug use and treatment inside prison

	Visit in the Last Month	Received Mental Health Medication	Police Use of Force	Writeups	Solitary Confinement
Past drug use	0.008	0.010	0.037***	0.106***	0.037***
	(.010)	(.007)	(.010)	(.011)	(.008)
Number of observations	14,037	14,037	14,037	14,037	14,037

*p<.1, **p<.05, ***p<.01

to be subjected to police use of force, more likely to be written up, and more likely to be placed in solitary confinement. The use of prison punishment, especially solitary confinement, is especially cruel. Many inmates have a drug dependence or abuse issue, which means they are unable to control their drug use. Then they are punished in prison for being unable to control their drug use. They may be sent to solitary confinement, which can cause or exacerbate mental illnesses, which may lead to drug use as a form of self-medication, which may lead to further punishment.

In some ways it is unsurprising that drug users in prison are punished disproportionately, since prisons have regulations forbidding drug use. However, we must keep in mind that many of these inmates are dependent on and/or addicted to drugs and that according to the *Diagnostic and Statistical Manual of Mental Disorders* substance abuse is a medical issue. It seems wrong to severely punish people for having a medical disorder. Even if the beginning of an inmate's drug use history was voluntary, by the time he or she is in prison, abuse or dependence can overcome an inmate's ability to quit or moderate use. Inmates who are drug users are punished for their vulnerability and their inability to overcome drug dependence and/or drug addiction.

Suggestions for Reform

The war on drugs is difficult to date precisely. However, the Harrison Narcotic Act dates to 1914, and the beginning of alcohol prohibition was in 1920. We can split the difference and say that law enforcement in the United States has actively waged battles against illegal substances for a hundred years. It has been an expensive struggle; the modern drug war costs over $51 billion a year. As a country, we have spent over $1 trillion on the war on drugs since Richard Nixon became president (Associated Press 2010). A greater expense, perhaps, has come from the destruction of human capital and the loss to families, neighborhoods, and communities caused by drug-related mass incarceration. The Federal Bureau of Investigation reported that 1.57 million people were arrested for drug violations in 2016. This number is about average; between 2007 and 2016, police arrested approximately 16 million people for drug violations.

In spite of an immense number of arrests and a tremendous public expenditure, the war on drugs has been largely ineffectual. In the last two decades, the price of cocaine, heroin, and cannabis has fallen while the potency of each drug has increased. This trend exists despite increasingly large annual drug seizures (Morin 2013). In 2009, customs agents seized 298 tons of drugs on the border with Mexico (Grillo 2012). In spite of such extraordinary efforts, the drug trade remains prolific and profitable. The United Nations has estimated that the global illicit drug trade is worth at least $350 billion a year (Morin 2013).

Profits are driven in part by illegality. The drug-trafficking industry in Mexico directly provides thousands of jobs and rivals the oil and tourism industries in size. A drug mule can make $1,000 to drive 60 pounds of cannabis into the United States, a process that takes about three hours of work. Drug mules can be paid more for transporting heroin, cocaine, or methamphetamine (Grillo 2012). Of course, money can also be made transporting and selling drugs inside the United States.

Iaon Grillo (2012) gives an example of the profitability of drug smuggling by analyzing cocaine. A Colombian peasant can sell a bundle of coca leaves from a two-acre field for about $80. After it goes through its first chemical process, it can be sold as a kilo of coca paste for about $800. A kilo of cocaine is worth about $2,100 in Colombian ports, $35,000 by the time it gets over the U.S. border, and $120,000 when it is sold on the streets of New York. The entire process represents a 150,000 percent profit (Grillo 2012). Although smuggling and distributing drugs has costs, it is still a very profitable industry. It is hard to imagine such a profitable market collapsing.

Similar to enforcement during Prohibition, enforcement in the drug war focuses on small-time dealers and drug users. As mentioned earlier, around 27 percent of inmates are in prison for either drug possession or street-level drug selling. Around 60 percent of inmates have a drug dependence or abuse issue and are in serious need of treatment. While in prison, a minority receive help, and some of that help is low quality. Many drug users are also subject to harsh punishments in prison. Punishing people with substance abuse issues has not ended the demand for drugs. Even if drug use is morally wrong, treatment is more effective than incarceration. American prisons are designed to be secure, not to be drug treatment centers. The demand for drugs may never completely end, but at the very least drug treatment could be performed more efficaciously and affordably outside of a prison setting.

Reforming drug laws would substantially decrease the state and federal prison populations. The more than 400,000 people in state and federal prisons on drug charges is nearly the same size as India's entire prison population and would rank as the sixth-largest prison population in the world. The number of inmates in American prisons for drug charges is larger than the *entire* prison populations in Mexico, South Africa, Colombia, Pakistan, and the United Kingdom. It is larger than the entire populations of Colombia, the Philippines, Egypt, and Canada, *combined.*

As evidenced by their lower prison populations, other countries have chosen different paths when regulating drug use. The government of Uruguay legalized cannabis in 2013 and has decriminalized drug possession for personal use since 1974. Holland has some of the most liberal drug laws in Europe but has low rates of drug use. Canada legalized recreational cannabis in late 2018 (Bilefsky 2018). Portugal decriminalized all drugs in 2001 in the midst of a heroin epidemic, and Portugal now has the second-lowest drug-related death rate in the European Union (Baer 2016). Under decriminalization, drug possession and use are legally prohibited, but violations are considered administrative violations.

Portugal's decriminalization process has been hailed as a success, and the country has one of the lowest drug use rates in Europe (Grillo 2012). Instead of court proceedings, people caught with drugs in Portugal are placed before a dissuasion commission. The commission can recommend that the offender be warned, fined, or required to take part in treatment. The commission is statutorily forbidden to impose a sanction on an alleged offender with no prior offenses who agrees to treatment. Since decriminalization in 2001, drug usage rates among youth have decreased, the spread of infectious diseases like HIV and AIDS has decreased, and the number of drug-related deaths has declined (Greenwald 2009). This is especially significant given the context of the European Union; the majority of EU states have drug usage rates that are double and triple that of Portugal (Greenwald 2009).

Legalization is also a viable option, at least for cannabis. As of November 2018, 33 states and the District of Columbia have legalized medical cannabis. 10 states, including the entire West Coast, have legalized recreational cannabis (Wu and Silva 2018). Legalization efforts are moving quickly; when I began writing this book, the penalty for possessing any amount of cannabis in the state of Michigan was a year in prison, and the penalty for cultivating a cannabis plant was four years. By the time this book is published in 2019, it will be legal to buy recreational cannabis in Michigan. It is worth noting that the first state to legalize medical cannabis was California in 1996 and the first states to legalize recreational cannabis were Colorado and Washington in 2012.

The effects of cannabis legalization have been less dramatic than either critics or proponents expected. Cannabis usage rates and crime rates have not changed significantly, although cannabis usage increased after medical cannabis became widely available (Dills, Goffard, and Miron 2016). There have been economic benefits, both to state governments and to private businesses. The legal cannabis industry in Colorado is estimated to have created 18,000 new full-time jobs and generated $2.4 billion in economic activity in 2015 (Ingraham 2016). Colorado, Oregon, and Washington all impose significant taxes on recreational cannabis, leading to significant revenue. In 2015, Colorado generated a total of $135 million in revenue, $35 million of which was earmarked for school construction projects. Washington state generated approximately $70 million in tax revenue in its first year of sales (Dill, Goffard, and Miron 2016).

Another broad approach is generally called harm reduction. An example is the use of needle exchanges and safe injection sites. Safe injection sites enable the consumption of drugs like heroin in a medically supervised environment. The first sites were established in Europe, and there are now at least 100 safe injection sites in the world, mostly in Europe, Canada, and Australia (Gordon 2018). The benefits of such sites include fewer overdoses, reduction in blood-borne diseases such as HIV, and a reduction in public disorder from people using drugs on the street (Bell and Globerman 2014). The lack of needle exchanges or safe injection sites can be catastrophic. In 2015, one town in rural Indiana experienced 190 new cases of HIV. The outbreak was spread by intravenous drug users who shared needles (Rudavsky 2016). The Centers for Disease Control and Prevention (2014) estimates that the lifetime cost for HIV treatment is $367,134; the treatment costs for the Indiana outbreak would be just under $70 million. While harm-reduction strategies do not eliminate problematic drug use, these strategies can reduce drug-related health problems. Currently, there are 39 states with needle exchange programs and there are attempts to open safe injection sites in several cities (Allyn 2018).

A comprehensive overview of all possible drug policy reforms is beyond the scope of this book. It is also difficult because we lump many different substances with many different impacts under the single heading of "illicit drugs." Drug policy reform will need a truly holistic, expert-driven approach. Fortunately, there are many activists and scholars working on this issue. The book's website (www.punishingthevulnerable.com) has links, literature, and further information about drug policy reforms.

I would recommend the following:

1. Treat drug dependence and abuse as a public health issue. All inmates with a drug dependence or abuse issue should be given access to a reputable treatment program. The most effective treatments are likely to be in a noncarceral setting.
2. Explore which drugs can effectively be legalized. The clearest candidate for legalization is cannabis; however, other relatively nonharmful drugs, such as psilocybin mushrooms and MDMA, should be considered for legalization.
3. All drugs not legalized should be decriminalized, borrowing best practices from Portugal and other decriminalizers.
4. Whether a drug is legalized or decriminalized, we should adopt harm-reduction policies related to those drugs. Harm-reduction policies are already in place for some illicit drugs (e.g., needle exchanges) as well as some legal drugs (DUI regulations and smoking cessation programs).

CHAPTER EIGHT

Punishing Families

> For a lot of young boys and young men in particular, they don't see an example of fathers or grandfathers, uncles, who are in a position to support families and be held up in respect. And so that means that this is not just a gun issue; it's also an issue of the kinds of communities that we're building. When a child opens fire on another child, there is a hole in that child's heart that government can't fill. Only community and parents and teachers and clergy can fill that hole.
>
> —President Barack Obama, speaking at a funeral in 2013

During his time as a candidate and as president, Barack Obama often spoke to majority African American crowds about what he perceived as the breakdown of African American families. The above quote was spoken at a funeral for a gun violence victim in Chicago (it is likely that the crowd came to mourn, not to be lectured), but such statements were common from President Obama. In a 2008 speech delivered on Father's Day at a church on Chicago's South Side, then candidate Obama lamented that too many African American fathers were missing from too many lives and too many homes. "They have abandoned their responsibilities, acting like boys instead of men" (Smith 2017, p. 1). In honor of the former president, the next time Mother's Day rolls around, I will bring my mother a list of complaints and disappointments in her parenting style. With friends like these . . .

Former first lady Michelle Obama, who has long been a hero to many liberals, has also engaged in paternalistic rhetoric. At a commencement speech for Bowie State University in 2013, Michelle Obama placed blame on African Americans and poor people. She stated, "If the school in your neighborhood isn't any good, don't just accept it. Get in there, fix it. Talk to the parents. Talk to the teachers. Get business and community leaders involved as well, because we all have a stake in building schools worthy of our children's promise. . . . And as my husband has said often, please stand up and reject the slander that says a black child with a book is trying to act white. Reject that." In the same speech, Michelle Obama chastised African American children for fantasizing about being "a baller or a rapper" instead of being a teacher, lawyer, or business leader.

The two strands of rhetoric have much in common. Both strands leave out government neglect or discriminatory behavior. Both strands blame poor people and racial minorities for their struggle (although interestingly, these messages are delivered at churches and college commencements, not exactly places with antisocial low achievers). Both strands are largely acts of victim blaming and feature the kind of rhetoric more commonly presented by strict conservatives like William Bennett. It clearly points to how negative the social construction of African American and impoverished communities in the United States has become. Rather than focus on the vulnerabilities and struggles that different communities face, the Obamas have spent a good deal of time blaming poor people for their poverty.

The rhetoric that President Obama repeatedly engaged in is symptomatic of a widespread cultural myth that African American men are less willing to parent than are other men. This has developed into a myth of the "missing black father" (Smith 2017). This pernicious myth blames problems in African American families on the pathology or voluntary neglect of African American fathers. This rhetoric is not only harmful and degrading but also empirically inaccurate. African American fathers are actually more likely than white or Latino fathers to feed their children or eat meals with them daily; to bathe, diaper, or dress their children; and to read to their children daily. African American fathers play with their children daily at essentially the same rates as white fathers (82.2 percent to 82.7 percent, respectively). African American fathers are less likely to be married but are more likely to engage in the actual raising of children (Blow 2015).

Our definitions of fatherhood can be self-serving. By pathologizing African American and poor fathers, we can avoid addressing structural barriers that those fathers may face. By picking out marriage rates rather than actual parenting behavior, we can paint African American and poor fathers as being less supportive of their children. However, judging someone's parenting skills is fraught with peril. During a 2005 interview with Howard Stern, Donald Trump discussed his child-rearing philosophy: "I mean, I won't do anything to take care of them. I'll supply the funds and she'll take care of the kids. It's not like I'm gonna be walking the kids down Central Park" (Kaczynski and Apper 2016). In the same interview, Trump bragged about never changing diapers (Kaczynski and Apper 2016). I am not suggesting that Donald Trump is a bad father because of his statements in that interview; however, I will suggest that if the phrase "I won't do anything to take care of them" was spoken by an African American inmate, we would probably have a very harsh judgment of that inmate.

Blaming poor parents with paternalistic rhetoric is common. There was a billboard on Interstate 75, between my home in Pontiac, Michigan, and my workplace at the University of Michigan, Flint, with a public service announcement sponsored by the government website Fatherhood.gov. On the billboard was a sad-looking child and the written message "Nothing can replace a father's love." The billboard always offended me, especially given its location close to the city of Flint, Michigan, where the government has failed to provide adequate health care, education, jobs, safety, and, infamously, safe drinking water. To imply that the fathers in Flint and Genesee County need to do a better job of loving their children, when the drinking water has lead in it and there are outbreaks of Legionnaires' disease, is remarkably tone deaf. If there is a need for more personal responsibility in the state of Michigan, I would argue that process should begin with Governor Snyder's office and spread to the Environmental Protection Agency and the Michigan Department of Environmental Quality. Yet there are not equivalent billboards shaming unethical bureaucrats or political officials.

Modern political rhetoric has a neoliberal, paternalistic tinge that focuses on personal responsibility. Much hand-wringing and lecturing focuses on poor neighborhoods and the commonality of single-parent households. The dominant rhetoric suggests that if only poor and minority communities had more self-control, less pathological behavior, and a stronger commitment to family, the problems of entrenched poverty would magically disappear. This ignores the very real role that the criminal justice system has played in destroying families, ruining marriages, separating parents from their children, and making communication from prison onerous and, in some cases, impossible. Our rhetoric about families does not match our treatment of prisoners.

Incarceration devastates families. It strains and ends marriages, greatly reduces and in some cases eliminates contact between children and parents, and leads to profound crises of identity for both mothers and fathers. Incarceration signals to inmates not just that they are bad people and viewed as disposable by the state but also that they are bad spouses and bad parents. Incarceration further disadvantages children, who are more likely to have behavioral problems, academic issues, and their own encounters with the criminal justice system. Millions of American children suffer due to the incarceration of their parents. These children suffer a cumulative disadvantage; the disadvantages of poverty and race combine with the disadvantage of having an incarcerated parent. Incarceration is a burden not just on the vulnerable but also on their families.

Incarceration, even for short periods, is associated with an increased likelihood of divorce and family dissolution and decreasing likelihood that children will reside with at least one of their biological parents (Arditti, Lambert-Shute, and Joest 2003; Arditti and Few 2006; Woldoff and Washington 2008). Parental incarceration is associated with lower levels of family income, parental education, parental socioeconomic status, and parental health, and higher levels of parental depression, inappropriate and inconsistent discipline, youth problem behaviors, and serious delinquency (Kjellstrand and Eddy 2011). Other harms from incarceration include traumatic separation issues, uncertain childcare, and negative child outcomes, such as poor academic performance, emotional suffering, alcohol and drug abuse, and involvement with the criminal justice system (Arditti, Lambert-Shute, and Joest 2003; Dallaire 2007).

Children with incarcerated parents are exposed to higher rates of mental illness and substance abuse. Incarceration can lead to placement in foster homes and siblings being separated from each other (Dallaire 2007). The incarceration of mothers seems to be more traumatic to children than the incarceration of fathers. Danielle Dallaire (2007, p. 443) explains, "When fathers go to prison, their children are more likely to remain in the care of their mothers; however, when mothers go to prison, not only are children separated from their mother but they more often transition to the care of a grandparent, or other family member, than to the care of their other parent."

Separation often leads to serious emotional and psychological problems. Woldoff and Washington (2008, p. 181) find that

> children of incarcerated parents often suffer in terms of psychological and emotional well-being, with many experiencing fear, anger, loneliness, guilt, resentment, depression and emotional withdrawal from friends and family. Some experience eating and sleeping disorders, diminished academic performance, and behavior problems such as truancy, aggressiveness, and disruptiveness.

Children of inmates are twice as likely to exhibit antisocial behaviors (Kjellstrand and Eddy 2011). The burdens of incarceration fall heavily on children and spouses, individuals who have little to nothing to do with their incarcerated family member's behavior.

About 1.7 million children currently have at least one parent in prison. Over 8 million minor children have been affected by parental incarceration (Kjellstrand and Eddy 2011). It is worth pausing and letting that number sink in. Eight million children. Eight million children who suffer because at least one parent has been incarcerated. There are more children affected by parental incarceration than there are people living in Washington, Massachusetts, Tennessee, or Colorado. Most of the parents who are incarcerated were sent away for minor crimes like drug possession, property crimes, or an immigration violation. Only a quarter of state inmates are incarcerated for murder or sexual assault. The idea that children are punished because their mother was caught with cannabis or their father was involved in a bar fight or their parent stole so that they could pay for life's necessities is simply tragic.

The number of children affected by incarceration has increased along with our nation's carceral binge. Between 1991 and 2007, the number of children under age 18 with a mother in prison more than doubled. In 2007, 2.3 percent of American children had a parent in prison. African American children (6.7 percent) were seven and a half times more likely than white children to have a parent in prison (Glaze and Maruschak 2008). Twenty-two percent of the children of state inmates were age 4 or younger. More than a third of minor children with a parent in prison will reach age 18 while their parent is incarcerated. In 2007, over 300,000 inmates were living with their minor children prior to either their arrest or incarceration. Forty-two percent of incarcerated mothers who were living with their minor children were living in single-parent households (Glaze and Maruschak 2008).

A majority of both male and female inmates are parents. Eighty percent of female inmates have at least one child, and close to 70 percent have children younger than 18. Most women plan on residing with their children and resuming their mothering role following release (Arditti and Few 2006). Most incarcerated men are fathers who lived with their children before entering prison, and most incarcerated fathers contributed to the well-being of their children and family prior to incarceration (Woldoff and Washington 2008). The stereotype of inmates may be that they are criminals and "deadbeats," but most inmates are parents who contributed positively to their children and desire a relationship with those children. Incarceration strains and sometimes severs those ties.

Incarceration further victimizes vulnerable families. Families were at risk economically before incarceration and became even more financially strained afterward. Incarceration is both an outcome of poverty and a contributor to financial challenges (Arditti, Lambert-Shute, and Joest 2003). Two-thirds of family members reported that they were financially worse off after their relative was incarcerated. Financial difficulties included a lack of child support and expenses related to incarceration, such as sending money to the inmate, attorney fees, and receiving collect calls. Other family members were more likely to take on extra work to make up for the reduction of income, which often led to childcare issues (Arditti, Lambert-Shute, and Joest 2003).

Financial burdens fall heavily on the disadvantaged and vulnerable, those least able to handle them. Kjellstrand and Eddy (2011, p. 20) write, "The incarceration of a family member is unlikely to mark the beginning of problems for a child and family. Rather, it is often a continuation or exacerbation of an already challenging situation in lives marked by little education, poverty, unstable home life, substance abuse difficulties, mental health problems, abuse, trauma and community violence." When governments target the most vulnerable members of society, they weaken the families of those inmates.

Vulnerable families have little support in managing the painful separation caused by incarceration. Incarceration creates a temporary, involuntary single-parent household. However, there is little sympathy for children or spouses who lose a family member to prison (unlike the sympathy a family would receive if a member died or was involuntarily separated due to behaviors like military service). Joyce Arditti (2005) argues that losing a family member to incarceration is a loss that is not socially validated. She argues that families of inmates face disenfranchised grief, a form of grief when people experience a loss that is not or cannot be openly acknowledged, publicly mourned, or socially supported. Families who lose a member to incarceration may even be stigmatized and tainted by their loved one's incarceration. It is yet another example of further punishments and penalties being placed on the vulnerable.

Society has little sympathy for the children and spouses of incarcerated family members, and public schools actively contribute to the stigmatization and marginalization of children with incarcerated parents. University of Michigan historian Heather Ann Thompson (2011) argues that American public schools have become criminalized since the 1960s. Schools have become heavily policed, often in response to social protest rather than the breaking of laws. When students pushed for civil rights in the 1960s and 1970s, the response by schools was to bring in thousands of police and security officers (Thompson 2011). Of course, schools do not say that they are bringing in police officers to squash dissent. Instead, echoing Dilulio's and the Clintons' super-predator rhetoric, by the 1990s public schools had internalized a rhetoric that suggests that inner-city youth are violent and need to be contained (Thompson 2011). More recently, concern over school shootings and school violence has prompted increased security in spite of the fact that school-related violence has steadily declined.

By 2011, the school district of Philadelphia employed 408 school police officers and 249 school security officers. In Chicago, a "zero tolerance" policy against loitering resulted in more than 42,000 arrests. Students have been expelled or arrested for acts such as smoking, talking back, having a cell phone in class, or having any sharp object in a backpack. Nearly all students expelled in Philadelphia between 2008 and 2009 were between the ages of 8 and 14, and the most common ages of the expelled students were 11 and 12 (Thompson 2011). Even students in preschool have been expelled, and African American preschoolers are disproportionately expelled (Anderson 2015). The moral panic about crime in the United States has gone off the rails to the point that we are afraid of violent four-year-olds and criminal eight-year-olds.

Although inner cities have become criminalized, it is not a result of higher levels of violence in those schools. Students in Philadelphia were twice as likely to be arrested for incidents than were students in the rest of Pennsylvania, although the rest of the state had five times as many incidents (Thompson 2011). Given the relatively minor incidents that can lead to an arrest and the stigmatization that children of incarcerated parents face, it is easy to see why the public school system has been criticized as a "school-to-prison pipeline." Thompson (2011, p. 26) writes that "literally tens of thousands of children across the nation have landed in jail cells instead of classrooms." Even if students are not arrested, school discipline can be severe. In the 2009–2010 school year, 2 million students were suspended in the state of Texas, 1.9 million for violating the "local code of conduct." Standardized testing has incentivized teachers to use arrests and suspensions to get rid of lower-performing students (Vitale 2017). These examples of systemic discrimination help highlight why so many of the vulnerable are punished by the prison system.

Incarceration severely limits contact between inmates and their family members. Prisons are designed to segregate inmates from the rest of society, which necessarily includes the inmate's family. More than 60 percent of mothers were incarcerated more than 100 miles from their child's home. Less than 9 percent of mothers were within 20 miles of their child's home (Law 2012). Even when children live relatively near, there is rarely public transportation to the prison (Law 2012).

Prisons are often located in remote areas, far from the major population centers where inmates are drawn from. For example, many inmates in Michigan state prisons are arrested in the Southeastern counties of Wayne and Oakland. Those inmates are then sent hundreds of miles away to prisons in the Upper Peninsula. This process not only separates inmates from their home counties but also serves to politically weaken cities like Detroit and politically strengthen rural Michigan towns. For purposes of the census, inmates are counted as residents of the county where they are incarcerated rather than the county where they are from. In Michigan, four state senate and five house districts meet their minimum population requirements because they count prisoners as residents (Thompson 2013). Felon disfranchisement also dilutes the political power of former inmates enough to swing congressional and presidential elections (Uggen and Manza 2002; Wacquant 2005).

Inmates are incarcerated far from home and have limited contact with their children while incarcerated (Arditti and Few 2006; Arditti 2005). Fifty-eight percent of fathers report never receiving visits from their children (Arditti 2005). Similarly, between 54 and 58 percent of mothers reported receiving zero to two visits per year (Arditti and Few 2006; Law 2012). It is difficult for parents to remain in contact with their children due to geographic distance, transportation and financial barriers, and a lack of child-friendly visiting contexts, including harsh and disrespectful treatment by correctional officers (Arditti 2005). Visitation requires a great deal of time, money, energy, and effort, and the vulnerable have fewer of those resources.

In addition to the time, money, and effort required to visit a family member in prison, the actual experience of prison visits can be difficult and in many ways demeaning. Arditti and colleagues (2003, p. 197) provide a description of visitation experiences at one prison:

> Visitors waited approximately 30–60 minutes before being called to visit their family member. Upon having their name called, family members went through a locked door and a metal detector before entering an elevator. After getting off the elevator on their respective floors, family members went through another locked door and into an area with several unenclosed booths. Jail regulations at this particular facility allowed each family member a 20-minute visit seated in a booth, using a telephone to talk to the inmate who was seated facing them in a separate booth behind a sealed Plexiglas wall. Physical contact was prohibited and impossible between the inmate and his or her family members.

Visitors pass through heavy security and must talk to their family members in unnatural and uncomfortable settings. After spending hours getting to the prison and another hour waiting and going through security, these family members had a short, 20-minute visit with their loved ones. We have created an environment where children can only see their mothers or fathers through a Plexiglas barrier. The ability to hug, kiss, or play with a loved one is limited in most American prisons. Our paternalistic, neoliberal state has come up with a system where fathers and mothers are separated from their children, unable to even touch their loved ones, and then those fathers and mothers are lectured about personal responsibility.

The official reasoning for the lack of contact visits and other restrictions is a concern for security and contraband. While it is possible that visitors will pass contraband, it is likely that we overestimate the risk. Visitors already pass through security checkpoints and are subject to surveillance before, during, and after their visit. The inmates they are visiting are also subject to searches and are closely watched. Both visitors and inmates are subject to harsh legal consequences if they are caught with contraband. The focus on security leaves inmates unable to hug their children or other loved ones. It is also worth pointing out that prison staff, volunteers, and lawyers have also smuggled contraband into prisons.

Family visitors experience heavy security and uncomfortable settings. Visitors sometimes experience negative treatment from prison guards. Family members often withstand humiliating and rude treatment by correctional officers (Arditti 2005). In one study, 27 percent of participants reported harsh or disrespectful treatment by prison staff (Arditti and Few 2006). Guards can be hostile during visitations, yelling at children and denying access for visits (Law 2012). Many families are uncomfortable bringing children into an environment where they will be abused by prison staff.

While working at a county detention facility, I was told that one of the easiest ways to "get" an inmate was to restrict his visitation rights. Visitation was the easiest "privilege" that could be taken away from an inmate. This echoes Victoria Law's (2012) finding that prison administrators use their control over visits to punish inmates who challenge existing prison conditions. Inmates are sometimes transferred to a facility farther from their families as a form of punishment (Law 2012). In these scenarios, inmates have little recourse for mistreatment. For example, if an inmate complains about a rude visitation guard, that visitation guard can limit the inmate's access to future visitors.

Other forms of contact between inmates and their families are also limited. As noted in chapter 3, inmates pay higher rates for stationery, envelopes, stamps, and phone calls than do members of the regular population. Stamps and envelopes cost more in jails and prisons than in the outside world. A 15-minute phone call can cost $3.15. Prior to Obama administration reforms in 2014, inmates could be charged as much as $17 for a 15-minute phone call. Those regulations were overturned in June 2017 (Kang 2017). In order to pay for these overpriced services and products, inmates must either rely on their subminimum-wage prison jobs or on family members who usually face significant financial difficulties.

The limitations and barriers to familial contact lead to serious identity issues for inmates. For both male and female inmates, their role as father or mother is a core part of their personal identity. Incarceration is a highly stigmatizing experience and one that has an impact on social roles. Male inmates view prison as an experience that strips a man of his fathering identity. Incarcerated fathers express feelings of helplessness and ambiguity. They also express frustration over an inability to have contact with their families, to provide for or protect their children, to help their families, and at being "out of the loop" regarding family information (Arditti 2005).

The literature on mothers in prison is more substantial than the literature on fathers in prison, which has a number of cultural implications in and of itself. Women's pains of imprisonment include separation from their children, the loss of the maternal role, and, sometimes, the legal termination of parental rights and concerns over placing children (Enos 2001). Under the 1997 federal Adoption and Safe Families Act, if an incarcerated parent does not have contact with his or her child for six months, the parent can be charged with abandonment and lose parental rights (Law 2012). The average sentence length for all sentences in the United States is 63 months (Justice Policy Institute 2011), and the average amount of time served behind bars rose by about five years from 2000 to 2014 (Williams 2017). We can therefore expect the average inmate to be at risk of losing his or her parental rights.

Incarcerated mothers often lose their parental rights during court sentencing. States have punished women who use drugs while pregnant by jailing them during their pregnancy, seizing custody of their babies at birth, and prosecuting them for crime. Thousands of low-income African Americans have lost their children on the basis of a single drug test. Even though there are not racial differences in drug use among pregnant women, African American women were 10 times more likely than white women to be reported to government authorities (Roberts 1997).

The hysteria over pregnant mothers using drugs is not based on empirical evidence of harm. Research has found that the harmful effects of prenatal cocaine use are temporary and treatable. There are no statistically significant differences in the long-term health of babies exposed to cocaine compared to those who were not. Researchers found that poverty was a greater influence than exposure to cocaine (McDonough 2013). Many of the health problems blamed on prenatal cocaine exposure were related to poverty and poor nutrition (Roberts 1997).

Dorothy Roberts (1997) argues that the United States suffered a moral panic over maternal crack cocaine use. Media depictions created two irredeemable characters: the pregnant addict and the crack baby. "Newspaper stories warned of a horde of Black children about to descend on inner-city kindergartens in need of high-cost special services" (Roberts 1997, p. 19). Politicians responded with harsh rhetoric and tough laws targeting African American mothers. Rather than focus on difficult, multicausal issues such as poverty and poor nutrition, governments in the United States punished the vulnerable.

Victim blaming is a common form of punishment for vulnerable families who deal with the pains of incarceration. Jill McCorkel (2013) studied drug treatment programs in an American women's prison. The program used "confrontational therapy" to break down and reform female inmates. The confrontational therapy program has its roots in Alcoholics Anonymous, a religion-based treatment program that views "addicts" as powerless. Counselors used derogatory terms to refer to female inmates, including the phrases "dogs," "crack hos," "uncaring," "selfish," and "diseased." The program's mission statement reads, "Drug abuse is a disorder of the whole person. The problem is the person, and not the drug, and addiction is a symptom and not the essence of the disorder" (McCorkel 2013, p. 126).

In addition to claiming that inmates were diseased, program counselors insisted that the women were failures as mothers. McCorkel (2013, p. 127) writes, "Counselors routinely report to the women that their 'worst' crime, and the one that reveals the most about their diseased selves, is the harm they inflict on their children through their 'lifestyles' and poor choices." Staff members posted an image of a tiny, sobbing, African American infant accompanied by the caption "Beat your drug problem instead." This demeaning treatment has very little basis in fact. Only 2 of the 170 female participants had a criminal record for child abuse or neglect (McCorkel 2013).

Counselors were likely responding to socially constructed stereotypes about female inmates rather than actual attributes. Indeed, the prison staff viewed women much more negatively as the prison population became less white. From 1986 to 2003, the incarceration rate for African American women increased by 800 percent. Prison staff referred to the new majority African American and Latina prison population as consisting of "real criminals" as opposed to the previous majority white population of "good girls" (McCorkel 2013). As African American women and Latinas have been increasingly incarcerated, prison treatment has become harsher and the rehabilitative emphasis has diminished (McCorkel 2013).

Even in cases where prison officials do not explicitly tell women that they are failures, many women think deeply about their role as mothers during the moments of isolation and solitude inherent in prison life. "Imprisonment engenders the feelings of loss and failure. Not only has she been ostracized by society for her criminal behavior, she has demonstrated a seeming failure as a mother. Whatever else prison does to or for a woman, it enables her to reflect for hours on end about herself and the consequences of her behavior on both herself and her children" (Baunach 1985). Incarceration can destroy family roles and crush a prisoner's identity as a parent.

The 2004 Survey has some information that sheds light on the experiences of incarcerated parents. Almost 80 percent of inmates were living with family members prior to their incarceration, and 41 percent had children. Sixty-eight percent of inmates were providing financially for their children before their incarceration. Overall, inmates were integrated with their families and were providing financial support before their incarceration. Inmates were highly connected to their families before their prison terms began.

Over 80 percent of inmates received a phone call from friends or family in the month that they were surveyed. A much smaller number, roughly 30 percent, received an in-person visit from their family or friends in the month that they were surveyed. In spite of expense, inmates are routinely called on the phone. This seems to suggest that there are people who would like to be involved in the inmates' lives. However, visits may be prohibitively expensive. Inmates are called at 2.7 times the rate they are visited. It is likely that the distance from the prison to their homes plays a role.

The 2004 Survey asked inmates how far their prison was from their residence at the time of their arrest. The variable is broken down into ordinal categories and does not include exact mileage. Fifteen percent of inmates are incarcerated less than 50 miles from their original residence. Even a distance of, say, 25 miles may be difficult logistically for economically disadvantaged families. Another 20 percent of inmates were incarcerated between 50 and 100 miles from their residence. Slightly over half are incarcerated between 101 miles and 500 miles from their residence. Smaller percentages were incarcerated between 501 and 1,000 miles from their residence (7 percent) or more than 1,000 miles from their residence (2 percent). It is not a common practice to locate inmates so far from their original home; however, some highly overcrowded prison systems, such as California's, have contracted out to other states for inmate bed space.

The distance from prison to their homes is one example of the cumulative disadvantage that many inmates face. We disproportionately incarcerate poor Americans from urban areas and then send those people to prisons in faraway rural areas. Because of their poverty, their families are less able to shoulder the significant financial burdens that visiting a prison causes. Imagine the difficulty that a poor family, possibly a poor family with small children, would have traveling over 100 miles to visit their loved one in prison. It is likely that those families will have to take a bus for hours to get to the prison. Long road trips are difficult even for wealthier families with reliable transportation; yet, because of disproportionate placements in rural prisons, over half of inmate families have to travel more than 100 miles to visit their loved one.

The full model estimations for whether an inmate has received a visit in the last month illustrate that the vulnerable are less likely to receive visits. Inmates who were relatively financially advantaged, those who were working full time before their incarceration, were more likely to receive visits. Those who are more financially disadvantaged, those who were forced to rely on a court-appointed attorney, and those who had experienced homelessness were less likely to receive visits. African American inmates were also less likely to receive visits. It is likely that African American inmates face the most hardship due to our system of incarcerating city residents in rural areas.

The federal government has emphasized the importance of family, and commentators sometimes bemoan the destruction of the nuclear family and the rise of divorce and single parenthood. This rhetoric is contradicted by our insistence on charging high amounts for phone calls, by locating prisoners far from their residences, and by having an unwelcoming environment during visitation. Some facilities do attempt to build ties between inmates and their families; when I worked at the Mecklenburg County Sheriff's Office, there was a program in which fathers were allowed to have their children sit on their laps while the fathers read to the children. However, such programs are not universally available and do not completely compensate for the difficulties involved in the visitation process. It is, perhaps, a sign of how unfriendly the prison visitation experience is that a simple program where fathers read to their children seems so welcoming.

Suggestions for Reform

Incarceration punishes not only the inmate but also the inmate's family. We don't know how many families would have stayed together were it not for incarceration; some would have fallen apart without imprisonment. We do know that millions of American children are unable to spend time with parents who deeply love them. Millions of husbands and wives are separated by the state, often for minor offenses. Paternalistic rhetoric about the importance of mothers and fathers is not matched by the actual behavior of government agents. While politicians and prison staff talk about the importance of parenting and the vital role of the American family on one hand, on the other hand those same actors imprison millions of parents and severely affect the lives of millions of children. We claim that "nothing can replace a father's love," but then we separate fathers and children with razor wire and Plexiglas walls. The punishment of the vulnerable extends far beyond prison walls and is one of the cruelest burdens of modern American incarceration.

I recommend the following:

1. Inmates should be incarcerated as close to their former homes as possible.
2. Phone calls to and from inmates should be free or as close to cost as possible. Stamps and envelopes should also be provided for free or as close to cost as possible.
3. The prison visitation environment should be as welcoming as possible. Other than basic security measures, visitors and especially children should not experience intrusive measures. Unless there is a specific reason, such as a past history of domestic or child abuse, to prevent it, all inmates should be allowed physical contact with their family members.
4. Prisons should work to identify temporary release policies that would enable inmates to work for and interact with their families. This will also help the inmate's eventual reintegration into society.

CHAPTER NINE

Instead of Prisons

> A lot are in here that don't need to be. Our criminal justice system isn't as good as people say it is. But that's not my place to say.
>
> —Correctional officer at Western Kentucky Correctional Complex

> I'm a scofflaw. I've been a fighter for the underdog all my life.
>
> —Arnold Abbott, South Florida advocate for the homeless

This book has documented the punishment of vulnerable American prisoners. Rather than punish "super predators," we tend to punish the poor, immigrants, the sick, the mentally ill, drug users, African Americans, Latino/as, and LGBT inmates. As a country, we disproportionately imprison these groups. While in prison, these groups continue to be disproportionately punished. Some of the punishments, such as solitary confinement, are quite severe and can cause or exacerbate mental illnesses. Other punishments are in some ways less severe but in other ways no less heartbreaking: a lack of visits can lead to depression or the dissolution of a family, the use of force may physically and psychologically scar an inmate, hard labor for minimal compensation can lead to feelings of disillusionment and exploitation. In our zeal for punishment, we have incarcerated millions of Americans and harmed even more of their family members. The harm is tremendous and long-lasting.

Our preference for punishment has led to an increased reliance on incarceration and harsh treatment in prison. The war on crime is a moral panic resulting from the domestic turmoil of the 1960s. Chapter 1 discussed how both crime and punishment have varied since the United States became an independent nation. Our conceptions of crime and acceptable punishment have changed multiple times, but since the 1960s we have engaged in a punitive crime-control model. This model deemphasizes rehabilitation and emphasizes punishment. These changes have led to the United States becoming the world's premier prison nation, with millions of people in jails and prisons, millions more on probation and parole, and still more millions devastated when their family members are sent to jail. Incarceration harms the emotional, physical, intellectual, and social capital of inmates and drains those same resources from the inmate's community.

When inmates are sent to prison, they are subject to modern American prison guards' high levels of discretion. American prison guards are outnumbered and short on resources. Further complicating matters, hundreds of stringent regulations mean that the number of potential violations is too large to ensure universal punishment. Prison guards have to sanction some inmates and help others but lack the resources to sanction or help everyone. I have argued that prison guards use heuristics to simplify their decision making. Rather than treat every inmate as an individual, prison guards view individual inmates as representative members of different groups. Original interviews and larger survey data suggest that correctional officers have differing views on rehabilitation and punishment and are able to place inmates in categories, and that some identifiers, such as race or mental illness, are more important than others.

The war on crime has not affected every community equally. In chapter 3, we saw that the war on crime is largely a war on the poor. With the theoretical backing of "broken windows" policing, a nationwide panic over crime, and the incentive of revenue generation, police officers target masses of poor people. Poor people are also less capable of posting bail, hiring an attorney, or managing a credible legal defense. Because of this, poor people are incentivized to plead guilty, even when they are innocent. When incarcerated, economically disadvantaged inmates have less access to rehabilitative services and are more likely to be punished. The poor are further exploited through prison labor, monetary sanctions, expensive commissary items, and a parole system that requires work in the meanest, least-well-compensated jobs. The vulnerable poor are sent to prisons and jails by the millions every year, and incarceration further decreases their economic capital and increases their social vulnerability.

Prisons are filled with the physically and mentally unwell. In chapter 4, I presented evidence that the prison population has higher rates of most physical and mental illnesses. Prisoners have rates of high blood pressure, stroke, diabetes, asthma, cirrhosis of the liver, tuberculosis, hepatitis, sexually transmitted diseases, HIV/AIDS, major depression, psychotic disorders, and heart-related problems that are much higher than the general public. Prisons have inadequate health care services, and some states, such as California, have lost control of their prison systems due to inadequate health care. Inmates have died due to poorly treated or untreated illnesses. With the deinstitutionalization of state mental health hospitals, many mentally ill people who would have been hospitalized are now placed in prisons. Prisons have become the provider of last resort for the mentally ill. While incarcerated, mentally ill inmates are frequently placed in solitary confinement, a punishment that both causes and exacerbates mental illness. Prisoners are in desperate need of mental and physical health care, another sign that points to their incredible vulnerability.

The war on crime has devastated African American and Latino/a communities. Racial discrimination in the American criminal justice system is one of the premier controversies of modern American society. Many measures of the war on crime were designed to target racial minorities and have been quite successful at that task. "Broken windows" policing has led to large-scale targeting of African American and Latino/a communities. It is becoming widespread knowledge that African Americans and Latino/as are subject to disproportionately harsh levels of arrest, sentencing, and imprisonment. Less well known is that significant racial discrimination exists inside American prisons as well. Prison guards engage in the use of race-based heuristics, and this profiling leads to disproportionate punishment. African Americans and Latino/as are more likely to be punished and less likely to receive rehabilitative services. Prisons are located far from the cities that most African Americans and Latino/as are arrested in, and African American inmates are less likely to receive visits from their family members. The "new Jim Crow" extends behind prison walls as well.

Immigration enforcement is the latest frontier for tough-on-crime policies. Both political parties are broadly supportive of harsh immigration policies. U.S. history shows that we have engaged in multiple moral panics regarding immigration. Current hysteria over Latino/a and Muslim immigrants matches previous hysteria about Catholics, Jews, Southern Europeans, and Asian immigrants. When placed in the criminal justice system, undocumented immigrants have fewer legal protections than do citizens. Immigration prisons use arbitrary decision making, immigration judges mass process cases, and prisons can get rich holding immigration detainees for the federal government. Immigration prisons are a Kafkaesque labyrinth of inhumane conditions. Enforcement disproportionately focuses on certain immigrants, mostly those from African or Latin American countries or those who practice stigmatized religions.

As part of the war on crime, the United States has waged an unsuccessful war on drugs for over 100 years, as the United States has prohibited drugs such as alcohol, cannabis, cocaine, opiates, and hallucinogens. Many of the excesses of the current drug war (e.g., civil forfeiture, mandatory minimum sentencing, police brutality, disproportionate enforcement against the poor and marginalized) have precedents in alcohol prohibition. Giving up the ghost of alcohol prohibition has saved billions of dollars and made alcohol consumption relatively safer. Yet the United States still fights a war on other drugs. After 100 years and over $1 trillion spent fighting the war on drugs, drug potency has increased and prices have declined. While the war on drugs has failed overall, it has succeeded in devastating vulnerable communities and is responsible for the placement of 400,000 Americans behind bars. Rather than incarcerating drug dealers or recreational users, American prisons are filled with inmates with a drug abuse or drug dependence issue, both of which are medical conditions. Drug users are disproportionately punished inside American prisons and lack access to necessary rehabilitative programs.

The final vulnerable victims of the United States' war on crime are the families of the incarcerated. Eight million children have a parent who has been incarcerated. Incarceration leads to family dissolution, the loss of custody, traumatic separation for both parents and children, disenfranchised grief, and a brutal questioning of identity. Prisons reinforce the trauma through degrading treatment of incarcerated parents and inconvenient and disrespectful visitation settings for their family members. Despite paternalistic rhetoric about the importance of family, American prisons place literal and figurative barriers between inmates and their loved ones, including expensive phone calls, stamps, and envelopes; humiliating searches; and a lack of physical contact during visits. Mass incarceration punishes not just the vulnerable but also the families of the vulnerable—families who did nothing wrong.

Even some prison staff are disillusioned with the process. Two separate correctional officers at Western Kentucky Correctional Complex expressed their dismay at the current American criminal justice system. One correctional officer said, "A lot are in here that don't need to be. Our criminal justice system isn't as good as people say it is. But that's not my place to say." A second officer said that, to him, the whole prison system is a joke. Wardens have also expressed the sentiment that the vast majority of prisoners can either be rehabilitated or do not belong in prison at all. It is commonly said that between 10 and 20 percent of inmates are actually dangerous or should be in prison, which of course implies that 80 to 90 percent should not be incarcerated.

Dissatisfaction with the prison system is nothing new, and ideas about how to reform prisons have abounded for decades. Prison abolition is an idea that goes back as long as prisons have existed. Charles Dickens bemoaned the existence of solitary confinement in the 1840s, and Jesus of Nazareth voiced his opposition to prisons 2,000 years ago. More recently, in the 1970s, a group of scholars joined together to form the Prison Research Education Action Project. The project produced a handbook for prison abolitionists entitled *Instead of Prisons* (1976). The handbook was republished by Critical Resistance, a prison abolition group. In some ways, the handbook is a better guide than my argument in this chapter. In other ways, it is a little disappointing that the prison state has expanded so vociferously in spite of the blood, sweat, and tears of dedicated antiprison activists. It is clear that support for prison reform and abolition will need to expand in order to pressure governments to reduce their reliance on incarceration.

For the most part, I would support the recommendations in *Instead of Prisons* (1976). One serious flaw was the call for mandatory sentences rather than the indeterminate sentencing of the 1970s. The call for mandatory sentencing was driven by a concern that indeterminate sentencing would allow for more discrimination against the poor and racial minorities. However, mandatory minimum sentencing has had a devastating impact and is one of the major causes of mass incarceration. Most scholars today prefer indeterminate sentencing. The discrepancy over mandatory minimum sentencing serves as an important warning: any prison reform is likely to have negative unintended consequences, which should give reformers pause. Other than their position on mandatory sentencing, I am largely in agreement with the recommendations, and I have named this chapter "Instead of Prisons" as a hat tip and nod of appreciation. I also assume that prison abolitionists are more likely to forgive my stealing and appropriating their title. The following are a series of proposals to replace the current predatory criminal justice system with something more humane.

Suggestions for Reform

First, there needs to be a realistic analysis of the costs of incarceration. In many, if not most, cases, the costs of incarceration are significantly higher than the damage inmates have done to society. Instead of criminalizing homelessness, we should provide housing for the homeless. Housing the homeless and providing them with support services is more cost-efficient than incarcerating the homeless. Over five years, New York City spent $129 million to jail 800 people, over half of whom were homeless. A study in Utah found that the cost of emergency treatment and jail time averaged over $16,000 a year, while the cost of a fully subsidized apartment is $11,000. A study in Central Florida found that providing the homeless with permanent housing and support services would save taxpayers $149 million (Vitale 2017).

A growing movement focuses on housing first. As the name implies, governments and nonprofits focus on finding stable housing before addressing other issues. Often, housing is temporary and/or comes with preconditions, such as drug treatment or work requirements. By focusing on housing first, some states have been able to greatly reduce homelessness. The state of Virginia uses rapid rehousing and permanent supportive housing, which has led to a 31 percent drop in homelessness. In 2015, Virginia became the first state to end veteran homelessness (Vitale 2017). A cost-benefit analysis is important for evaluating other petty crimes as well. The average cost of incarceration is $91 per inmate per day, or around $33,000 a year. Anyone who is incarcerated should have caused more than $33,000 in harm (or perhaps significantly more, given the amount of damage that prison does to the average person's mental health and earning potential). This would lead to most nonviolent offenders and most property crime offenders being released from prison.

A second reform goes along with the first: we need new goals for the prison system as a whole. Retribution is the main goal of contemporary American criminal justice. I recommend a switch to a restorative justice model. Restorative justice is a "philosophy that moves from punishment to reconciliation, from vengeance against offenders to healing for victims, from alienation and harshness to community and wholeness, from negativity and destructiveness to healing, forgiveness and mercy" (Goulding, Hall, and Steels 2008, p. 234). Restorative justice requires offenders to take responsibility for the harm they have done and to apologize and make amends to their victims. Restorative justice involves active victim participation and seeks to strike a balance between the victim, the offender, and the community (Goulding, Hall, and Steels 2008).

In the current system, offenders are removed from the community and no longer take part in society. This violates norms of social inclusion. A democratic society benefits when all members participate in the full range of community affairs. If we want everyone to become full members of society, we need to include everyone in society (Osgood, Foster, and Courtney 2010). Ironically, by removing offenders from society, we are negating any personal responsibility they should take for their actions. The current approach fails both victims and offenders. Restorative justice seeks to "bring all parties (victims, offenders and communities of interest) together with a view to achieving some form of reconciliation through a mutually acceptable outcome" (Goulding, Hall, and Steels 2008, p. 234).

Restorative justice programs already exist in multiple countries. There are restorative justice prison programs in England, Belgium, and Australia. The entire prison system in Belgium uses a restorative justice framework. Even maximum security prisons have used a restorative justice model; HMP Grendon in the United Kingdom has more than 200 high-security inmates, all of whom participate in restorative justice programming. Restorative justice programs are also effective at reducing recidivism. With effective therapeutic interventions, restorative justice models have reduced reoffending by 31 percent (Goulding, Hall, and Steels 2008).

Third, I advocate the abolishment of cash bail. Eighty-three percent of people in American jails are there because they cannot afford to pay bail. Jails are pretrial detention facilities, which means that the people in jail have not been convicted of a crime. Jails sever people from their community, their job, and their sanity. In the most tragic of cases, such as that of Djibril Niyomugabo, inmates have committed suicide. Over 700,000 people are in local jails at any given time; over 600,000 would be released with the abolishment of cash bail. Along with the elimination of cash bail, there should be an abolishment of monetary sanctions, or at the very least monetary sanctions should be based on a sliding scale. In addition to reforming these financial aspects, there needs to be an abolishment of or at least a severe restriction of plea bargaining. Plea bargaining strengthens the hand of the state and pressures the innocent into accepting guilty pleas. We must get back to the norm of jury trials for criminal offenses. If a criminal offense is not serious enough to require a jury trial, it is not serious enough to require jail time.

Fourth, I recommend diverting all inmates with a significant mental illness to alternate treatment facilities. The American health care system lacks adequate mental health care facilities, and as such, prisons have become de facto providers. Eighty-one percent of state prison inmates have a mental health issue and/or a substance abuse issue. This represents 1.58 million state prison inmates who should be receiving specialized treatment. It cannot be stressed enough that prisons are designed to segregate people from society, and the number-one priority of modern American prison administrators is security. Prisons and prison staff do not have the training, knowledge, skills, or abilities to provide adequate mental health care. With their reliance on solitary confinement, American prisons cause and exacerbate mental illnesses rather than solve them. Deinstitutionalization was in part an effort to remove patients from corrupt and unethical mental health hospitals; therefore, it is important to make sure that whatever alternative form of treatment is decided on is protective of the mentally ill.

Fifth, solitary confinement must be abolished. Solitary confinement places inmates in physical isolation for 22 to 23 hours a day in a 54-square-foot cell. Solitary confinement has been decried as torture by the United Nations, the American Civil Liberties Union, Human Rights Watch, the American Friends Service Committee, Critical Resistance, the National Religious Campaign Against Torture, and Pope Francis. Reforming solitary confinement is impossible. Human beings are social creatures and need social interaction. As many as 100,000 inmates are presently in solitary confinement, an issue that should be a national scandal.

In addition to ending cash bail, abolishing solitary confinement, and finding alternative treatment for the mentally ill, it is necessary to reclassify the vast majority of criminal law to civil violations. There are more than 4,500 offenses in the federal criminal code and 300,000 more regulations that carry criminal consequences. The plethora of offenses and regulations should horrify both liberals concerned about equality and conservatives worried about government overreach. Any action that does not have an identifiable victim should not be a criminal violation. Even if some laws are reclassified as civil penalties, it should be illegal to send anyone to prison for failure to pay a government fine. Alternative punishments under a restorative justice framework should be used instead.

Another type of offense that needs to be reclassified are immigration offenses. Undocumented immigrants come to the United States in search of better opportunities and are often fleeing the negative consequences of inhumane U.S. policies. Citizenship is mostly an accident of birth. If you believe that all humans are created equal and are of equal worth, it is inconsistent to claim that any human does not have the right to live in the United States. Someone born in Juarez, Mexico; or Bogota, Colombia; or Beijing, China, has the same worth as someone born in New York or Alabama. Borders are in part a human construction. These statements may represent my libertarian/anarchist fantasies, but I think they have some validity. Even if we agree that borders are important and that people need to be deported, indefinite detention is unnecessary and expensive. Undocumented immigrants could be subject to surveillance outside of prison during their trials and, if necessary, prior to their deportation. Unless an undocumented immigrant is a specific flight risk, it is unnecessary to lock him or her up.

Serious drug reform is also necessary. If Americans can navigate a world where tobacco and alcohol are legal, they can surely navigate a world with legal cannabis and possibly other substances as well. Assuming all drugs will not be legalized tomorrow (with apologies to the fine folks at *Reason* magazine), drug policy experts should meet and discuss which drugs can be legalized. Cannabis is the most likely early candidate and is already effectively legal in many parts of the country. Other drugs, like MDMA and psilocybin mushrooms, may follow close behind. Experts should recommend what to do with "harder" drugs like heroin or cocaine. However, even those drugs should be decriminalized, following the example of decriminalizers like Portugal.

Along with any liberalization to laws related to mental health, immigration, bail, or drug usage, we must figure out what to do with people currently incarcerated for those crimes. A team of experts must determine which prisoners are potential threats to public safety and which inmates can be safely released. This team should include not just prison security staff but also psychologists, social workers, and other experts. The goal should be individualized plans for each inmate's eventual reentry into the community. The parole system could be reformatted to provide more credible reintegration opportunities for former inmates and could work in a more collaborative than adversarial way. This model of social services and social reintegration was largely the model practiced in the United States between the 1870s and the 1960s.

Under the plan suggested by these recommendations, most prisoners will be either released or temporarily placed in specialized mental health care centers. There may be a number of violent offenders who cannot be safely returned to society. Abolitionists refer to this group as the "dangerous few." The small number of truly dangerous inmates should be placed in the lowest possible custody setting. A number may need to remain in secure facilities while some may be placed in alternative custody arrangements, which may include electronic monitoring or community custody. To the largest extent possible, these inmates should have interactions with their families and communities.

The ultimate goal should be the closing of the vast majority of prisons in the United States. Experts will determine if any existing prisons need to remain, or remain for a short time. Mass incarceration is a modern phenomenon; we can visualize its disappearance with a little imagination. Institutions are created by societies; whatever a society can create, it can destroy. Prisons deprive inmates of their liberty, autonomy, security, goods and services, and healthy relationships (Mathiesen 1986). As such, prisons are inhumane institutions. Prisons have existed long enough for their flaws to be clearly known. Whatever negative unintended consequences occur because of decarceration, and there are sure to be some, those consequences are unlikely to be worse than keeping millions of vulnerable people in cages.

There are two final issues that need to be addressed. Once the vulnerable are released from prison, we must be vigilant to make sure that more vulnerable people do not take their place. This will require a radical reform of policing in the United States. As currently constructed, the job of police in the United States is impossible. There are too many conflicting priorities. The police maintain the law, investigate crime, keep the peace, direct traffic, monitor events, give first aid, settle domestic disputes, and interact with the homeless, the mentally ill, and the community in myriad ways (Ferguson 2014). All the while, police officers are under pressure from supervisors and politicians to make more arrests, to raise revenue, and to symbolically represent the state. Finally, the police are required to manage vulnerable populations that have been effectively abandoned by the state.

Alex Vitale (2017, p. 16) discusses the impossibility of any form of community policing, given the tensions between the police and the public inherent in modern policing.

> When their job is to criminalize all disorderly behavior and fund local government through massive ticketing-writing campaigns, their interactions with the public in high-crime areas will be at best gruff and distant and at worst hostile and abusive. The public will resist them and view their efforts as intrusive and illegitimate; the police will react to this resistance with defensiveness and increased assertiveness. Community policing is not possible under these conditions.

Police forces, just like prisons, are a historical, social creation, and a relatively new creation at that. The majority of people, for the majority of our species' existence, have managed without a formal police force. Vitale discusses several possibilities to reform policing in his book *The End of Policing*. Even if policing is not ended, it can be dramatically reformed. Part of that reform may involve the fragmentation and specialization of current policing tasks. Some may specialize in traffic control, others in responding to domestic disputes, others in community relations, others in investigations, and others in disaster relief. Those who specialize in less dangerous jobs should not be armed. Very few police officers in other countries are armed, which must at least partially explain the difference in police homicide rates. Police should also limit themselves to responding to calls rather than going through neighborhoods looking for, and sometimes manufacturing, trouble. In addition, police must be held accountable for any use of force. Currently, a small minority of aggressive officers worsen the reputation of entire departments.

Finally, we must acknowledge that the criminal justice system has devastated many communities across this country. Many neighborhoods have been damaged by overly aggressive police forces and mass incarceration. The United States must provide economic aid for communities and individuals harmed by incarceration. The criminal justice system has often proclaimed the need for restitutions for victims. Restitution should also extend to victims of government violence. Indeed, government officials should be held to a higher standard than regular citizens. Luke 12:48 states, "From everyone who has been given much, much will be demanded; and from the one who has been entrusted with much, much more will be asked."

Here is a list of my summarized reforms:

1. Rational analysis of the costs of incarceration
2. Embracing a restorative justice model
3. Abolition of cash bail and reform of monetary sanctions
4. Alternative treatment for the mentally ill
5. Abolition of solitary confinement
6. Reclassification of most criminal laws
7. Reclassification of immigration laws
8. Drug reform, including decriminalization, legalization, and a public health approach
9. Mass decarceration
10. Policing reform
11. Economic investment, including restitution for those harmed by mass incarceration

What conditions will allow prison reform to take place? There may need to be a profound culture shift. Poor economic conditions have proven insufficient, as have poor prison conditions. There is a nationwide prison reform movement led by groups like Critical Resistance and the American Friends Service Committee along with allied groups working for drug policy and immigration reform. These and similar organizations will need to expand their activities. This book's website (www.punishingthevulnerable.com) has some links and resources for prison reform organizations. Although groups are helpful, brave individuals, both inside and outside of prison, are needed to help shine a light on the inhumane conditions of American prisons.

Prisoners themselves must be key to any eventual prison abolition. There is a rich history of prison memoirs and prison protests. In spite of their difficulties and multiple disadvantages, American prison inmates are not passive recipients of punishment. Currently, in August 2018, there are hunger and work strikes in both American and Canadian prisons. The strikes have occurred at prisons in Washington, California, Florida, and Nova Scotia in response to a deadly riot in South Carolina that led to the death of seven inmates (Pilkington 2018). This strike comes after the largest prison strike in U.S. history, a 2016 event that saw protests in at least 12 states (Lopez 2016).

The strikers have released a set of 10 demands, including an immediate improvement in prison conditions, payment for prison labor that is commensurate with state labor laws, a rescission of the Prison Litigation Act, sentencing reform, additional rehabilitative services, and the restoration of voting rights (Press Release 2018). The strike is scheduled to run for 19 days. Even if it does not receive much publicity, it is a signal to prison officials and politicians that prisoners are politically active. A massive prison strike would be very disruptive of prisons. Much of the day-to-day work of inmates, from food preparation to cleaning to providing services for local communities, is vital to maintaining the viability of prisons. Prisoners should take a major role in any reform effort.

Individuals not in prison also have an important role to play. This chapter began with a quote from Arnold Abbott, the 93-year-old advocate for the homeless whose charity, Love Thy Neighbor, provides food for the indigent in Florida. Abbott said, "I'm a scofflaw. I've been a fighter for the underdog all my life." Abbott and his fellow advocates managed to shame the city of Fort Lauderdale after police arrested him for feeding the homeless. While we should never doubt the power and reach of the government, it is possible to achieve real changes by speaking truth to power. So many of the excesses in prison run toward the absurd, and by shining a light we can better illustrate the inhumanity of modern American criminal justice. Much of that inhumanity flourishes in the shadows.

Robert Ferguson (2014, p. 13) writes of this shadowy nature and the ultimate denial of responsibility when he claims that "no single official ever has to look directly into the abyss. No one punisher need feel the full burden of creating suffering." Ferguson argues that the average person does not like to think about or witness punishment. As Americans we have become accustomed to ignoring the realities of war, of migration, of punishment, of poverty. We have a hard time empathizing with others because we ignore others. We might see the panhandler asking for change, but we don't see that same man sleeping in an unheated, abandoned house. We might think about the migrant who crossed the border "illegally," but we do not think about the terrors she is running from or the difficulties of her journey. We might think of a mentally ill person being placed in prison, but we do not think about the isolation and emotional torment that comes from being placed in solitary confinement. We must think about what goes on behind prison walls—the everyday deprivation, isolation, fear, anger, sadness, and hopelessness. Individuals can help shine a light on these issues. If enough individuals dedicate themselves to prison reform, it'll no longer be avoidable.

It may be difficult to find the imagination to end mass incarceration. It may also be difficult to know where to begin. Karl Weick (1984) argues that we should focus on "small wins," which are concrete outcomes of moderate importance. The advantage of these small wins is that they build on each other and are less overwhelming than trying to fix a massive problem all at once. While none of my recommendations are necessarily small, some are larger than others, and some are likely less politically feasible than others. Scholars and activists should continue to debate which areas of prison reform are likely to be most fruitful. However, I would argue that pushing for a ban on cash bail and monetary sanctions, or at least developing a sliding scale for monetary sanctions, is perhaps the most fruitful area.

The cash bail and monetary sanctions systems are clearly inequitable and unfair. In addition, criticizing cash bail and monetary sanctions is not considered "soft on crime" in the same way that legalizing or decriminalizing drugs is. Criticizing cash bail and monetary sanctions is not as politically controversial as many reforms related to racial discrimination. New Jersey essentially ended cash bail in 2017, while California is posed to pass a bill virtually eliminating cash bail, and a half dozen other states have limited the use of cash bail. U.S. senators, including Cory Booker and Sherrod Brown, have criticized cash bail and the bail bond industry (Neff 2018; Ulloa 2018). Reforming the cash bail system would tremendously reduce the size of jail populations, and jail populations are the feeder to prisons. I would recommend that activists focus on reforming the cash bail and monetary sanctions system. A focus on cash bail and monetary sanctions is also beneficial since so much focus is already placed on racial discrimination and drug law reform.

As we consider the possibilities of reform, we should keep in mind that real people are suffering. Our prisons are full of the poor, the sick, the marginalized, and the vulnerable. While there are some dangerous people currently incarcerated, and there may be a need to continue the incarceration of a small number of people, our prisons are not full of "super predators." Until there are significant reforms, the vulnerable will continue to suffer punishment for being vulnerable in a country that refuses to dedicate adequate resources to issues of poverty, discrimination, and mental health. Until there are significant reforms, 8 million American children will live in a world where their loved ones are locked up. It is time to lessen the burden faced by vulnerable Americans. The vulnerable have carried their burdens for long enough.

This book is for the vulnerable.

Technical Appendix

The CJ-DATS Survey

The Criminal Justice Drug Abuse Treatment Studies (CJ-DATS) was conducted by the National Institute on Drug Abuse between 2002 and 2008. The CJ-DATS selected a nationally representative, cross-sectional sample of 150 adult prison facilities. Fifty-eight facilities were chosen for their focus on drug and alcohol treatment, while the other 92 prisons were selected randomly. From this set of 150 adult prison facilities, a random sample of frontline workers was selected. In all, 734 frontline workers from adult facilities responded to the survey. The survey, which was estimated to take one hour to complete, was mailed and self-administrated with a response rate of 34 percent. The survey included security, administrative, and treatment staff. The CJ-DATS offers significant advantages over previous work (Jurik 1985), including a larger sample of female, African American, and Latino/a workers.

Each question asks respondents for their level of agreement with various crime-reduction strategies on a five point scale (from 1=strongly disagree to 5=strongly agree). Three corresponding additive indices were developed as dependent variables. All three indices are included in the CJ-DATS survey. Confirmatory factor analysis was performed, with punishment, deterrence, and rehabilitation factors emerging. Each factor had an Eigenvalue above 2, and collectively explained 93 percent of the variation in questions. Four questions are related to rehabilitation, three to deterrence, and two to "just desserts" punishment. The question wording for the three categories is reproduced below.

Rehabilitation:

1. Make sure criminals get effective treatment for addictions and other problems while they're in prison/jail, or on supervision in the community.

2. Provide criminals with treatment to address addiction, mental health problems, or other problems.
3. Make sure that the treatment provided is matched to the offender's needs.
4. Provide more treatment, jobs, and educational programs to address problems that often contribute to crime.

Deterrence:

1. Show people who use drugs they will be punished severely if they don't stop.
2. Deter future offenders by severely punishing criminals who are caught and convicted.
3. Deter future criminals by severely punishing drug users who are caught and convicted.

Just Desserts Punishment:

1. Use the eye for an eye, tooth for a tooth principle.
2. Punish addicts in prison/jail to stop them from using drugs.

Explanatory variables focused on the demographic characteristics of the survey respondents. Racial and ethnic categories consist of African American, Latino/a, and other race, with white Americans as the reference category. Gender is coded as a one for female respondents and a zero for male respondents. Education is measured by a series of dummy variables for associate, college, and graduate degrees with a high school education as the reference category. Age is a series of dummy variables broken down (by the survey originally) into 10-year increments to capture cohort differences. Table A.1 in the Appendix reports the results for the CJ-DATS survey. Standard errors are shown in parentheses underneath the reported coefficients. Significance levels are designated by asterisks next to the coefficients.

The 2004 Survey

The data on treatment inside prisons comes from the Bureau of Justice Statistics' "Survey of Inmates in State and Federal Correctional Facilities, 2004" (2004 Survey). A new version of the survey is set to be released in 2019. As soon as that dataset is available, I will rerun the analysis presented below to see what relationships may or may not have changed. The analysis will be published on this book's website (www.punishingthevulnerable.com). Readers can access the 2004 Survey, including the codebook and dataset, at https://www.bjs.gov/ index.cfm?ty=dcdetail&iid=275.

The 2004 Survey involved personal interviews in both state and federal prisons that provided information about the inmate's offense, criminal history, pre-incarceration life, participation in treatment programs, and punishment inside prison. This analysis uses only state prison inmates. The 2004 Survey is a nationally representative sample of inmates, selected in a two-stage process. Prisons were selected in the first stage, and inmates within the sampled prisons were selected in the second. In the first stage, 290 state prisons were selected,

Table A.1 CJ-DATS results

	Support for Rehabilitation	Support for Deterrence	Support for Just Desserts
African American	0.136***	-0.078	-0.201***
	0.051	0.08	0.074
Latino/a	0.099	-0.358*	-0.387**
	0.118	0.187	0.178
Other race	0.006	-0.195	0.068
	0.12	0.19	0.178
Female	-0.092*	0.323***	0.159**
	0.047	0.075	0.07
Associate's degree	0.038	-0.076	0.041
	0.092	0.146	0.135
Bachelor's degree	0.142**	-0.253**	-0.189**
	0.063	0.1	0.094
Some graduate school	0.248***	-0.166	-0.183
	0.089	0.14	0.131
Master's degree	0.291***	-0.628***	-0.432***
	0.087	0.137	0.128
Age: thirties	0.025	-0.051	-0.078
	0.061	0.096	0.089
Age: forties	0.139**	-0.197*	-0.143
	0.068	0.107	0.1
Age: fifties plus	0.078	-0.294**	-0.392***
	0.077	0.122	0.114
Number of observations	622	625	627
Adjusted r-squared	0.0356	0.0693	0.0504

*p<.10, **p<.05, ***p<.01

including 225 male facilities and 65 female facilities. The 14 largest male prisons and 7 largest female prisons were selected with certainty. The remaining facilities were selected based on probability proportional to size. From the 290 state prisons, approximately 1 in every 85 males and 1 in every 24 females were selected. There were 14,499 complete interviews for the state survey.

The 2004 Survey contains a wide-ranging list of questions. In some cases, I have reported only summary statistics (e.g., the percentage of inmates who have used cocaine or the percentage of inmates who have received a phone call from friends or family members). The full model estimations include 23 independent variables and 5 dependent variables. The model estimations were produced using the Stata statistical software program and include fixed effects for each prison. The fixed effects are necessary because it is likely that vulnerable inmates, overall, are sent to worse prisons. I have sought to isolate the impact of variables unique to the inmates rather than variables related to the prison itself. I would encourage other researchers to explore some of the prison-level determinants of treatment. The Bureau of Justice Statistics does publish statistics about prison-level data.

The vast majority of the variables are dichotomous in nature (e.g., has an inmate been diagnosed with depression, is the inmate African American). Only two variables included in the full model estimations are nondichotomous—a control variable for how many total incarcerations the inmate has received and a variable measuring the highest grade the inmate attended. A number of other potentially confounding variables may be accounted for by including fixed effects at the prison level.

In addition to the 2 nondichotomous variables are 21 dichotomous variables. Along with the total incarceration variable is a variable measuring whether the inmate was convicted of a violent offense. Another control variable measures whether the inmate was sent to prison due to a probation or parole violation. Seven variables measure demographic information about the inmate—whether they are female, African American, Latino/a, American Indian, Asian American, Hawaiian Pacific, or other race. There were not significantly different results for female prisoners, but this is likely because of the prison-level fixed effects. Most women are incarcerated in gender-segregated prisons, and therefore the "female" variable measures very little in terms of differences. Analyses run with and without the female variable are nearly identical. In addition, some of the race/ethnicity variables were insignificant, likely because of the relatively small number of Asian American, Hawaiian Pacific, and other race inmates. Analyses with and without those groups were also virtually identical. I have included the racial groups in part because it makes the interpretation of results easier (because the reference category is white inmates rather than white/Asian American/Hawaiian Pacific/other race inmates).

A set of variables measures socioeconomic status. There is a variable for whether the inmate is married. There are also four variables that measure economic status: whether the inmate had a court-appointed attorney (signaling

Table A.2 Full model estimations

	Visit in the Last Month	Received Mental Health Medication	Police Use of Force	Writeups	Solitary Confinement
Total incarcerations	−0.006***	0.000	0.001	0.003*	0.003***
	(.001)	(.001)	(.001)	(.001)	(.001)
Violent offender	0.021***	0.024***	−0.014*	0.100***	0.033***
	(.009)	(.006)	(.008)	(.009)	(.007)
Past drug use	0.008	0.010	0.037***	0.106***	0.037***
	(.010)	(.007)	(.010)	(.011)	(.008)
Probation or parole violation	−0.005	−0.012	0.013*	−0.024***	0.001
	(.008)	(.005)	(.008)	(.009)	(.006)
Court-appointed attorney	−0.171***	0.004	−0.012	0.018**	0.006
	(.009)	(.006)	(.008)	(.009)	(.007)
Experienced homelessness	−0.045***	−0.010	0.025**	0.026*	0.018*
	(.013)	(.009)	(.013)	(.014)	(.010)
Worked full time	0.023***	−0.012**	−0.010	−0.049***	−0.017***
	(.008)	(.006)	(.008)	(.009)	(.006)
Worked part time	0.021	−0.013	−0.013	−0.002	0.009
	(.014)	(.009)	(.013)	(.015)	(.011)
Highest grade attended	0.009***	0.001	−0.001	−0.004**	−0.003**
	(.002)	(.001)	(.002)	(.002)	(.001)

(continued)

Table A.2 *(continued)*

	Visit in the Last Month	Received Mental Health Medication	Police Use of Force	Writeups	Solitary Confinement
Married	0.102***	−0.003	0.004	−0.069***	−0.024***
	(.010)	(.007)	(.010)	(.011)	(.008)
African American	−0.064***	−0.027***	0.048***	0.056***	0.030***
	(.009)	(.006)	(.008)	(.010)	(.007)
Latino/a	−0.008	−0.027***	0.029***	−0.014	0.020**
	(.012)	(.008)	(.012)	(.013)	(.009)
American Indian	0.003	−0.009	0.048***	0.031*	−0.001
	(.017)	(.011)	(.016)	(.018)	(.013)
Asian American	−0.006	−0.013	0.043	0.001	−0.024
	(.040)	(.026)	(.038)	(.042)	(.031)
Hawaiian Pacific	−0.022	−0.030	0.017	−0.009	−0.011
	(.044)	(.029)	(.042)	(.047)	(.034)
Other race	0.026	−0.022	0.027	0.019	−0.009
	(.022)	(.014)	(.021)	(.023)	(.017)
Female	−0.146	−0.102	−0.241	−0.116	−0.043
	(.165)	(.109)	(.158)	(.176)	(.128)
Sexual assault before prison	−0.022*	0.026***	0.031***	0.049***	0.013
	(.013)	(.008)	(.012)	(.013)	(.010)

Depression	0.014	0.349***	0.025**	0.053***	−0.002
	(.011)	(.008)	(.011)	(.012)	(.009)
Manic depression, bipolar	−0.022	0.133***	0.031**	−0.003	0.017
	(.012)	(.009)	(.014)	(.015)	(.011)
Schizophrenia	−0.049***	0.204***	0.000	−0.015	0.015
	(.019)	(.013)	(.018)	(.020)	(.015)
Personality disorder	−0.024	0.065***	0.049***	0.065***	0.041***
	(.017)	(.011)	(.016)	(.018)	(.013)
Suicide attempt	−0.004	0.115***	−0.012	0.042***	0.027***
	(.012)	(.008)	(.011)	(.013)	(.009)
Number of observations	14,037	14,037	14,037	14,037	14,037
R-squared within	0.058	0.357	0.009	0.040	0.014
R-squared between	0.015	0.650	0.296	0.140	0.160
R-squared overall	0.034	0.379	0.022	0.054	0.024

*p<.1, **p<.05, ***p<.01

higher poverty), whether the inmate was working full time or part time, and whether the inmate had ever experienced homelessness. Finally, a set of variables measures mental health and substance abuse issues. One is a variable measuring whether the inmate has used drugs in the past. Two other variables measure whether the inmate was sexually assaulted before prison and whether the inmate had attempted suicide. The remaining mental health variables measure whether the inmate was diagnosed with specific mental health disorders: depression, manic depression/bipolar disorder, schizophrenia, and/or a personality disorder.

The dependent variables are all dichotomous, measuring whether the inmate received a visit in the last month, whether the inmate received mental health medication, whether the inmate was subject to police use of force during arrest (an admittedly rough proxy for use of force inside prison), whether the inmate was written up for any infraction, and whether the inmate was ever placed in solitary confinement. Table A.2 in the Appendix shows the results of the full model estimation from the 2004 Survey variables. The results for all 23 independent variables and all 5 dependent variables are reported in Table A.2 in the Appendix. Standard errors are shown in parentheses underneath the reported coefficients. Significance levels are designated by asterisks next to the coefficients.

Readers who have any questions about the analysis are welcome to contact me through the book's website at www.punishingthevulnerable.com.

References

Aday, L. 1994. "Health Status of Vulnerable Populations." *Annual Review of Public Health* 15:487–509.

Alexander, M. 2010. *The New Jim Crow*. New York: New Press.

Allyn, B. 2018. "Cities Planning Supervised Drug Injection Sites Fear Justice Department Reaction." *NPR*, July 12, 2018.

American Friends Service Committee. n.d. "Solitary Confinement Facts." Accessed July 14, 2017. https://www.afsc.org/resource/solitary-confinement-facts.

Anderson, M. 2015. "Why Are So Many Preschoolers Getting Suspended? The Frequency of Punishment Has a Troubling Racial Skew." *Atlantic*, December 7, 2015.

Andreas, P. 2013. *Smuggler Nation: How Illicit Trade Made America*. New York: Oxford University Press.

Applegate, B., F. Cullen, and B. Fisher. 1997. "Public Support for Correctional Treatment: The Continuing Appeal of the Rehabilitative Ideal." *Prison Journal* 77:237–58.

Arditti, J. 2005. "Families and Incarceration: An Ecological Approach." *Families in Society: The Journal of Contemporary Social Services* 86(2):251–60.

Arditti, J., and A. Few. 2006. "Mothers' Reentry into Family Life Following Incarceration." *Criminal Justice Policy Review* 17(1):103–23.

Arditti, J., J. Lambert-Shute, and K. Joest. 2003. "Sunday Morning at the Jail: Implications of Incarceration for Families and Children." *Family Relations: Interdisciplinary Journal of Applied Family Studies* 52(3):195–204.

Associated Press. 2010. "AP Impact: After 40 Years, $1 Trillion, US War on Drugs Has Failed to Meet Any of Its Goals." *Associated Press*, May 13, 2010.

Association of State Correctional Administrators. 2010. "ASCA Responses: Staff to Inmate Ratio Survey (June 2010)." Accessed July 12, 2017. https://www.prisonlegalnews.org/media/publications/ASCA%20Responses%20Staff%20to%20Inmate%20Ratio%20Survey%2C%20Association%20of%20State%20Correctional%20Administrators%2C%202010.pdf.

Avila, M. 2016. "18-Year-Old at Kent County Jail Found Hanging in Cell, Dies." WGVU Public Media, January 18, 2016. http://wgvunews.org/post/18-year-old-kent-county-jail-found-hanging-cell-dies.

Baer, D. 2016. "5 Countries Experimenting with Liberal Drug Laws." *Business Insider*, March 30, 2016. http://www.businessinsider.com/countries-experimenting-with-liberal-drug-laws-2016-3/#the-country-most-closely-associated-with-drug-use-and-drugged-out-tourists-is-probably-the-netherlands-1.

Banks, C. 2005. *Punishment in America: A Reference Handbook (Contemporary World Issues)*. Santa Barbara, CA: ABC-CLIO.

Barrilleaux, C., and E. Bernick. 2003. "Deservingness, Discretion, and the State Politics of Welfare Spending, 1990–96." *State Politics and Policy Quarterly* 3(1):1–22.

Bauer, Shane. 2012. "Solitary in Iran Nearly Broke Me. Then I Went Inside America's Prisons." *Mother Jones*, November/December 2012. http://www.motherjones.com/politics/2012/10/solitary-confinement-shane-bauer/.

Baumeister, R. 1997. *Evil: Inside Human Violence and Cruelty*. New York: Henry Holt and Company.

Baunach, P. 1985. *Mothers in Prison*. New Brunswick: Transaction.

Beccaria, Cesare. 1764. *On Crimes and Punishments*. Philadelphia: Seven Treasures.

Beckett, K. 1997. *Making Crime Pay: Law and Order in Contemporary American Politics*. Oxford: Oxford University.

Beckett, K., and B. Western. 2001. "Governing Social Marginality: Welfare, Incarceration, and the Transformation of State Policy." *Punishment and Society* 3:43–59.

Beckett, K., and T. Sasson. 2000. *The Politics of Injustice: Crime and Punishment in America*. Thousand Oaks, CA: Pine Forge.

Bell, Stephanie, and J. Globerman. 2014. "Rapid Response: What Is the Effectiveness of Supervised Injection Services?" Ontario HIV Treatment Network, May 2014. http://www.ohtn.on.ca/Pages/Knowledge-Exchange/Rapid-Responses/Documents/RR83-Supervised-Injection-Effectiveness.pdf.

Berg, M., and M. DeLisi. 2006. "The Correctional Melting Pot: Race, Ethnicity, Citizenship, and Prison Violence." *Journal of Criminal Justice* 34:631–42.

Berger, P., and T. Luckmann. 1966. *The Social Construction of Reality: A Treatise in the Sociology of Knowledge*. Garden City, NY: Anchor Books.

Bilefsky, D. 2018. "Legalizing Recreational Marijuana, Canada Begins a National Experiment." *New York Times*, October 17, 2018. https://www.nytimes.com/2018/10/17/world/canada/marijuana-pot-cannabis-legalization.html.

Binswanger, I., M. Stern, R. Deyo, P. Heagerty, A. Cheadle, J. Elmore, and T. Koepsell. 2007. "Release from Prison: A High Risk of Death for Former Inmates." *New England Journal of Medicine* 356:157–65.

Blackmon, D. 2008. *Slavery by Another Name: The Re-Enslavement of Black Americans from the Civil War to World War II*. New York: Anchor Books.

Blair, I., C. Judd, and K. Chapleau. 2004. "The Influence of Afrocentric Facial Features in Criminal Sentencing." *Psychological Science* 15(10):674–79.

Blalock, H. M. 1967. *Toward a Theory of Minority Group Relations*. New York: Wiley.

Blomberg, T., and K. Lucken. 2010. *American Penology: A History of Control*, 2nd ed. New Brunswick, NJ, and London, UK: Aldine Transaction.

Blow, C. 2015. "Black Dads Are Doing Best of All." *New York Times*, June 8, 2015.

Bobo, L., and D. Johnson. 2004. "A Taste for Punishment: Black and White Americans' Views on the Death Penalty and the War on Drugs." *Du Bois Review* 1(1):151–80.

Booth, M. 2015. *Cannabis: A History*. New York: Macmillan.

Bosworth, M., and E. Kaufman. 2011. "Foreigners in a Carceral Age: Immigration and Imprisonment in the United States." *Stanford Law and Policy Review* 22(2):429–54.

"The Bracero Program." 2003. *Rural Migration News* 9, no. 2 (April). https://migration.ucdavis.edu/rmn/more.php?id=10.

Bradbury, M., and J. Kellough. 2011. "Representative Bureaucracy: Assessing the Evidence of Active Representation." *American Review of Public Administration* 41:157–66.

Brehm, J., and S. Gates. 1997. *Working, Shirking and Sabotage: Bureaucratic Response to a Democratic Public*. Ann Arbor: University of Michigan Press.

Bronson, J., J. Stroop, S. Zimmer, and M. Berzofsky. 2017. "Drug Use, Dependence, and Abuse among State Prisoners and Jail Inmates, 2007–2009." U.S. Department of Justice, Office of Justice Programs, Bureau of Justice Statistics, June 2017. https://www.bjs.gov/content/pub/pdf/dudaspji0709.pdf.

Brown, G. 2010. "Autocastration and Autopenectomy as Surgical Self-Treatment in Incarcerated Persons with Gender Identity Disorder." *International Journal of Transgenderism* 1:31–39.

Brown, G., and E. McDuffie. 2009. "Health Care Policies Addressing Transgender Inmates in Prison Systems in the United States." *Journal of Correctional Health Care* 15(4):280–91.

Brown, R., and K. Severson. 2011. "Enlisting Prison Labor to Close Budget Gaps." *New York Times*, February 24, 2011.

Bump, P. 2016. "The Facts about Stop-and-Frisk in New York City." *Washington Post*, September 26, 2016.

Bureau of Justice Statistics. 2004. "Data Collection: Survey of Inmates in State Correctional Facilities (SISCF)." https://www.bjs.gov/index.cfm?ty=dcdetail&iid=275.

Bureau of Prisons. 2016. "Annual Determination of Average Cost of Incarceration." *Federal Register* 81(138):46957.

Calacal, C. 2016. "This Is How Many People Police Have Killed So Far in 2016." *ThinkProgress*, July 5, 2016. https://thinkprogress.org/this-is-how-many-people-police-have-killed-so-far-in-2016-7f1aec6b7098.

Calavita, K., and V. Jenness. 2013. "Inside the Pyramid of Disputes: Naming Problems and Filing Grievances in California Prisons." *Social Problems* 60:50–80.

Cao, L., J. Zhao, and S. Van Dine. 1997. "Prison Disciplinary Tickets: A Test of the Deprivation and Importation Models." *Journal of Criminal Justice* 25(2):103–13.

Carmon, I. 2016. "The Allegations Women Have Made against Donald Trump." *NBC News*, October 27, 2016. https://www.nbcnews.com/politics/2016-election/allegations-women-have-made-against-donald-trump-n665731.

Carson, E. 2015. "Prisoners in 2014." U.S. Department of Justice, Office of Justice Programs, Bureau of Justice Statistics, September 2015. https://www.bjs.gov/content/pub/pdf/p14.pdf.

Center for Constitutional Rights. 2012. "Stop and Frisk, the Human Impact: The Stories behind the Numbers, the Effects on Our Communities." July 2012. https://ccrjustice.org/sites/default/files/attach/2015/08/the-human-impact-report.pdf.

Centers for Disease Control and Prevention (CDC). 2014. "2014 National Diabetes Statistics Report." Accessed December 18, 2018. https://www.cdc.gov/diabetes/pdfs/data/2014-report-estimates-of-diabetes-and-its-burden-in-the-united-states.pdf.

Centers for Disease Control and Prevention (CDC). 2015a. "Economic Trends in Tobacco." Last modified May 4, 2018. https://www.cdc.gov/tobacco/data_statistics/fact_sheets/economics/econ_facts/index.htm.

Centers for Disease Control and Prevention (CDC). 2015b. "Heart Disease Facts." Last modified November 28, 2017. https://www.cdc.gov/heartdisease/facts.htm.

Centers for Disease Control and Prevention (CDC). 2016a. "Fact Sheets—Alcohol Use and Your Health." Last modified January 3, 2018. https://www.cdc.gov/alcohol/fact-sheets/alcohol-use.htm.

Centers for Disease Control and Prevention (CDC). 2016b. "High Blood Pressure Fact Sheet." Last modified June 16, 2016. https://www.cdc.gov/dhdsp/data_statistics/fact_sheets/fs_bloodpressure.htm.

Chang, B., S. Bakken, S. Brown, T. Houston, G. Kreps, R. Kukafka, C. Safran, and Z. Stavri. 2004. "Bridging the Digital Divide: Reaching Vulnerable Populations." *Journal of the American Medical Information Association* White Paper.

Chasmar, J. 2014. "Florida Pastors Face 60 Days in Jail for Feeding Homeless." *Washington Times*, November 4, 2014. https://www.washingtontimes.com/news/2014/nov/4/florida-pastors-face-60-days-in-jail-for-feeding-h/.

Chen, K., and J. Shapiro. 2007. "Does Prison Harden Inmates?" *American Law and Economics Review* 9(1):1–29.

Chomsky, A. 2014. *Undocumented: How Immigration Became Illegal*. Boston: Beacon.

Close, B., and P. Mason. 2006. "After the Traffic Stops: Officer Characteristics and Enforcement Actions." *Topics in Economic Analysis and Policy* 6:1–41.

Close, B., and P. Mason. 2007. "Searching for Efficient Enforcement: Officer Characteristics and Racially Biased Policing." *Review of Law and Economics* 3(2):263–321.

Coates, T. 2013. "How the Obama Administration Talks to Black America." *Atlantic*, May 20, 2013.

Comaroff, J., and J. Comaroff. 2016. *The Truth about Crime: Sovereignty, Knowledge, Social Order*. Chicago: University of Chicago Press.

Conlon, D., and N. Hiemstra. 2014. "Examining the Everyday Micro-Economies of Migrant Detention in the United States." *Geographica Helvetica* 69:335–44.

Crenshaw, K. 1989. "Demarginalizing the Intersection of Race and Sex: A Black Feminist Critique of Antidiscrimination Doctrine, Feminist Theory and Antiracist Politics." *University of Chicago Legal Forum* 140:139–67.

Cullen, F., B. Fisher, and B. Applegate. 2000. "Public Opinion about Punishment and Corrections." *Crime and Justice* 27:1–79.

Cullen, F., E. Latessa, B. Velmer, and L. Lombardo. 1993. "The Correctional Orientation of Prison Wardens: Is the Rehabilitative Ideal Supported?" *Criminology* 31:69–92.

Daley, K. 2017. "'We Are Completely Broken,' NOPD Detective Says of Struggling Homicide Unit." *Times-Picayune*, April 14, 2017.

Dallaire, D. 2007. "Incarcerated Mothers and Fathers: A Comparison of Risks for Children and Families." *Family Relations* 56(5):440–53.

Davis, A. 1998. "Masked Racism: Reflections on the Prison Industrial Complex." Article reprinted from Colorlines. *Indigenous Law Bulletin* 4(27):4.

Davis, A. 2003. *Are Prisons Obsolete?* New York: Seven Stories.

DelReal, J., and S. Sullivan. 2016. "Trump Calls Women's Claims of Sexual Advances 'Vicious' and 'Absolutely False.'" *Washington Post*, October 13, 2016.

Devine, P., and A. Elliot. 1995. "Are Racial Stereotypes Really Fading? The Princeton Trilogy Revisited." *Personality and Social Psychology Bulletin* 21(11):1139–50.

Dills, A., S. Goffard, and J. Miron. 2016. "Dose of Reality: The Effect of State Marijuana Legalizations." *Cato Institute*, no. 799.

Dodes, L., and Z. Dodes. 2014. *The Sober Truth, Debunking the Bad Science behind 12-Step Programs and the Rehab Industry*. Boston: Beacon.

Dow, M. 2004. *American Gulag: Inside U.S. Immigration Prisons*. Berkeley and Los Angeles: University of California Press.

Drago, F., R. Galbiati, and P. Vertova. 2008. "Prison Conditions and Recidivism." IZA Discussion Paper no. 3395, March 2008.

Eberhardt, J., P. Goff, P. Atiba, V. Purdie, and P. Davies. 2004. "Seeing Black: Race, Crime and Visual Processing." *Journal of Personality and Social Psychology* 87(6):876–93.

Economist. 2015a. "Police Fail to Make an Arrest in More Than a Third of the Nation's Killings." July 4, 2015.

Economist. 2015b. "This Land Is Our Land." November 28, 2015.

Edwards, B. 2017. "Mass. Sheriff Offers Free Inmate Labor to Build Trump's US-Mexico Border Wall." *Root*, January 5, 2017.

Eisinger, J. 2014. "Why Only One Top Banker Went to Jail for the Financial Crisis." *New York Times Magazine*, April 30, 2014. https://www.nytimes.com/2014/05/04/magazine/only-one-top-banker-jail-financial-crisis.html.

Engel, R. 2005. "Citizens' Perceptions of Distributive and Procedural Injustice during Traffic Stops with Police." *Journal of Research in Crime and Delinquency* 42(4):445–81.

Enos, S. 2001. *Mothering from the Inside: Parenting in a Women's Prison*. New York: SUNY Press.

Epp, C., S. Maynard-Moody, and D. Haider-Markel. 2014. *Pulled Over: How Police Stops Define Race and Citizenship*. Chicago: University of Chicago Press.

Escobar, M. 2016. *Captivity Beyond Prisons: Criminalization Experiences of Latina (Im)Migrants*. Austin: University of Texas Press.

Everett, R., and R. Wojtkiewicz. 2002. "Difference, Disparity, and Race/Ethnic Bias in Federal Sentencing." *Journal of Quantitative Criminology* 18(2):189–211.

Fahrenthold, D. 2016. "Trump Recorded Having Extremely Lewd Conversation about Women in 2005." *Washington Post*, October 8, 2016.

Fang, M. 2015. "Nearly 90 Percent of People Killed in Recent Drone Strikes Were Not the Target." *Huffpost*, October 15, 2015. https://www.huffingtonpost.com/entry/civilian-deaths-drone-strikes_us_561fafe2e4b028dd7ea6c4ff.

Fassin, D. 2013. *Enforcing Order: An Ethnography of Urban Policing*. Malden, MA: Polity.

Feldscher, K. 2017. "Trump Continues to Slam Lewis, Calls cities 'Burning and Crime Infested.'" *Washington Examiner*, January 14, 2017. https://www.washingtonexaminer.com/trump-continues-to-slam-lewis-calls-cities-burning-and-crime-infested.

Ferguson, R. 2014. *Inferno: An Anatomy of American Punishment*. Cambridge, MA: Harvard University Press.

Ferner, M., and N. Wing. 2016. "Here's How Many Cops Got Convicted of Murder Last Year for On-Duty Shootings." *Huffington Post*, January 13, 2016. http://www.huffingtonpost.com/entry/police-shooting-convictions_us_5695968ce4b086bc1cd5d0da.

Finn, M. 1995. "Disciplinary Incidents in Prison: Effects of Race, Economic Status, Urban Residence, Prior Imprisonment." *Journal of Offender Rehabilitation* 22(1–2):143–56.

Fisher, G. 2014. "The Drug War at 100." *Stanford Law School Blogs*, December 19, 2014. https://law.stanford.edu/2014/12/19/the-drug-war-at-100/.

Fisher, W., J. Geller, and J. Pandiani. 2009. "The Changing Role of the State Psychiatric Hospital." *Health Affairs* 28(3):676–84.

Flynn, C. 1996. "Normative Support for Corporal Punishment: Attitudes, Correlates, and Implications." *Aggression and Violent Behavior* 1(1):47–55.

Frank, R., and S. Glied. 2006. *Better but Not Well: Mental Health Policy in the United States since 1950*. Baltimore, MD: Johns Hopkins Press.

Frankovich, N. 2015. "Sunday Is for Football." *National Review*, January 31, 2015. http://www.nationalreview.com/article/397635/sunday-football-nicholas-frankovich.

Freudenberg, N. 2002. "Adverse Effects of US Jail and Prison Policies on the Health and Well-Being of Women of Color." *American Journal of Public Health* 92(12):1895–99.

Ganim, S. 2017. "Flint Water Crisis Likely the Cause of Deadly Legionnaires Outbreak." *CNN*, March 30, 2017. http://www.cnn.com/2017/03/30/health/legionnaires-disease-flint-water-crisis-study/index.html.

Garland, David. 2001. *The Culture of Control*. Urbana, IL: University of Chicago Press.

Gavula, A. 2014. "Pope Francis: Solitary Confinement Is Torture." American Civil Liberties Union of Ohio, November 12, 2014. http://www.acluohio.org/archives/blog-posts/solitary-confinement-is-torture.

Gibson, L., and C. Hensley. 2013. "The Social Construction of Sexuality in Prison." *Prison Journal* 93, no. 3.

Glaze, L., and L. Maruschak. 2008. "Parents in Prison and Their Minor Children." U.S. Department of Justice, Office of Justice Programs, Bureau of Justice Statistics.

Goode, E., and N. Ben-Yehuda. 1994. "Moral Panics: Culture, Politics, and Social Construction." *Annual Review of Sociology* 20:149–71.

Goode, E., and N. Ben-Yehuda. 2009. *Moral Panics: The Social Construction of Deviance*, 2nd ed. West Sussex, UK: Blackwell.

Gordon, E. 2018. "What's the Evidence That Supervised Drug Injection Sites Save Lives?" *NPR*, September 7, 2018. https://www.npr.org/sections/health-shots/2018/09/07/645609248/whats-the-evidence-that-supervised-drug-injection-sites-save-lives.

Goulding, D., G. Hall, and B. Steels. 2008. "Restorative Prisons: Towards Radical Prison Reform." *Current Issues in Criminal Justice* 20(2):231–45.

Graham, S., and B. Lowery. 2004. "Priming Unconscious Racial Stereotypes about Adolescent Offenders." *Law and Human Behavior* 28(5):483–504.

Gramlich, J. 2017. "Most Violent and Property Crimes in the U.S. Go Unsolved." *Pew Research Center*, March 1, 2017. http://www.pewresearch.org/fact-tank/2017/03/01/most-violent-and-property-crimes-in-the-u-s-go-unsolved/.

Grant, R. 2013. "VC Firm Hopes for High Returns with Fund for Marijuana." *Venture Beat*, June 5, 2013. https://venturebeat.com/2013/06/05/vc-firm-hopes-for-high-returns-with-1-million-fund-for-marijuana/.

Grassian, S. 2006. "Psychiatric Effects of Solitary Confinement." *Washington University Journal of Law and Policy* 22(1):325–83.

Green, E. 2016. "It's Hard to Go to Church." *Atlantic*, August 23, 2016. https://www.theatlantic.com/politics/archive/2016/08/religious-participation-survey/496940/.

Greenberg, D., and V. West. 2001. "State Prison Populations and Their Growth, 1971–1991." *Criminology* 39:615–53.

Greenberg, G., and R. Rosenheck. 2008. "Jail Incarceration, Homelessness, and Mental Health: A National Study." *Psychiatric Service* 59(2):170–77.

Greenwald, A., D. McGhee, and J. Schwartz. 1998. "Measuring Individual Differences in Implicit Cognition: The Implicit Association Test." *Journal of Personality and Social Psychology* 74(6):1465–80.

Greenwald, G. 2009. "Drug Decriminalization in Portugal: Lessons for Creating Fair and Successful Drug Policies." Cato Institute. Accessed December 18, 2018. http://www.midcoastforum.org/wp-content/uploads/greenwald_whitepaper.pdf.

Grillo, I. 2012. *El Narco: Inside Mexico's Criminal Insurgency.* New York: Bloomsbury.

Hagan, J., R. Levi, and R. Dinovitzer. 2008. "The Symbolic Violence of the Crime-Immigration Nexus: Migrant Mythologies in the Americas." *Criminology and Public Policy* 7(1):95–112.

Hager, E. 2015. "Job Opening: No Training, Low Pay, High Turnover." The Marshall Project, June 5, 2015. https://www.themarshallproject.org/2015/06/05/job-opening-no-training-low-pay-high-turnover#.uc5tRcIpi.

Haley, S. 2016. *No Mercy Here: Gender, Punishment and the Making of Jim Crow Modernity.* Chapel Hill: University of North Carolina Press.

Hamblin, J. 2013. "Why We Took Cocaine out of Soda." *Atlantic*, January 31, 2013.

Hannah, A., and D. Mallinson. 2017. "How to Tell Whether Your State Is Ripe for Legalizing Medical Marijuana." *Newsweek*, October 26, 2017.

Hardman, R. 2015. "New Yale Survey Estimates Nearly 100,000 in Solitary Confinement in the U.S." WNPR All Things Considered, September 2, 2015.

Harris, A. 2016. *A Pound of Flesh: Monetary Sanctions as Punishment for the Poor.* New York: Russell Sage Foundation.

Hassan, M. 2017. "US Planning to Return 5,000 Somali Migrants to Their Homeland." *VOA News*, April 18, 2017.

Heaney, M., and F. Rojas. 2011. "The Partisan Dynamics of Contention: Demobilization of the Antiwar Movement in the United States, 2007–2009." *Mobilization: An International Journal* 16(1):45–64.

Heinzmann, D. 2016. "As Chicago Killings Surge, the Unsolved Cases Pile Up." *Chicago Tribune*, September 9, 2016.

Henderson, M., F. Cullen, L. Cao, S. Browning, and R. Kopache. 1997. "The Impact of Race on Perceptions of Criminal Injustice." *Journal of Criminal Justice* 25(6):447–62.

Hennessy-Fiske, M. 2015. "Paid $1 to $3 a Day, Unauthorized Immigrants Keep Family Detention Centers Running." *Los Angeles Times*, August 3, 2015.

Hess, A. 2018. "California Is Paying Inmates $1 an Hour to Fight Wildfires." *CNBC*, November 12, 2018. https://www.cnbc.com/2018/08/14/california-is-paying-inmates-1-an-hour-to-fight-wildfires.html.

Hewitt, J., E. Poole, and R. Regoli. 1984. "Research Note: Self-Reported and Observed Rule-Breaking in Prison: A Look at Disciplinary Response." *Justice Quarterly* 1:437–447.

Hill, M. 2016. *Nobody: Casualties of America's War on the Vulnerable, from Ferguson to Flint and Beyond.* New York: Atria.

Hinton, E. 2016. *From the War on Poverty to the War on Crime: The Making of Mass Incarceration in America.* Cambridge, MA: Harvard University Press.

Howard, C., T. Winfree, L. Mays, M. Stohr, and D. Clason. 1994. "Processing Inmate Disciplinary Infractions in a Federal Correctional Institution: Legal and Extralegal Correlates of Prison-Based Legal Decisions." *Prison Journal* 74(5):5–31.

Human Rights Watch. 2008. "Targeting Blacks: Drug Law Enforcement and Race in the United States." Accessed April 3, 2012. http://www.hrw.org/sites/default/files/reports/us0508_1.pdf.

Human Rights Watch. 2009. "Decades of Disparity: Drug Arrests and Race in the United States." March 2, 2009. https://www.hrw.org/report/2009/03/02/decades-disparity/drug-arrests-and-race-united-states.

Huntington, S. 2009. "The Hispanic Challenge." *Foreign Policy*, October 28, 2009.

Hurwitz, J., and M. Peffley. 1997. "Public Perceptions of Race and Crime: The Role of Racial Stereotypes." *American Journal of Political Science* 41:374–401.

Ingraham, C. 2015. "The U.S. Has More Jails Than Colleges. Here's a Map of Where Those Prisoners Live." *Washington Post*, January 6, 2015.

Ingraham, C. 2016. "The Marijuana Industry Created More Than 18,000 New Jobs in Colorado Last Year." *Washington Post*, October 27, 2016.

Ingraham, C. 2017. "Officer Who Shot Philando Castile Said Smell of Marijuana Made Him Fear for His Life." *Washington Post*, June 21, 2017.

Jacobs, D., and A. Jackson. 2010. "On the Politics of Imprisonments: A Review of Systematic Findings." *Annual Review of Law and Social Science* 6:129–48.

Jacobs, D., and J. Carmichael. 2001. "The Politics of Punishment across Time and Space: A Pooled Time-Series Analysis of Imprisonment Rates." *Social Forces* 80:61–91.

Jacobs, D., and R. Helms. 1996. "Toward a Political Model of Incarceration: A Time Series Examination of Multiple Explanations for Prison Admission Rates." *American Journal of Sociology* 102:323–57.

James, D., and L. Glaze. 2006. "Mental Health Problems of Prison and Jail Inmates." U.S. Department of Justice, Office of Justice Programs, Bureau of Justice Statistics.

Jedra, C. 2015. "Forty-Four Charged in Baltimore Jail Scandal; Here's How Cases Ended." *Baltimore Sun*, July 11, 2015.

Jiang, S., and M. Fisher-Giorlando. 2002. "Inmate Misconduct: A Test of the Deprivation, Importation and Situational Models." *Prison Journal* 82:335–58.

Johnson, C., and B. Chappell. 2014. "Solitary Confinement Costs $78K per Inmate and Should Be Curbed, Critics Say." *NPR*, February 25, 2014. http://www.npr.org/blogs/thetwoway/2014/02/25/282672593/solitary-confinement-costs-78k-per-inmate-and-should-be-curbed-critics-say.

Jolls, C., and C. Sunstein. 2006. "The Law of Implicit Bias." *California Law Review* 94(4):969–96.

Jones, B. 2011. "BP Profits Hit $5.3 Billion, Year on from Gulf Spill." *CNN*, July 26, 2011. http://edition.cnn.com/2011/BUSINESS/07/26/bp.profits.dudley/index.html.

Jurik, N. 1985. "Individual and Organizational Determinants of Correctional Officer Attitudes toward Inmates." *Criminology* 23(3):523–39.

Justice Policy Institute. 2011. "Factsheet: Sentencing." April 2011. http://www.justicepolicy.org/uploads/justicepolicy/documents/sentencing.pdf.

Kaczynski, A., and M. Apper. 2016. "Donald Trump Thinks Men Who Change Diapers Are Acting 'Like the Wife.'" *BuzzFeed News*, April 24, 2016.

Kaeble, D., L. Glaze, A. Tsoutis, and T. Minton. 2015. "Correctional Population in the United States, 2014." U.S. Department of Justice, Office of Justice Programs, Bureau of Justice Statistics. Revised January 21, 2016. http://www.bjs.gov/content/pub/pdf/cpus14.pdf.

Kahneman, D. 2003. "A Perspective on Judgment and Choice: Mapping Bounded Rationality." *American Psychologist* 58(9):697–720.

Kahneman, D. 2011. *Thinking, Fast and Slow.* New York: Farrar, Straus and Giroux.

Kang, C. 2017. "Court Strikes Obama-Era Rule Capping Cost of Phone Calls from Prison." *New York Times*, June 13, 2017.

Karnowski, S., and A. Forliti. 2017. "Newly-Released Dashcam Video Shows Minnesota Officer Shooting Philando Castile." *Time*, June 20, 2017.

Kaste, M. 2015. "How Many Crimes Do Your Police 'Clear'? Now You Can Find Out." *NPR*, March 30, 2015. http://www.npr.org/2015/03/30/395799413/how-many-crimes-do-your-police-clear-now-you-can-find-out.

Kautt, P. 2009. "Heuristic Influences over Offense Seriousness Calculations: A Multilevel Investigation of Racial Disparity under Sentencing Guidelines." *Punishment and Society* 11(2):191–218.

Keiser, L., and J. Soss. 1998. "With Good Cause: Bureaucratic Discretion and the Politics of Child Support Enforcement." *American Journal of Political Science* 42(4):1133–56.

Key, V. O. 1949. *Southern Politics: In State and Nation*. New York: Vintage

Kincaid, J. 2009. "WeedMaps Wants to Be a Yelp for Cannabis Clubs." *TechCrunch*, March 12, 2009. https://techcrunch.com/2009/03/12/weedmaps-wants-to-be-a-yelp-for-cannabis-clubs/.

Kjellstrand, J., and J. Eddy. 2011. "Parental Incarceration during Childhood, Family Context, and Youth Problem Behavior across Adolescence." *Journal of Offender Rehabilitation* 50(1):18–36.

Klapper, B., D. Butler, and D. Reichmann. 2017. "Trump Says Torture Works as His Government Readies a Review." *AP News*, January 26, 2017.

Kubrin, C., S. Zatz, and R. Martinez. 2012. *Punishing Immigrants: Policy, Politics, and Injustice*. New York: New York University Press.

Lamb, H. Richard, and Leona L. Bachrach. 2001. "Some Perspectives on Deinstitutionalization." *Psychiatric Services* 52(8):1039–45.

Lamb, H. Richard, and Linda E. Weinberger. 1998. "Persons with Severe Mental Illness in Jails and Prisons: A Review." *Psychiatric Services* 49(4):483–92.

Lartey, J. 2015. "By the Numbers: US Police Kill More in Days Than Other Countries Do in Years." *Guardian*, June 9, 2015. https://www.theguardian.com/us-news/2015/jun/09/the-counted-police-killings-us-vs-other-countries.

Law, V. 2012. *Resistance Behind Bars: The Struggles of Incarcerated Women*. Oakland, CA: PM Press.

Lee, M., and R. Martinez. 2009. "Immigration Reduces Crime: An Emerging Scholarly Consensus." *Immigration, Crime and Justice* 13:3–16.

Leerkes, A., and D. Broeders. 2010. "A Case of Mixed Motives?: Formal and Informal Functions of Administrative Immigration Detention." *British Journal of Criminology* 50(5):830–50.

Lerman, A. 2014. *The Modern Prison Paradox*. New York: Cambridge University Press.

Liebler, C. 2010. "Me(di)a Culpa? The 'Missing White Woman Syndrome' and Media Self-critique." *Communication, Culture and Critique* 3(4):549–65.

Liebling, A. 2000. "Prison Officers, Policing and the Use of Discretion." *Theoretical Criminology* 4(3):333–57.

Lipsky, M. 1980. *Street-Level Bureaucracy*. New York: Russell Sage Foundation.

Liptak, A. 2011. "Justices, 5-4, Tell California to Cut Prisoner Population." *New York Times*, May 23, 2011.

LoBianco, T. 2016. "Report: Aide Says Nixon's War on Drugs Targeted Blacks, Hippies." *CNN*, March 24, 2016. https://www.cnn.com/2016/03/23/politics/john-ehrlichman-richard-nixon-drug-war-blacks-hippie/index.html.

Lommel, J. 2004. "Turning Around Turnover." *Corrections Today* 66(5):54–58.

Lopez, G. 2015. "You Could Fit 19 Solitary Confinement Cells in a Typical 1-Bedroom Apartment." *Vox*, June 11, 2015. https://www.vox.com/2015/6/11/8765977/solitary-confinement-cells-small.

Lopez, G. 2016. "We're in the Midst of the Biggest Prison Strike in US History." *Vox*, October 19, 2016. https://www.vox.com/identities/2016/10/19/13306178/prison-strike-protests-attica.

Loss, S., T. Will, and P. Mara. 2013. "The Impact of Free-Ranging Domestic Cats on Wildlife of the United States." *Nature Communications* 4:1–7.

Lovell, D., and R. Jemelka. 1996. "When Inmates Misbehave: The Costs of Discipline." *Prison Journal* 76:165–79.

MacAlister, T. 2012. "BP's $25bn Annual Profit Sees Confidence and Dividends Soar." *Guardian*, February 7, 2012. https://www.theguardian.com/business/2012/feb/07/bp-announces-25bn-annual-profit.

Macias-Rojas, P. 2016. *From Deportation to Prison: The Politics of Immigration Enforcement in Post-Civil Rights America*. New York: New York University Press.

Mack, J. 2017a. "See Number of Medical Marijuana Cardholders in Your Michigan County." *MLive*, July 24, 2017. http://www.mlive.com/news/index.ssf/2017/07/see_number_of_medical_marijuan.html.

Mack, J. 2017b. "Marijuana Is 9% of All Michigan Arrests, and Other Facts on Marijuana Arrests." *MLive*, July 31, 2017. http://www.mlive.com/news/index.ssf/2017/07/marijuana_is_9_of_all_michigan.html.

Mack, J. 2017c. "Michigan Announces New Fees, Transition Rules for Medical Marijuana Businesses." *MLive*, November 17, 2017. http://www.mlive.com/news/index.ssf/2017/11/michigan_announces_new_fees_tr.html.

Martinez, O. 2013. *The Beast: Riding the Rails and Dodging Narcos on the Migrant Trail*. New York: Verso Books.

Martinez, R., J. Stowell, and M. Lee. 2010. "Immigration and Crime in an Era of Transformation: A Longitudinal Analysis of Homicides in San Diego Neighborhoods, 1980–2000." *Criminology* 48(3):797–829.

Martinez, R., R. Rosenfeld, and D. Mares. 2009. "Social Disorganization, Drug Market Activity, and Neighborhood Violent Crime." *Urban Affairs Review* 43(6):846–74.

Maruschak, L., M. Berzofsky, and J. Unangst. 2015. "Medical Problems of State and Federal Prisoners and Jail Inmates, 2011–12." U.S. Department of Justice, Office of Justice Programs, Bureau of Justice Statistics.

Mathiesen, T. 1986. "The Politics of Abolition." *Contemporary Crises* 10:81–94.

Mauer, M., and R. King. 2007. "Uneven Justice: State Rates of Incarceration by Race and Ethnicity." The Sentencing Project, July 2007. http://www.sentencingproject.org/wp-content/uploads/2016/01/Uneven-Justice-State-Rates-of-Incarceration-by-Race-and-Ethnicity.pdf.

Maynard-Moody, S., and M. Musheno. 2003. *Cops, Teachers, Counselors: Stories from the Front Lines of Public Service*. Ann Arbor: University of Michigan Press.

McCarthy, J. 2016. "One in Eight U.S. Adults Say They Smoke Marijuana." *Gallup*, August 8, 2016. http://www.gallup.com/poll/194195/adults-say-smoke-marijuana.aspx.

McCorkel, J. 2013. *Breaking Women: Gender, Race and the New Politics of Imprisonment*. New York: New York University Press.

McCoy, T. 2014. "The 'Unverifiable' Legacy of Chris Kyle, the Deadliest Sniper in American History." *Washington Post*, July 30, 2014.

McDonough, K. 2013. "Long-Term Study Debunks Myth of the 'Crack Baby.'" *Salon*, July 23, 2013. http://www.salon.com/2013/07/23/longterm_study_debunks_myth_of_the_crack_baby/.

McGirr, L. 2016. *The War on Alcohol: Prohibition and the Rise of the American State*. New York: W. W. Norton.

McKenna, T. 1999. *Food of the Gods: The Search for the Original Tree of Knowledge*. New York: Random House.

McNiel, D., R. Binder, and J. Robinson. 2005. "Incarceration Associated with Homelessness, Mental Disorder and Co-occurring Substance Abuse." *Psychiatric Services* 56(7):840–46.

Mears, D., X. Wang, C. Hay, and W. Bales. 2008. "Social Ecology and Recidivism: Implications for Prisoner Reentry." *Criminology* 46(2):301–40.

Mechanic, D., and J. Tanner. 2007. "Vulnerable People, Groups, and Populations: Societal View." *Health Affairs* 26(5):1220–30.

Meier, K., and J. Nicholson-Crotty. 2006. "Gender, Representative Bureaucracy, and Law Enforcement: The Case of Sexual Assault." *Public Administration Review* 66(6):850–60.

Metraux, S., and D. Culhane. 2004. "Homeless Shelter Use and Reincarceration Following Prison Release." *Criminology and Public Policy* 3(2):139–60.

Metraux, S., and D. Culhane. 2006. "Recent Incarceration History among a Sheltered Homeless Population." *Crime and Delinquency* 52(3):504–17.

Milman, O. 2018. "Deepwater Horizon Disaster Altered Building Blocks of Ocean Life." *Guardian*, June 28, 2018. https://www.theguardian.com/environment/2018/jun/28/bp-deepwater-horizon-oil-spill-report.

Mitchell, S. 1988. *Tao Te Ching*. New York: Harper Perennial.

Moore, J. 2016. "Donald Trump vs. Hillary Clinton in Final U.S. Presidential Debate: Full Transcript." *Newsweek*, October 20, 2016. http://www.newsweek.com/donald-trump-hillary-clinton-us-presidential-debate-full-transcript-511916.

Morin, M. 2013. "Illegal Drug Prices Falling as Purity, Potency Rise, Research Finds." *Los Angeles Times*, October 1, 2013.

Muhammad, K. 2010. *The Condemnation of Blackness: Race, Crime and the Making of Modern Urban America*. Cambridge, MA: Harvard University Press.

Mustard, D. 2001. "Racial, Ethnic, and Gender Disparities in Sentencing: Evidence from the U.S. Federal Courts." *Journal of Law and Economics* 44(1):285–314.

National Association of State Budget Officers. 2011. "2010 State Expenditure Report." Accessed December 18, 2018. https://higherlogicdownload.s3.amazonaws.com/NASBO/9d2d2db1-c943-4f1b-b750-0fca152d64c2/UploadedImages/SER%20Archive/2010%20State%20Expenditure%20Report.pdf.

Neff, J. 2018. "Senators Take Aim at Bail Industry Backers." The Marshall Project, August 6, 2018. https://www.themarshallproject.org/2018/08/06/senators-take-aim-at-bail-industry-backers?ref=collections.

New York Civil Liberties Union (NYCLU). 2017. "Stop-and-Frisk Data." Last modified April 2, 2018. https://www.nyclu.org/en/stop-and-frisk-data.

New York Times Editorial Board. 2013. "Mental Illness in California Prisons." *New York Times*, April 10, 2013.

Ngai, M. 2004. *Impossible Subjects: Illegal Immigrants and the Making of Modern America*. Princeton: Princeton University Press.

Nicholson-Crotty, J., and S. Nicholson-Crotty. 2004. "Social Construction and Policy Implementation: Inmate Health as a Public Health Issue." *Social Science Quarterly* 85(2):240–56.

Norman, B. 2017. "Arnold Abbott Vows to Continue Feeding Homeless in Fort Lauderdale Despite Dwindling Funds." *ABC Local News*, 10, April 11, 2017. https://www.local10.com/news/local/fort-lauderdale/arnold-abbott-vows-to-continue-feeding-homeless-in-fort-lauderdale-despite-dwindling-funds.

Nurse, J., P. Woodcock, and J. Ormsby. 2003. "Influence of Environmental Factors on Mental Health within Prisons: Focus Group Study." *Primary Care* 327:1–5.

Obama, Barack. 2006. *The Audacity of Hope: Thoughts on Reclaiming the American Dream*. New York: Crown.

O'Connor, I. 2014. "Visuals Sealed Adrian Peterson's Fate." *ESPN*, November 18, 2014. http://www.espn.com/nfl/story/_/id/11897549/minnesota-vikings-rb-adrian-peterson-was-done-horrific-visuals-child-abuse-case.

Olson, Jeremiah. 2016. "Race and Punishment in American Prisons." *Journal of Public Administration Research and Theory* 26(4):758–68.

Osgood, D., E. Foster, and M. Courtney. 2010. "Vulnerable Populations and the Transition to Adulthood." *The Future of Children* 20(1):209–29.

Palsha, R. 2016. "Pregnant in Prison: What Happens to a Baby Born in Prison." NBC2 KTUU, October 27, 2016. http://www.ktuu.com/content/news/Pregnant-in-prison-What-happens-to-a-baby-born-in-prison--398959951.html.

Pascoe, P. 2010. *What Comes Naturally: Miscegenation Law and the Making of Race in America*. New York: Oxford University Press.

Patrick, M., P. Wightman, R. Schoeni, and J. Schulenberg. 2012. "Socioeconomic Status and Substance Use among Adults: A Comparison across Constructs and Drugs." *Journal of Studies on Alcohol and Drugs* 73(5):772–82.

Pauly, M. 2017. "How a Private Prison Company Used Detained Immigrants for Free Labor." *Mother Jones*, April 3, 2017.

Peffley, M., and J. Hurwitz. 2010. *Justice in America: The Separate Realities of Blacks and Whites*. Cambridge: Cambridge University Press.

Peffley, M., J. Hurwitz, and P. Sniderman. 1997. "Racial Stereotypes and Whites' Political Views of Blacks in the Context of Welfare and Crime." *American Journal of Political Science* 41(1):30–60.

Pelissero, T. 2014. "Adrian Peterson: 'I Won't Ever Use a Switch Again.'" *USA Today*, November 20, 2014. https://www.usatoday.com/story/sports/nfl/vikings/2014/11/20/adrian-peterson-roger-goodell-child-abuse-switch-minnesota-vikings/70025476/.

Penrose, L. 1939. "Mental Disease and Crime: Outline of a Comparative Study of European Statistics." *British Journal of Medical Psychology* 18(1):1–15.

Peterson, R., and L. Krivo. 2005. "Macrostructural Analyses of Race, Ethnicity, and Violent Crime: Recent Lessons and New Directions for Research." *Annual Review of Sociology* 31:331–56.

Pew Research Center. 2017. "Changing Attitudes on Gay Marriage." June 26, 2017. http://www.pewforum.org/fact-sheet/changing-attitudes-on-gay-marriage/.

Philliber, S. 1987. "Thy Brother's Keeper: A Review of the Literature on Correctional Officers." *Justice Quarterly* 4(1):9–37.

Phillips, A. 2017. "'They're rapists.' President Trump's Campaign Launch Speech Two Years Later, Annotated." *The Washington Post*, June 16, 2017. https://www.washingtonpost.com/news/the-fix/wp/2017/06/16/theyre-rapists-presidents-trump-campaign-launch-speech-two-years-later-annotated/?utm_term=.1496cd6fc8b9.

Phippen, J. 2016. "Australia's Controversial Migration Policy." *Atlantic*, April 29, 2016.

Pilkington, E. 2018. "Major Prison Strike Spreads Across US and Canada as Inmates Refuse Food." *Guardian*, August 23, 2018.https://www.theguardian.com/us-news/2018/aug/23/prison-strike-us-canada-forced-labor-protest-activism.

Poole, E., and R. Regoli. 1980. "Race, Institutional Rule Breaking and Disciplinary Response: A Study of Discretionary Decision Making in Prison." *Law and Society Review* 14(4):931–46.

Press Release. 2018. "Press Release: National Prisoners Strike August 21st–September 9th 2018." https://www.dropbox.com/s/r5cr546jlscgkhj/Prison%20Strike.pdf?dl=0.

Prison Policy Initiative. 2017. "Section III: The Prison Economy." Accessed July 13, 2017. https://www.prisonpolicy.org/prisonindex/prisonlabor.html.

Prison Research Education Action Project. 1976. "Instead of Prisons." Syracuse, Fay Knopp. https://www.prisonpolicy.org/scans/instead_of_prisons/.

Quillian, L., and D. Pager. 2001. "Black Neighbors, Higher Crime? The Role of Racial Stereotypes in Evaluations of Neighborhood Crime." *American Journal of Sociology* 107(3):717–67.

Rafter, N. 1983. "Prisons for Women, 1790–1980." *Crime and Justice* 5(1):29–181.

RAINN (Rape, Abuse and Incest National Network). 2017. "The Criminal Justice System: Statistics." Accessed July 17, 2017. https://www.rainn.org/statistics/criminal-justice-system.

Reaves, B. 2013. "Felony Defendants in Large Urban Counties, 2009, Statistical Tables." U.S. Department of Justice, Office of Justice Programs, Bureau of Justice Statistics, December 2013. https://www.bjs.gov/content/pub/pdf/fdluc09.pdf.

Reinarman, C., H. Nunber, F. Lanthier, and T. Heddleston. 2011. "Who Are Medical Marijuana Patients? Population Characteristics from Nine California Assessment Clinics." *Journal of Psychoactive Drugs* 43(2):128–35

Reiter, K. 2012. "Parole, Snitch or Die: California's Supermax Prisons and Prisoners, 1997–2007." *Punishment and Society* 14(5):530–63.

Richie, B. 2012. *Arrested Justice: Black Women, Violence, and America's Prison Nation*. New York: New York University Press.

Ridgeway, G. 2006. "Assessing the Effect of Race Bias in Post-traffic Stop Outcomes Using Propensity Scores." *Journal of Quantitative Criminology* 22(1):1–29.

Riley, R. 2014. "13 Mainstream Corporations Benefiting from the Prison Industrial Complex." *Atlanta Black Star*, October 10, 2014.

Roberts, D. 1997. *Killing the Black Body: Race, Reproduction, and the Meaning of Liberty*. New York: Vintage Books.

Robinson, N. 2016. "Bill Clinton, Superpredator." *Jacobin*, September 8, 2016. https://www.jacobinmag.com/2016/09/bill-clinton-hillary-superpredators-crime-welfare-african-americans/.

Rodriguez, M. 2007. "More Than Whiteness: Comparative Perspectives on Mexican American Citizenship from Law and History." *Berkeley La Raza Law Journal* 18(6):79–86.

Roelofs, T. 2016. "The Price of Michigan's Cash Bail System." *Bridge Magazine*, November 15, 2016. http://www.mlive.com/news/index.ssf/2016/11/the_price_of_michigans_cash_ba.html.

Rothman, L. 2015. "When Spousal Rape First Became a Crime in the U.S." *Time*, July 28, 2015.

Rudavsky, S. 2016. "An Indiana Town Recovering from 190 HIV Cases." *Indy Star*, April 8, 2016. https://www.indystar.com/story/news/2016/04/08/year-after-hiv-outbreak-austin-still-community-recovery/82133598/.

Schaufeli, W., and M. Peeters. 2000. "Job Stress and Burnout among Correctional Officers: A Literature Review." *International Journal of Stress Management* 7(1):19–48.

Schneider, A., and H. Ingram. 1993. "Social Construction of Target Populations: Implications for Politics and Policy." *American Political Science Review* 87(2):334–47.

Schram, S., J. Soss, R. Fording, and L. Houser. 2009. "Deciding to Discipline: A Multi-Method Study of Race, Choice, and Punishment at the Frontlines of Welfare Reform." *American Sociological Review* 74(3):398–422.

Scott, E. 2016. "Black Lives Matter Protesters Confront Clinton at Fundraiser." CNN, February 25, 2016. https://www.cnn.com/2016/02/25/politics/hillary-clinton-black-lives-matter-whichhillary/index.html.

Segura, L. 2012. "In Sentencing Criminals, Is Norway Too Soft? Or Are We Too Harsh?" *Nation*, August 28, 2012. https://www.thenation.com/article/sentencing-criminals-norway-too-soft-or-are-we-too-harsh/.

Shoichet, C., and A. Kessler. 2016. "Trump's Plan to Deport Criminals Won't Be Easy. Just Ask Obama." CNN, November 11, 2016. http://www.cnn.com/2016/11/29/politics/trump-obama-criminal-deportations/index.html.

Simon, H., G. Dantzig, R. Hogarth, C. Plott, H. Raiffa, H. Schelling, K. Shepsle, R. Thaler, A. Tversky, and S. Winter. 1987. "Decision Making and Problem Solving." *Interfaces* 17(5):11–31.

Simon, J. 2007. *Governing through Crime: How the War on Crime Transformed American Democracy and Created a Culture of Fear.* New York: Oxford University Press.

Smith, K. 2004. "The Politics of Punishment: A Political Model of Punishment." *Journal of Politics* 66:925–38.

Smith, M. 2017. "The Dangerous Myth of the 'Missing Black Father.'" *Washington Post*, January 10, 2017.

Solitary Watch. 2011. "Fact Sheet: The High Cost of Solitary Confinement." Accessed July 14, 2017. http://solitarywatch.com/wp-content/uploads/2011/06/fact-sheet-the-high-cost-of-solitary-confinement.pdf.

Sorensen, J., and D. Stemen. 2002. "The Effect of State Sentencing Policies on Incarceration Rates." *Crime and Delinquency* 48:456–75.

Soss, J., R. Fording, and S. Schram. 2008. "The Color of Devolution: Race, Federalism, and the Politics of Social Control." *American Journal of Political Science* 52(3):536–53.

Soss, J., R. Fording, and S. Schram. 2011. *Disciplining the Poor: Neoliberal Paternalism and the Persistent Power of Race*. Chicago: University of Chicago Press.

St. John, P. 2015. "California Regains Control over Healthcare at Folsom Prison." *Los Angeles Times*, July 13, 2015.

Stack, L. 2016. "Donald Trump Featured Paula Jones and 2 Other Women Who Accused Bill Clinton of Sexual Assault." *New York Times*, October 9, 2016.

Steffensmeier, D., J. Ulmer, and J. Kramer. 1998. "The Interaction of Race, Gender, and Age in Criminal Sentencing: The Punishment Cost of Being Young, Black and Male." *Criminology* 36(4):763–98.

Stephan, J. 2008. "Census of State and Federal Correctional Facilities, 2005." U.S. Department of Justice, Office of Justice Programs, Bureau of Justice Statistics, October 2008. https://bjs.gov/content/pub/pdf/csfcf05.pdf.

Straus, M., and J. Stewart. 1999. "Corporal Punishment by American Parents: National Data on Prevalence, Chronicity, Severity, and Duration, in Relation to Child and Family Characteristics." *Clinical Child and Family Psychology Review* 2(2):55–70.

Stucky, T., K. Heimer, and J. Lang. 2005. "Partisan Politics, Electoral Competition and Imprisonment: An Analysis of States over Time." *Criminology* 43(1):211–48.

Substance Abuse and Mental Health Services Administration (SAMSHA). 2010. "Results from the 2009 National Survey on Drug Use and Health: Volume 1. Summary of National Findings." Office of Applied Studies, NSDUH Series H-38A, HHS Publication No. SMA 10-4586 Findings. Rockville, MA.

Theobald, N., and D. Haider-Markel. 2008. "Race, Bureaucracy and Symbolic Representation: Interactions between Citizens and Police." *Journal of Public Administration Research and Theory* 19:409–26.

Thompson, H. 2011. "Criminalizing Kids: The Overlooked Reason for Failing Schools." *Dissent* 58(4):23–27.

Thompson, H. 2012. "The Prison Industrial Complex—A Growth Industry in a Shrinking Economy." *New Labor Forum* 21(3):39–47.

Thompson, H. 2013. "Unmaking the Motor City in the Age of Mass Incarceration." *Journal of Law in Society* 15(1):41–61.

Torrey, E. 1995. "Editorial: Jails and Prisons: America's New Mental Hospitals." *American Journal of Public Health* 85(12):1611–13.

Tversky, A., and D. Kahnemen. 1974. "Judgment under Uncertainty: Heuristics and Biases." *Science* 185(4157):1124–31.

Udechukwu, I., W. Harrington, T. Manyak, S. Segal, and S. Graham. 2007. "The Georgia Department of Corrections: An Exploratory Reflection on Correctional Officer Turnover and Its Correlates." *Public Personnel Management* 36(3):247–68.

Uggen, C., and J. Manza. 2002. "Democratic Contraction? Political Consequences of Felon Disenfranchisement in the United States." *American Sociological Review* 67(6):777–803.

Ulloa, J. 2018. "California Senate Sends Landmark Bail Reform Bill to Gov. Jerry Brown." *Los Angeles Times*, August 21, 2018. http://www.latimes.com/politics/essential/la-pol-ca-essential-politics-may-2018-california-senate-sends-landmark-bail-1534892792-htmlstory.html.

UN News Centre. 2011. "Solitary Confinement Should Be Banned in Most Cases, UN Expert Says." October 18, 2011. https://news.un.org/en/story/2011/10/392012-solitary-confinement-should-be-banned-most-cases-un-expert-says.

Unnever, J. 2008. "Two Worlds Far Apart: Black-White Difference in Beliefs about Why African-American Men Are Disproportionately Imprisoned." *Criminology* 46(2):511–38.

Unnever, J., F. Cullen, and C. Johnson. 2008. "Race, Racism and Support for Capital Punishment." *Crime and Justice* 37(1):45–96.

Unnever, J., F. Cullen, and J. Jones. 2008. "Public Support for Attacking the 'Root Causes' of Crime: The Impact of Egalitarian and Racial Beliefs." *Sociological Focus* 41(1):1–33.

U.S. Department of Justice, Bureau of Justice Statistics. 2006. "Justice Expenditure and Employment Extracts, NCJ 224394, Table 2 [Online]." Accessed March 5, 2014. https://www.bjs.gov/index.cfm?ty=pbdetail&iid=1022.

Vera Institute of Justice. 2017. "The Price of Prisons." May 23, 2017. https://www.vera.org/publications/price-of-prisons-2015-state-spending-trends.

Vitale, A. 2017. *The End of Policing*. New York: Verso.

Wacquant, L. 1999. "'Suitable Enemies' Foreigners and Immigrants in the Prisons of Europe." *Punishment and Society* 1(2):215–22.

Wacquant, L. 2005. "Race as Civic Felony." *International Social Science Journal* 57(183):127–42.

Wacquant, L. 2009. *Punishing the Poor: The Neoliberal Government of Social Insecurity*. Durham: Duke University Press.

Wade-Olson, J. 2016. "Race, Staff and Punishment: Representative Bureaucracy in American State Prisons." *Administration and Society*, October 2016:1–28.

Walmsley, R. 2016. *World Prison Population List*, 11th ed. London: Institute for Criminal Policy Research.

Weaver, V., and A. Lerman. 2010. "Political Consequences of the Carceral State." *American Political Science Review* 104(4):817–33.

Weick, K. 1984. "Small Wins: Redefining the Scale of Social Problems." *American Psychologist* 39(1):40–49.

Welch, K. 2007. "Black Criminal Stereotypes and Racial Profiling." *Journal of Contemporary Criminal Justice* 23(3):276–88.

Welch, M. 2002. *Detained: Immigration Laws and the Expanding INS Jail Complex*. Philadelphia: Temple University Press.

Western, B. 2006. *Punishment and Inequality in America*. New York: Russell Sage Foundation.

Wilkins, V., and L. Keiser. 2006. "Linking Passive and Active Representation by Gender: The Case of Child Support Agencies." *Journal of Public Administration Research and Theory* 16:87–102.

Williams, J. 2017. "Serving Time: Average Prison Sentence in the U.S. Is Getting Even Longer." *Newsweek*, July 22, 2017. https://www.newsweek.com/prison-sentences-increased-2017-jail-639952.

Williams, K. 2015. *Our Enemies in Blue: Police and Power in America*, 3rd ed. Oakland, CA: AK Press.

Wilper, A., S. Woolhandler, J. Boyd, K. Lasser, D. McCormick, D. Bor, and D. Himmelstein. 2009. "The Health and Health Care of US Prisoners: Results of a Nationwide Survey." *American Journal of Public Health* 99(4):666–72.

Wilson, D., and S. Neville. 2009. "Culturally Safe Research with Vulnerable Populations." *Contemporary Nurse: A Journal for the Australian Nursing Population* 33(1):60–79.

Wilson, J., and G. Kelling. 1982. "Broken Windows." *Atlantic*, March 1982.

Winsor, M. 2017. "2017 in Review: The Biggest Stories of the Year." ABC News, December 23, 2017. http://abcnews.go.com/International/2017-review-biggest-stories-year/story?id=51792152.

Woldoff, R., and H. Washington. 2008. "Arrested Contact: The Criminal Justice System, Race, and Father Engagement." *Prison Journal* 88(2):179–206.

World Atlas. 2017. "World's Largest Cities." Last modified January 17, 2018. http://www.worldatlas.com/citypops.htm.

Wright, T. 1993. "Correctional Employee Turnover: A Longitudinal Study." *Journal of Criminal Justice* 21:131–42.

Wu, J., and D. Silva. 2018. "MAP: See the States Where Marijuana Is Legal." *NBC News*, November 20, 2018. https://www.nbcnews.com/news/us-news/map-see-if-marijuana-legal-your-state-n938426.

Yates, J., and R. Fording. 2005. "Politics and State Punitiveness in Black and White." *Journal of Politics* 67(4):1099–121.

Yee, V. 2017. "Judge Blocks Trump Effort to Withhold Money from Sanctuary Cities." *New York Times*, April 25, 2017. https://www.nytimes.com/2017/04/25/us/judge-blocks-trump-sanctuary-cities.html.

Zeitchik, S. 2015. "'American Sniper' Box Office: Why It Will Probably Never Happen Again." *Los Angeles Times*, March 9, 2015.

Index

Abbott, Arnold, 51, 121, 131
African Americans, xiv, xv, xviii–xxvi, 4, 6–8, 16–18, 25, 30–31, 34, 43, 69–78, 83, 95–100, 108–110, 112–113, 117–119, 123
Aid to Families with Dependent Children (AFDC), 42
Alcoholics Anonymous, 19, 102, 117
Alexander, Michelle, 17, 19–20, 39–40, 44–46, 52, 72–73, 75, 100,
American Civil Liberties Union, 64, 127
American Friends Service Committee, 62–64, 127, 131
American Indians, xv, xxvi, 69, 75–78
American Prisons: brief history, 13–19; modern prisons, 19–22
American Sniper, 1–2
Anslinger, Harry, 97–98
Anti-Terrorism and Effective Death Penalty Act, 87
Asian Americans, xv, 75, 99
Average prison sentence, 11, 116
Audacity of Hope, The, xiv
Australia, xx, 86, 107

Baltimore, Maryland, 39, 62
Beccaria, Cesare, 15
Biblical texts, xxiii, 2, 4, 15, 16, 19
Bipolar disorder, 65–66
Black Lives Matter movement, xiii, 13, 54
Bracero program, 83–84
"Broken windows" policing, 36–38, 122–123. *See also* "Stop and frisk"
Bureau of Justice Statistics, xiii, xx, xxii, xxv, 21, 33, 42, 51, 56–57

Canada, xix–xx, 12, 105, 107
Cannabis, xxvi, 8–9, 11, 30, 38, 40, 44, 95–100, 103–107, 112, 123, 128
Capital punishment, xxiii, 4, 14
Cash bail system, xxvii, 19, 36, 44, 50, 54–55, 67, 90, 122, 126–128, 130, 132
Castile, Philando, 43, 95–96
Catholic Church, 64
Children of inmates, xxvi, 87–88, 90–91, 110–115, 119–120, 124, 133
CJ-DATS (Criminal Justice Drug Abuse Treatment Studies), 33–34, 75, 78, 135–137
Clinton, Bill, xiii–xiv, xvii, 6, 80
Clinton, Hillary, xiii, xiv, 80, 82
Cocaine, 8, 100, 103–105, 117, 123, 128
Cognitive biases, xxiii–xxiv, 28–29, 35, 70–71, 73–75, 78, 89, 122–123. *See also* heuristics

Colonial prisons, 13–16, 19
Convict leasing, 16–19, 47
Corporal punishment, 2
Corporations using prison labor, 16–17, 47–48, 92
"Crack epidemic," xiv, xvii–xviii, 8, 117
Crime clearance rates, xxii
Crime control model, xviii, 18–19, 91
Crime rates, xviii, xx, 39, 70, 106
Criminal history, 48, 74, 77, 89
Criminal Justice Drug Abuse Treatment Studies (CJ-DATS), 33–34, 75, 78, 135–137
Critical Resistance, 64, 124, 127, 131

Davis, Angela, 47, 62
Deinstitutionalization of mental healthcare, 60, 122, 127
Department of Justice, xvi, xxv, 10–11, 62, 89
Department of State, 10, 96
Depression, 57–58, 65–66, 83, 111, 121–122
Diagnostic and Statistical Manual of Mental Disorders, 101, 104
Dilulio, John, xiii, xx, 113
Disciplinary process, 24, 27, 31, 33, 72, 75–76,
Discretion of prison guards, xxiv, 22–24, 26–28, 33–34, 58, 122; in searches, xxv, 25, 38, 63, 88, 115, 124
Domestic violence, xxv
Drone strikes, 43
Drug(s), xv, xxvi, 21, 34, 96, 100–101, 125; abuse and dependence, 50, 64–65, 101–104, 111, 117; decriminalization and legalization, 106–107; war on, 40, 81, 98, 100, 103–105, 123
Drug Enforcement Agency, 40, 70

Economist, xxii, 85

Families of inmates, xiv, xxvi–xxvii, 53, 79, 91, 104, 108, 110, 112–113, 117–118, 120, 124, 129; visitation by, xxvi, 26, 28, 52–53, 62, 66, 76, 103, 114–116, 119–120, 124
Fathers in prison, 59, 111–112, 114–116, 119
Federal Adoption and Safe Families Act, 116
Federal Bureau of Investigation, 104
Federal Bureau of Prisons, xvi, 24, 42, 47–48, 64
Ferguson, Missouri, 39, 43
Flint, Michigan, xvi, 3, 77, 102, 110
Folk devils, 9, 18, 81

Gangs, xiii–xiv, 31, 63, 74, 79, 81, 97

Harm reduction, 106
Harrison Narcotics Tax Act, 96
Health of inmates, xv, xxv, 16, 30–31, 56–59, 100, 107, 112, 122; mental health, xxi, xxiii, xxv, 19, 27, 52–53, 56–58, 64–68, 76, 78; physical health, xxv, 56–58, 65–66
Heroin, 8, 98, 100, 103–106, 128
Heuristics, xxiii–xxiv, 29, 71, 73–75, 78, 122–123. *See also* cognitive biases
HIV/AIDS, 56–59, 106–107, 122
Homelessness, xxiv, 36, 50–53, 119, 125
Human Rights Watch, 25, 64, 72, 100, 127

Illegal Immigration Reform and Responsibility Act (IIRIRA), 87
Immigration, xiv–xv, xxi, xxiv, xxvi, 7–8, 20–21, 44, 79–80, 82–84, 87–91, 93, 96–97, 111, 123, 128, 131; prisons, 49, 58, 81–82, 87, 92
Implicit bias, xxiv, 71
Inadequate education, xv–xvi, 34, 50, 110, 112

Incarceration rates, xvi, xix–xx, 73, 81, 92
Intersectionality, xiv, 54
Investigations, 21–22, 39, 72, 129–130
Islam, xxvi, 85

Johnson, Lyndon, xvii
Johnson-Reed Immigration Act, 82

Kahneman, Daniel, 4, 29, 71
Kentucky Department of Corrections, 24
Kentucky field work and interviews, 23, 25, 30, 33, 75, 121, 124
Kyle, Chris, 1–2

Lafler v Cooper
Latino/as, xv, xxvi, 4, 7, 22, 30–31, 34, 69–70, 73–78, 90, 97–100, 109, 118, 121, 123
Life without parole sentence, xx–xxi
Lipsky, Michael, 27–28
LSD, 8

Mandatory minimums, 44, 97, 123, 125
Marriage, 4–5, 109–110
Maynard-Moody, Steven, 28–29, 39, 70, 72
MDMA, 107, 128
Media portrayals of crime, xiv, 8, 10, 17, 69, 117
Mental health treatment: counseling, 65, 102; medication, 52–53, 58, 61, 65–66, 76, 103
Methamphetamine, xviii, 8, 103, 105
Mexico, xix–xxi, xxvi, 5, 47, 81, 83, 85, 88, 91, 93, 104–105
Monetary sanctions, xxvii, 45–46, 48, 54, 97, 122, 127, 130, 132
Moral panics, xxiv, 1, 7–11, 13, 81, 83, 85–86, 90, 96, 113, 117, 121, 123
Mothers in prison, 46, 59, 110–112, 114–118, 120
Muhammad, Khalil, 69, 73–74
Musheno, Michael, 28–29

National Institute on Drug Abuse, 33
National Religious Campaign Against Torture, 64, 127
Nativism, 85
Needle exchange, 106–107
Neoliberal paternalism, 41, 58, 110, 115
New Jim Crow, The, 39
New York Police Department, 37–39, 70, 125
New York Times, 11, 61
Nixon, Richard, xvii, 98, 104
Niyomugabo, Djibril, 36, 40, 44, 67, 127

Obama, Barack, xiv, 50, 79–80, 89, 108–109, 116

Parents in prison, xxvi, 87, 90–91, 110–114, 118, 120, 124
PCP, 8
Personality disorder, 65–67
Peterson, Adrian, 2
Phone calls from prison, xxvi, 62, 116, 119–120, 124
Police, xvi, 20, 37, 39–40, 43, 59, 70, 95, 100, 104, 129–130; brutality, 3–4, 9, 11–13, 95, 97, 100, 123; social order function of, 18, 21–22, 37–39, 44, 70, 86, 97, 113
Policing in schools, 113
Portugal, 105–107, 128
Poverty, xii, xv, xxiv–xxv, 3, 8, 13, 18, 22, 36, 40–41, 43, 46, 51–54, 59, 68–69, 73, 88, 100, 103, 109–110, 112, 117, 119, 132–133
Prison(s): abolition of, 124-125, 129, 131; commissary, 38, 48–50, 59, 122; cost of, xvi, 3, 31, 48, 64, 92,

Prison(s) (*cont.*)
102, 125–126, 130; labor, 15–18, 45, 47–48, 122, 131; overcrowding of, 24, 28, 57, 97; pregnancy in, 117; private, 58, 92; strikes in, 47, 90, 131
Prison guard turnover, 26
Prison Litigation Reform Act, 27
Prison Policy Initiative, 47, 102
Prison Research Education Action Project, 124
Prohibition of alcohol, xx, xxvi, 96–98, 100, 104–105, 123
Property crime, xviii, xx–xxii, 36, 51, 62, 111, 126
Protests, 9, 12, 80, 86, 100, 113, 131
Psilocybin mushrooms, 107, 128
Public order crime, xx–xxi, 21
Punishing the Poor, 41–42

Race, xv, xvii, xxv–xxvi, 2, 5, 30, 34, 54, 66, 69–70, 73–78, 82, 98, 100, 103, 110, 122–123
Racial discrimination, xxvi, 17, 41, 67, 69, 71–72, 74, 76–77, 100, 123, 132
Racial threat theory, 69
RAINN (Rape, Abuse and Incest National Network), xxii
Reagan, Ronald, xvii
Recidivism, 64, 126
Reform suggestions, 54–55, 67–68, 77–78, 93–94, 104–107, 119–120, 125–133
Rehabilitation, xvi–xvii, 9, 18–19, 32–34, 41, 56, 67, 75, 102, 121–122
Representative bureaucracy, 77
Rioting, xvii–xix, 25, 84, 131

Sanctuary cities, 91
Scapegoat, 9–10, 16, 81, 86, 92
Schizophrenia, 65–66,
Scott, Keith Lamont, 95
Searches, 25, 38, 62–63, 88, 115, 124
Sentencing disparities, 123, 125
Sexual assault, xx–xxii, 17, 62, 65–67, 81, 112
Slavery, 1, 4–5, 10, 14, 16
Social construction: of crime, xxiv, 22, 29, 68; of drug use, xiv, xviii–xix, xxiv, 7–8, 31, 74, 79–80, 96; of immigration, 81, 84–86, 96; of race 5, 30, 70, 74, 109
Solitary confinement, xiv, xvi, xviii, xxv–xxvi, 16, 25–26, 28, 31–32, 52–53, 60–68, 76–77, 90, 92, 103–104, 121, 123–124, 127, 130, 132
"Stop and frisk." xxii, 21, 38–39. *See also* "Broken windows" policing
Street level bureaucracy, 26–29, 33–35, 70, 88, 102, 105
Suicide, 61, 65–67, 86, 127
"Super predators," xiv, xvii, xx, 7, 57, 65, 68, 121, 133
Supervised drug injection, 106–107
Survey of Inmates in State and Federal Correctional Facilities, 2004, 51–52, 58, 63, 65, 67, 74–77, 93, 102–103, 118, 136–138, 142

Tao Te Ching, xii
Temporary Assistance to Needy Families (TANF), 42
Tobacco, xxvi, 8, 128
Torture, 64, 127
Traffic stops, 20, 40, 43, 54, 72, 79, 95, 129–130
Trump, Donald, xiv, 7, 64, 79–80, 85, 89, 91, 109

Violent crime, xx, xxii, 73, 94, 98
Vulnerable, definition of, xiv–xv
Wacquant, Loic, xviii–xxiv, 11, 19–20, 41–44, 47–48, 56, 86, 114
"War on Drugs," 8, 71, 96, 104, 123–124

Washington Post, 11–12
WeedMaps, 99
Welfare benefits (Temporary Assistance to Needy Families), xvi, 28–29, 41–42
White-collar crime, 11, 43
Wilson, James Q., 36–37
Women's health care, 58–59
Writeups, 52–53, 66–67, 76, 103–104

Yanez, Jeronimo, 95

About the Author

Jeremiah Wade-Olson is an assistant professor at the University of Michigan, Flint. He has a PhD in political science from the University of Kentucky and an MPA from the University of North Carolina at Charlotte. His work focuses on prisons and the social construction of crime. He has been published in the *Journal of Public Administration Research and Theory* and in *Administration and Society*.